Understanding Children

UNDERSTANDING CHILDREN

Dr Richard C Woolfson

CB
Caring Books

First published in 2003 by
Caring Books, PO Box 1565,
Glasgow G46 6SX.

Reprinted in 2004

Printed and bound in Great Britain
by Bell & Bain Ltd.

British Library in Cataloguing Publication Data.

ISBN 0-9523649-5-6

Understanding Children

Richard Woolfson is a child psychologist, working with young children and their families. He appears regularly on radio and television. He is also an author and writes on child and family development for many magazines and newspapers – including Practical Parenting, Young Parents, Who Minds? and The Herald – as well as a member of the Guardian newspaper's Parents Panel. Richard runs training workshops on managing children's behaviour, for early years professionals throughout the country.

His books – many of which have been translated into other languages – include 'Children With Special Needs' (1991), 'An A-Z Of Child Development' (1993), 'Starting School' (1995), 'Sibling Rivalry' (1995), 'Body Language' (1996), 'The Professional Nanny Handbook' (1997), 'From Birth To Starting School' (1998), 'Bright Baby' (2001), 'Bright Toddler' (2001), 'Bright Child' (2001), 'Small Talk' (2002), 'Fact File for First Time Fathers' (2003), 'Siblings: Encouraging Your Children To be Friends' (2003), 'Start Right' (2003) and 'Why Do Kids Do That?' (2004).

Richard is a Fellow of the British Psychological Society. He is married to a child psychologist, and they have two daughters, aged 24 and 22.

Other books by the same author

Starting School
From Birth To Starting School

These titles are available from
Caring Books, PO Box 1565, Glasgow G46 6SX
email: caring.books@ntlworld.com

In memory of my father and grandfather

CONTENTS

Introduction

Understanding Children

This course book is a supplementary reader for your ICS course. Students of this particular course come from all walks of life, each with their own knowledge of child psychology and each with their own background and experience with children. For instance, you might be:

- a child carer – perhaps working as a childminder, au pair, nanny or nursery nurse – wanting to improve your current level of training and understanding of child development.
- a school pupil with an interest in child psychology, and you may want to study this course in order to help you decide your long-term plans for your future career.
- a parent at home raising your children, determined to further your understanding of your own children and to widen your grasp of child development issues in general.
- a play-leader who works with children every day and although you already have had training in aspects of child development, you would like to improve your knowledge and understanding.
- working in a career that has absolutely nothing to do with children or families at all and you simply want to learn more about this fascinating topic of child psychology.

Or your own personal profile might not fit into any of these categories. All that really matters is that you have chosen to further your knowledge of child psychology through studying this ICS course.

The course material that will be supplied to you through regular mailings gives a thorough overview of the key theories within child psychology and also examines the main research findings. By the time you complete this course – including all the written assessments and the coursework – you will have a good grasp of the central strands of child psychology and the research this has generated.

This course book, however, will add a further strand to your understanding by turning the theory and evidence of child development into practice, by looking at the practical application of child psychology for stimulating child development and for managing many of the routine challenges that are faced when involved with growing children. Therefore, this course book concentrates on the application of theories and evidence, not on the theories themselves.

Book Structure

This course book is divided into six sections. The first five cover the pre-school years, namely, General Development, Personal Development, Emotional Development. Social Development and Intellectual Development. The sixth section, The Older Child, covers middle childhood and adolescence. During your study of the Course Units you will be directed to specific sections of the book, but you may also want to read other sections out of sequence – it's entirely up to you. (Advice is given in the book, based on the assumption that you are a parent yourself or that you have the opportunity to work with children. Don't worry if that doesn't apply to you – the book is still an important part of your course study.)

Section 1: General Development

This section examines the progress that a child is expected to achieve during the pre-school years. Chapter 1 looks at general strategies and techniques for stimulating young children, while Chapters 2-5 outline the major developmental milestones between birth and five years, and at the same time offer ways of testing a child's progress as well as encouraging it. At times it is difficult to know whether a child's behaviour is normal or abnormal, and this question is closely examined in Chapter 6.

1

Stimulating Child Development

"I know lots of children but there have been times when I was not sure what they should be doing at a specific age. A baseline for judging child development would be useful, rather than just comparing them with each other. That would be reassuring."

Normal development in childhood is varied. You'll already have noticed that the children you know develop at different rates from each other (even though they may be the same age). Don't be concerned about these individual differences.

There is no need to worry, for instance, that one child doesn't talk in sentences yet she is three years old, while another talks fluently and she hasn't even reached her second birthday – both these ages are within the normal range in which children acquire language. The same applies to every other area of child development. And that's why it is normal, for instance, for one child to learn elementary reading skills only once she has started school, while another child arrives at school already able to read a few words or for one child to want to watch television while another prefers to do her homework immediately after school. Individual differences like these are nearly always a normal part of growing up.

Testing & Helping

In this ICS course, the focus is on child development throughout childhood, and therefore issues affecting both preschool children and older children are considered in detail. The lists in Chapters 2-5 outline the major skills that a child usually achieves during the periods birth-one year, one-two years, two-three years, three-five years, and suggest ways you can test these.

These tests fulfil two purposes. First, they can help you pinpoint her level of development, identifying her strengths and weaknesses, so you know how well she progresses. Second, they can help you promote her development by providing her with stimulation and suitable activities to encourage further progress.

You'll soon realise that the child already does a lot of the things associated with her age, while there are others that she cannot manage on her own. The fact that she might not be able to complete all of them at the moment really doesn't matter, however; it simply means she's not at the stage of maturity to have the necessary skills – the chances are that she'll soon get there. Checklists of development, such as those given in Chapters 2-5, are useful, however, because they will give you guidelines to the approximate rate of progress that a child is expected to make during the first five years.

Providing Encouragement

A child's drive to grow and progress during the pre-school years is spontaneous and instinctive. But any help and encouragement given by her parents and carers can make a difference to her rate of development. She needs **varied experiences** to use the skills that she already has. True, she is going to investigate her surroundings whether or not she is helped - her need to discover is innate. But more opportunities for exploration available to her (eg toys and games, books and discussions, playing freely with other children who are with her at the same time) means more opportunities for her to learn new concepts and skills, and therefore more opportunities to progress.

One characteristic of young children is that they know no bounds. They will try to go wherever they want, whenever they want, totally oblivious to the hazards that might be waiting for them (such as falling down stairs, burning on gas fires, choking on swallowed objects, jamming a hand in the closing door). So **she must know where she is (and isn't) allowed to venture** in her house and what she is (and isn't) allowed to touch. Her parents or carers have to draw the line somewhere, and then clearly explain what that line is. The fact that she may challenge these limits should not stop the adults in her world from setting them – her personal safety is at stake.

Playing with a child, rather than just direct her towards play activities, is very effective. You only need to look at the delighted expression on her face when her parent joins in her play activities to realise that adult involvement makes the activity much more fun. Of course, adults need to remember that it's her game, not theirs, so they should participate but not dominate. And she can play with the same toy, game or activity again and again if she wants. To an adult, repetition is boring, but to a young child repetition can be exciting. For instance, suppose she is already able to put the shapes into the correct holes in the shape sorter. Continued play with this toy lets her consolidate her knowledge of shapes (which builds her confidence) and provides her with a chance to learn about, say, colour matching.

Watching a child struggle at an activity that you know other children her age can complete without any problem can be very frustrating. But **avoid putting her under too much pressure**, as this could turn off her interest altogether. Try to find a learning task that is more demanding than the one she can manage already but that is not so hard that she feels totally overwhelmed by it. It's a matter of knowing each child individually, and then identifying the right activity that is suited to her needs. If she is upset because she can't solve a puzzle or make a toy go the way she wants it to, it's best for her to leave it for the moment and then to come back to it later.

There will be times when you can help a child learn a new skill by **showing her what to do.** This is a very effective form of learning. Young children are often fiercely independent and resist all efforts for help. However, giving her support in the form of a friendly helping hand – especially when her frustration begins to bubble up – may be just what she needs to get over this particular hurdle. Once you have shown her what to do, suggest that in turn she shows you how to do it. It's more a matter of your sharing with her, rather than simply teaching her. Providing a demonstration that takes her part of the way to the correct solution can help her make her own way to the end point.

Q & A

Q. *Is there a danger that an adult will reduce a child's spontaneity by joining in?*

A. This can happen if the adult becomes too dominant and starts to make choices for the child, for instance by suggesting toys that would be more fun, and so on. Adult involvement of this sort devalues play in the eyes of the child. However, sensitive involvement – in which an adult lets the child take the lead and yet still participates along with her – may encourage her to play for longer. Never underestimate the positive effect attention from a caring adult can have on a child; she loves it.

Q. *What is the best way to stop a two-year-old from playing with the same construction blocks all the time? She has no interest in any other activity.*

A. Aim for gradual change, rather than sudden change. If you try, for example, to hide her favourite blocks, then you may find she becomes even more determined to play with them! Select a couple of toys that you think may interest her, and then bring her over to play with them, just for a couple of moments. Reassure her that she can return to the construction blocks very soon. When a minute or two has passed, put the new toys away. Then bring them out again the next day, only this time ask her to play with them for a little longer. Gradually introducing new play ideas in this way will eventually harness her interest in them.

Q. *Why is it young girls are more interested in quiet activities that involve co-operation, while young boys prefer rough-and-tumble play?*

A. This question has vexed psychologists for decades, and there is still no definitive answer. Some argue that this sex difference in play preferences is due to innate biological differences which are seen in all aspects of life, including play. Others argue that children behave this way because adults in particular, and society in general, expect them to. Irrespective of the underlying theories of gender differences, it is important that all children are encouraged to have as broad a range of play and learning experiences as possible. This is the best way of enhancing their development during the pre-school years.

Q. *Is it normal for a four-year-old who is bright to have a two-year-old brother who is developing at a slower rate?*

A. In the same way that any two children of the same age develop at different rates, any two siblings can progress at varying speeds even though they are both brought up in the same family. Research shows that identical twins usually have different rates of development too. All these differences between siblings are common and rarely signify any cause for concern. The only time to worry is when a child's progress is well below that normally expected for a child her age, irrespective of her sibling's progress.

2

Child Development: Birth-One Year

"Young babies are fascinating because they change so quickly, from week to week and even from day to day. It's amazing how they grow and grow. Sometimes it's frustrating that they can't speak and that they can't tell anyone what's wrong."

The first year of life is a time of enormous change and development, both physically and psychologically. From being a screaming baby who has arrived into this world – perhaps with ease, perhaps with difficulty – he gradually becomes transformed into a thinking, feeling, sensitive infant who is completely fascinated by all that happens around him.

Some of these changes are visible to anyone who comes into contact with the young baby. For instance, his birth weight doubles by the age of five months and triples by the end of the first year; that's quite a growth spurt by anybody's standards! And his length also increases significantly. At birth, the typical baby is around 20 inches (50 cm) long, but is around 30 inches (75 cm) long a year later. One of the signs of this physical growth is that he needs more and more milk during the early months, and that eventually he requires solid food not long after that, in order to satisfy his ever-increasing hunger.

Although a new baby has little control over his limbs and body at birth, by his first birthday he can control his head and arm movements, reach out for objects in front of him, sit up independently and possibly even walk a few steps without support. He is altogether more mobile than he was a few months earlier.

Other changes are more subtle. He has control over his attention by the age of 12 months and can choose what he looks at or ignores. Concentration has improved too, as has his ability to anticipate routine events that he experiences every day, such as bathtime or a story before he has a nap.

Testing Child Development at Three Months

Baby Skill: Reaches for a toy in front of him.
What To Do: Prop the baby up in a comfortable seat and then place a small toy just out of his reach. Encourage him as he stretches his hand towards it in an attempt to grasp it.

Baby Skill: Shows a greater interest in the faces of people.
What To Do: When talking to a baby of this age, keep your face approximately 10 inches away from his so that he can see your facial expression very clearly.

Baby Skill: Focuses his attention on a specific sound source.
What To Do: Sing lullabies and play music to him, as this will give him an incentive to concentrate. You can also start reciting nursery rhymes to him at this age.

Baby Skill: Tracks a moving object with his eyes.
What To Do: Hold a small toy in your hand and attract the baby's attention to it. Then, gently move it round and round in a large, slow circular movement.

Baby Skill: Smiles when he sees a familiar face.
What To Do: Enter his line of vision with a big smile across your face. Let him know how pleased you are with him when he responds with a large smile himself.

Baby Skill: Closes his fingers round a small object.
What To Do: Put a small rattle in his hand and very gently shake it back and forth a few times. The baby will want to continue holding it for at least a couple more seconds.

Baby Skill: Starts to anticipate familiar events.
What To Do: Let him see you start to prepare his next feed; do this in full view so that he can see everything you do. He'll become excited at the beginning of this sequence.

Baby Skill: Shows fascination with his hands.
What To Do: When you watch him playing quietly in his cot or pram, you'll notice he wiggles his hands and fingers about, fanning the air with them or bringing them to his mouth to chew.

Testing Child Development at Six Months

Baby Skill: Starts to sit up independently without support.
What To Do: Give the baby opportunities to sit on the carpeted floor, propping him up with cushions on all sides if necessary to stop him falling over.

Baby Skill: Babbles when you speak to him.
What To Do: Talk to the baby in your normal voice, pausing regularly

to let him babble, as if you are having a conversation with him. Show your pleasure when he babbles back at you.

Baby Skill: Holds a small toy in each hand.
What To Do: When you see him holding an object or small toy in one of his hands, gently place another object in his other hand so that he holds them both simultaneously.

Baby Skill: Watches a toy even when it slips from his grasp.
What To Do: Reach out to give him a toy, then gently drop it just as his hand starts to touch it. Look puzzled, then ask him "Where is the toy?" You may have to repeat the question.

Baby Skill: Gets actively involved if his interest is stimulated.
What To Do: Place a rattle or other noisy toy just out of his reach, then shake it in order to attract his attention. When he looks at the rattle, ask him to try to take it.

Baby Skill: Shows the first signs that he is starting to crawl.
What To Do: Place the baby face down on a clean, carpeted floor and put an attractive toy beyond his reach. Encourage him in his efforts as he desperately tries to grab the toy.

Baby Skill: Produces consistent babbling sounds.
What To Do: Listen to his speech closely. At this age, he may be able to make at least four or five different babbling sounds, such as "aa", "goo", "da", and so on.

Baby Skill: Shows that he enjoys playing with an adult.
What To Do: If you go towards the baby, and put your hands out as though you are about to lift him up, he'll start to get excited at the prospect of playing with you.

Testing Child Development at Nine Months

Infant Skill: Pinpoints the source of a particular sound.
What To Do: Bring a ticking watch up to his ear, making sure that he does not see it, and react positively when he turns his head round to look directly at it.

Infant Skill: Controls hand movements with more co-ordination.
What To Do: When you see that he holds a small toy in each of his hands, pass him a third. He'll realise that he needs to drop one of the other toys in order to take it from you.

Infant Skill: May use his first word at this age.
What To Do: Talk to the growing infant whenever you are with him, and make a big fuss of him when you think you have heard him say his first word.

Infant Skill: Knows he is a separate individual.
What To Do: Hold a mirror up to the infant's face; he will probably smile at his own reflection, and he might even reach out to try to touch what he sees in the mirror.

Infant Skill: Plays purposefully with two toys together.
What To Do: Give him a plastic cup and a plastic saucer, or two small wooden blocks. He'll try to place one on top of the other, or else try to thump them together.

Infant Skill: Looks for an object that has been covered up.
What To Do: Let the infant watch you closely as you place a sweet under an upturned cup, right in front of him. The chances are that he will lift the cup up straight away.

Infant Skill: Distinguishes a stranger from a familiar person.
What To Do: When you are out with him and you meet someone that he doesn't know, his shyness will become apparent; he might burst into tears or scowl or even pull you anxiously towards him.

Infant Skill: Loves crumpling up paper.
What To Do: If you ever make the mistake of letting him get hold of an important letter, it is highly likely that you will return to find that he has crushed it.

Testing Child Development at One Year

Infant Skill: Follows basic directions.
What To Do: Give him a simple instruction that he can carry out on his own, such as "Please give me the cup" or "Please sit down on the floor beside me."

Infant Skill: Imitates the actions of other people.
What To Do: Stand in front of the infant so that he can see you, and then bang two wooden bricks together to make a noise. Hand him the two bricks and ask him to do the same.

Infant Skill: Becomes more curious about how things work.
What To Do: Put a couple of small wooden bricks into a small box with

a lid on it. Rattle the box and then hand it to him. He'll try to open it in search of the mysterious contents.

Infant Skill: Likes to play with other children and adults.
What To Do: Play singing games with him, such as "Pat a cake, pat a cake" or "Round and round the garden". He anticipates the actions and tries to join in.

Infant Skill: Has at least three clear words.
What To Do: Talk to him and listen closely to the language he uses. Count the number of single words that he uses in the proper context during a typical day.

Infant Skill: Has greater manipulation of his fingers.
What To Do: While the infant is in his highchair, place a sweet on the tray in front of him. He will pick it up with his thumb and forefinger in a pincer grasp.

Infant Skill: Crawls around the floor with more co-ordination.
What To Do: When put face down, he will crawl effectively round the room using his hands and knees. However, some children prefer to "bottom shuffle" instead.

Infant Skill: Uses toys constructively in play.
What To Do: Give him a plastic cup, saucer and spoon to hold. He plays with them appropriately, by putting the cup on the saucer or the spoon into the cup.

How to Enhance a Baby's Progress from Birth-One Year

There is lots that can be done to help a baby's progress during the first year, particularly by providing him with a stimulating environment even when he lies in his cot. A mobile hung on the ceiling, for example, so that it dangles in his line of vision, or an activity-centre attached to the side of his cot but within his reach, will encourage him to look, to reach out and to touch. He is pre-programmed to learn and discover. It's important he gets positive feedback from his parent or carer when he does react; a pleasurable response encourages him to repeat the action, because he likes approval.

And don't forget that talking to a young baby is very important. Some adults feel this is silly, since a baby can't talk back. However, the more people use language with a young baby then the more likely he is to see that language has a purpose and is a useful way of communicating. The more other children and adults talk to him, the better.

When it comes to toys, the best ones are those that have good play value (in other words, toys that he will enjoy playing with again and again). Suitable toys at this age are those that are brightly coloured, noisy when shaken, and with a variety of textures – this means that the baby can play with them regularly and yet have new experiences each time. He needs good positioning wherever he is. Because he can't yet walk, or find a good seating position on his own, he is dependent on others to position him in a way that he can see clearly and can reach toys comfortably. This includes sitting him in his high chair, or propping him up on the floor.

Get him involved in play. Of course, you can bring toys over to the infant and show him how they can be used. But get him involved, rather than doing things for him. For instance, if he is not interested in reaching for a toy, then place his hands on it.

(If you do practise some of these items on a young child while studying for this course, it is very important to obtain his parent's permission and also to share the information with them afterwards. They want to know how he reacted.)

Q & A

Q. *What is likelihood of a child becoming more attached to his childminder than to his mother?*

A. The chances are that the baby will form a close emotional bond with his childminder – and indeed, there would be concern if he didn't, given that she looks after him for much of the day. However, all children are capable of forming more than one emotional attachment during the early years, and therefore the attachment to the mother is not at risk as long as she herself makes a point of spending as much time as she can with her baby when she is at home with him. The growing infant will benefit from each of these relationships in his young life.

Q. *What can a baby see and hear when he is born?*

A. A baby's senses are already highly tuned the moment he enters the world. For instance, a newborn baby will pay more attention to the drawing of a real face than to the drawing of a scrambled face. Many newborns show colour preferences, and are able to discriminate between two-dimensional drawings of a triangle, cross, circle and square. Hearing, too, is highly developed at birth. When a new baby hears another baby cry he continues to cry, but when he hears a recording of his own cry, he stops crying; this suggests he can distinguish between the sound of his own voice and other voices. And a baby prefers human voices to any other sounds.

Q. *If a baby weighs less than six pounds when he is born, is that much lighter than he should be?*

A. Full-term babies (ie those born after a full 40-week pregnancy) vary in their birthweight. While the average birthweight is about seven and a half pounds, the range of normal weight stretches from around five pounds to around 14 pounds – quite a spread! So a baby's weight of six pounds is probably normal. Generally, parents who are small themselves tend to have smaller babies and parents who are large tend to have larger babies, boys are frequently larger than girls, and first babies are often lighter than their brothers and sisters. Birthweight doesn't have any connection with weight in later childhood.

Q. *What is an Apgar assessment for a new baby?*

A. Devised during the 1950s by an American doctor, the Apgar system gives a rating of two, one or zero to the following physical characteristics: heart rate, breathing, muscle tone, reflexes and colour. The higher the score, the better. A healthy baby will probably score at least seven; a score of less than seven indicates he may be at risk, and a score of four or under indicates the baby may be in a critical condition. The Apgar assessment is made at birth, then repeated five minutes later – in most instances, a low first score is replaced by a higher second score.

3

Child Development: One-Two Years

"Life certainly becomes more hectic once the child is up on her feet, toddling about independently at home! She gets into absolutely everything, not because she is naughty or anything like that, but just because she is determined to explore new territory."

During this period in an infant's life, her size changes considerably, in several different ways. For instance, she grows taller, she weighs more and she is generally more robust than she was, say, just six months ago. These changes are very noticeable.

The toddler's growth continues at a fast rate during this period. If you compare the sideways-on outline of a toddler's tummy with that of an older child, you'll see that she looks as though she is fat. But she's not. This physical characteristic is due to fact that her liver and bladder are disproportionately large in relation to the rest of her body, causing her stomach to appear as though it sticks out. Sometimes when parents see this apparent overweight in their toddler, they mistakenly put her on a mini-diet – this is completely unnecessary.

Another feature of this stage in a child's life is that she learns to walk. Of course, she may have achieved this skill when she was younger (some children are able to walk at nine or ten months), but for many it is between the age of 15 and 18 months. Being able to 'toddle' around means she can now venture into previously unreachable areas of her house and garden! One minute, she's sitting on the carpet playing quietly, and so her parents think this is a good time to get on with that long-overdue household chore – but the next minute she's howling hysterically because she has crawled onto the sofa and is too afraid to move any further. Such is the curiosity of the inquiring, determined toddler.

And her play changes, too. Of course, she still likes to discover new things, to explore new places, and to play with new toys, but she doesn't simply put everything into her mouth. This need to explore objects orally has passed, and instead she manipulates objects and visually inspects them until she is satisfied that she has learned enough.

Testing Child Development at 15 Months

Infant Skill: Takes her first few steps on her own.
What To Do: Let her stand upright, while you face her holding her

hands. Then let go gently, take a few steps back and encourage her to walk towards you. Give her time.

Infant Skill: Grips two objects in each hand without letting go.
What To Do: Place two small wooden cubes in her left hand and two in her right hand. She may hold all four, even if only just for a few seconds, before dropping them.

Infant Skill: Recognises her own name.
What To Do: In the infant's presence, while talking to another adult, introduce her name into the conversation without specifically emphasising it. Watch to see if she turns round in recognition.

Infant Skill: Is fascinated by a box that contains something inside.
What To Do: Take a small box with a lid, and let her see you put a couple of small toys inside. Hand her the closed box and ask her to get the toys out. She'll tug away forcefully at the lid.

Infant Skill: Loves familiar songs and nursery rhymes.
What To Do: Sing songs to her, and tell her popular nursery rhymes, such as "This little piggy went to market." Her expression of delight indicates she knows what is coming next.

Infant Skill: Wants to become more independent.
What To Do: Give her a spoon so that she can feed herself, although do expect some of the contents to spill. She may also want to help you when you get her dressed or undressed.

Infant Skill: Is able to complete elementary inset boards.
What To Do: Many infants at this age are able to complete a one-piece or two-piece inset board, assuming the shape is not too irregular. You may have to demonstrate the solution the first time.

Infant Skill: Indicates her preference for a particular hand.
What To Do: Although she still uses her left hand and her right hand for manual tasks, you'll start to notice that she now uses one more consistently than the other.

Testing Child Development at 18 Months

Toddler Skill: Doesn't fall over as easily as she did before.
What To Do: If you hand her a doll but drop it before she can get a firm hold of it, she will look down for the doll on the floor. Then she'll reach for it and pick it up, while remaining steady.

Toddler Skill: Uses words to tell you what she wants.
What To Do: She has six or more different words, but these depend on whether or not her parents use "baby talk" eg she might say "bow wow" instead of "dog".

Toddler Skill: Completes a request when asked only once.
What To Do: Wait until she has just finished a drink of juice and say to her "Give me the cup, please" – she'll respond positively almost straight away by handing the item to you.

Toddler Skill: Understands that her actions affect objects.
What To Do: Place a biscuit on a large tissue in such a way that she can reach the edge of the tissue but not the biscuit. The chances are she'll know to tug at the tissue to get the biscuit.

Toddler Skill: Is more able to grip objects firmly in her hand.
What To Do: One day, when the child is already playing with bricks, show her how to make a tower with them. She'll copy you and will build a tower with up to three bricks before it topples.

Toddler Skill: Shows signs that her memory is expanding.
What To Do: If she is in the habit of watching a television programme regularly at the same time each day, she may tell you the programme's name as soon as you switch the set on.

Toddler Skill: Wants to hold a drink by herself.
What To Do: Many toddlers are able to lift up a cup on their own, without adult help, and then to take a drink from it without making a terrible mess everywhere.

Toddler Skill: Walks around the room more confidently.
What To Do: When she's having a tantrum, she'll stomp about the house furiously. When she's in a better mood, she may enjoy "marching" to the sound of loud music.

Testing Child Development at 21 Months

Toddler Skill: Manages more complex tasks.
What To Do: Ask her to go to the water tray, then to pour some of the water from one cup into another. The toddler will try this, though some of the water spills into the tray.

Toddler Skill: Recognises pictures of everyday objects.
What To Do: Pick out her favourite story book, one that has lots of

simple pictures in it. Point to the picture of a table and ask her to tell you what it is.

Toddler Skill: Has steadier hand control.
What To Do: Her tower of bricks contains five or more before it falls over, although she might need a couple of attempts. The more she practises this, the better she becomes at it.

Toddler Skill: Likes to discover new places.
What To Do: Accompany her as she climbs the stairs to go to the bathroom or bedroom. She may go on her hands and knees to climb them, or just climb normally.

Toddler Skill: Likes to tell you what has happened to her.
What To Do: Listen when she tries to engage you in conversation. She loves telling you her news, especially if something has upset her. Most times, you'll understand what she says to you.

Toddler Skill: Uses two words together.
What To Do: Whereas before she used one word at a time, her language has developed to the point where she uses two-word phrases or sentences, eg "Want sweet" or "Mummy gone".

Toddler Skill: Is ready to begin toilet training.
What To Do: The child may show that she is ready to gain bowel and bladder control. But there's plenty of time for toilet training. There is no need to rush the process.

Toddler Skill: Learns the names of some body parts.
What To Do: When a toddler is playing with one of her dolls, say to her "Where is dolly's head?" or "Where is dolly's nose?" She'll point out these body parts accurately.

Testing Child Development at Two Years

Toddler Skill: Loves playing outdoors.
What To Do: Now that her leg muscles are stronger, she likes to drag a pull-along toy across the grass using the cord attached to it, or to sit astride a large toy that has foot pedals.

Toddler Skill: Realises her name is different from other names.
What To Do: She starts to talk about herself using her own name. Instead of saying, for instance, "Want doll" she might say "Debbie want doll." This is a significant step forward.

Toddler Skill: Takes part in imaginative play.
What To Do: Give her some hats to play with, such as a toy policeman's helmet, a toy postman's hat, and so. She has great fun using these in her pretend-play.

Toddler Skill: Likes to manage without your help.
What To Do: Your attempts at toilet training are probably proving to be successful, although she still needs to wear a nappy at night. She responds well to praise for success.

Toddler Skill: Continues to improve her speech and language.
What To Do: Now, if you take a note of the number of words she says over a two-day period, you'll discover she uses at least two dozen, usually in short sentences.

Toddler Skill: Can pick up very small objects.
What To Do: When she is sitting at a table, put a small piece of soft food (the size of her fingernail) in front of her. She won't have a problem lifting it to her mouth.

Toddler Skill: Is fascinated by jigsaws.
What To Do: Let her play with an inset-board, the type of small infant jigsaw that has its own outer frame to hold the pieces steady. She'll persist until she's successful.

Toddler Skill: Begins to show hand preference.
What To Do: You'll notice that she usually favours one hand over the other. Watch her pick up finger-food from her plate, or pass you a toy - she uses one hand in preference to the other.

How to Enhance an Infant's Progress from One-Two Years

There is lots that can be done to help a child's progress when she is a toddler, particularly by providing her with plenty of stimulation. But safety is a top priority too, so she requires very careful supervision when playing. She will want to empty drawers, to go into dark cupboards, to stick her finger in that tantalising opening at the front of the video player, and to do all the sorts of things that fill her parents with dread. However, too much restriction will make her lose interest and become passive which in turn could diminish her desire to learn.

From the moment she stands on her own two feet, she sees the world in a different and more interesting way. Further improvement in her balance and co-ordination will be encouraged by playing on climbing frames, balancing logs and so on. Fortunately, there are lots of safe park playgrounds, full of this type of outdoor equipment (though some remain unsafe, and so each one needs to be checked very carefully). Seeing other children her age playing is an added incentive for her to join in. Independence in play activities spurs on her independence in other areas of her life as well (and vice-versa), though she still needs adult encouragement to do more for herself. She should be encouraged to help when getting dressed, and to try to use a fork when eating. Don't expect too much of her, though, or she'll just give up.

When stopped from doing something that is potentially dangerous, she responds best when told why her behaviour is being restricted. In many instances, she might not care what is said to her because the excitement of the activity is what matters to her, not the danger that goes with it. Keep telling her the reasons anyway.

Playing with other children is important at this stage, despite the fact they aren't yet mature enough to play games with rules, or even to play together – you may already have discovered that children this age spend more time staring at each other than they do interacting with each other. Even so, she'll build up her self-confidence and begin to develop vital social skills for use later on.

Toddlerhood is marked by a massive increase in a child's use of language. This brings her a lot of pleasure because she can communicate more easily and more accurately, and this in turn reduces her frustration. Her speech skills also develop through singing and poems. She will adore joining in with action rhymes that combine words with body movements. All of these enhance her interest in language.

Making the Home Safe

Safety is always a priority when considering young inquisitive children. Here are some basic safety measures:

- **medicines.** Keep all medicines and other dangerous substances in high cupboards, well out of the toddler's reach. If cleaning fluids are kept under the kitchen sink, fit childproof locks to each cupboard door in the house.
- **electric sockets.** These are at the perfect height for a toddler - she needs very little effort to reach out and stick her finger into the enticing holes. Make sure that every unused electric socket has a plastic safety cover fitted.
- **kitchen.** There should be a cooker guard, to stop the toddler from pulling pots off the hob. In addition, always turn pot handles inwards. Flexes from other electrical items, such as the kettle, should be clipped to the wall.
- **stairs.** Toddlers love going up and down stairs as fast they can, but they are not very steady on their feet and easily fall when doing so. If

there are stairs in the house, fit safety gates at the top and bottom so that she can't gain entry without your help.

- **fireguard.** Every coal fire or open gas fire should have a fireguard that completely encloses it, because a child can fall against it or even just touch it out of curiosity. The fireguard should be firmly attached to the wall with a proper fastening.
- **windows.** You'd be amazed how agile young children can be – and an open window is very enticing. She may be able to reach the window handle more easily than you think. Fit special childproof locks to each window in the house, so that only adults can open them.
- **bath.** Wet surfaces are slippery, and a toddler is vulnerable when climbing into, or out of, the bath. A non-slip rubber mat attached temporarily to the base of the bath will provide stability and increase her confidence.
- **smoke alarms.** Most rooms in a house should be fitted with a smoke alarm. These are widely available and there are many instances where they have saved lives. Once fitted, they should be checked regularly as the battery may have expired.

Q & A

Q. *I know a two-year-old girl who is too afraid to try anything new. How can I make her more confident?*

A. Although the desire to explore appears to be innate, there are some children who are so timid that they are afraid to venture into new areas – and the toddler you know appears to be one of them. As a first step, take her hand and lead her gently around your house. She'll be more likely to explore when you are by her side. Next, while staying in the room with her, tell her to open a cupboard or to take a lid off a box. These explorations with you by her side, or near her, will give her the extra confidence she needs to be more curious.

Q. *What should I do with a 15-month-old who is very passive, preferring to sit and watch rather than get actively involved?*

A. Some children are like this – it's not that they are disinterested, just that they like to stand back and observe. Almost certainly, however, she is picking up new skills this way, despite her apparent inactivity, and she will probably surprise you every so often by showing she can do something you don't expect. Remember also that if she won't go over to toys and games to play with them, then you can bring the toys and games over to her.

Q. *What's the best way to deal with a toddler who gets so frustrated when trying to do something that she often erupts in temper?*

A. Her frustration stems from the fact that her belief in her own ability to complete a task is ahead of the reality. In other words, she expects too much of herself and rages when she can't achieve it. Watch her closely when she is engaged in a task, and when you see that the boiling point is soon to be reached, stop her and calm her. Then let the child continue. Each time you see her frustration building up, stop her and calm her. This stop-start approach, with regular rests, will help her gain control over her feelings of frustration.

Q. *What can be done with a 21-month-old toddler who still likes to put everything into her mouth?*

A. Try to avoid confrontations with her over this. Toddlers can be very determined, and the more you try to stop her from mouthing objects the keener she will be to continue the practice. She will probably grow out of the habit very soon anyway, even if you do nothing at all. However, if you are bothered, you can try to distract her attention to another object every time you see that she's about to put the object she's holding into her mouth.

4

Child Development: Two-Three Years

"Children can become very determined at this age. Everything has to be done their way, and has to be done immediately. If it isn't, then they can fly into a rage. Yet at other times they can be so caring towards each other."

By now you'll have realised that children aged two or three years like to get their own way, and they don't give up easily! Flashpoint is quickly reached, and before you know it he's screaming furiously at you. This escalation in his temper is just one part of the changes that occur as he experiences new feelings, new abilities and new ideas.

Two-year-olds believe that the world should – and does – revolve around them. Parents should do as they are told, thinks the typical young child, and he doesn't like it at all when they lay down rules and regulations for him to follow. When they do set a limit that he mustn't breech, he goes haywire with rage. Tantrums are very typical (and very draining, both for adult and child). This phase of egocentricity and lack of co-operation will pass.

An infant becomes even more inquisitive than before, partly because he is physically able to reach places that he couldn't previously. He's ingenious enough to use a chair as a stepping stone to reach the crystal vase on the middle shelf, and he's dextrous enough to be able to pull a safety plug out of the electric wall socket. He's not being naughty when he does these things, just giving vent to his naturally inquiring mind.

There are also physical changes during this period. He puts on approximately five pounds (2.25 kg), and grows approximately four inches (10 cm) taller. Most, if not all, of his 20 'baby' teeth have broken through his gums and he munches away quite happily with them. He might even eat a more varied diet than before, although sometimes a child becomes a fussy eater between the ages of two and three years. Much depends on the individual child.

Testing Child Development at 30 Months

Child Skill: Takes great pleasure from looking at books.
What To Do: He likes you to read a story to him, either at bedtime or during the day, and he probably prefers stories that he's heard many times before. Familiarity is comforting.

Child Skill: Has increased co-ordination.
What To Do: He can stand on his tip-toes for a moment or two, which really is quite a difficult task for him, requiring good muscle strength and fine balance.

Child Skill: Completes complex manual activities.
What To Do: Provide him with a lacing card – the type with a picture on it and holes round the perimeter – and a strong, coloured lace to thread in and out the holes.

Child Skill: Uses words other than names to identify people.
What To Do: Listen for personal pronouns (eg "her", "him", "it", "me") beginning to appear in his speech. This is linked to his increased ability to understand symbolism.

Child Skill: Gives sensible answers to personal questions.
What To Do: Arrange so that a visitor to your house asks him his name (if you ask him, he may think you're silly because he realises you already know).

Child Skill: Knows that he is a different child from others.
What To Do: He can pick himself out from a group photo; he may also be able to point out other people that he knows well and to tell you their names.

Child Skill: Is more independent when dressing for outside.
What To Do: He shows an interest in putting his coat on when it's time to go outside. He still needs help, of course, but at least he makes an effort to manage on his own.

Child Skill: Grasps the connection between coins and money.
What To Do: When he sees you bring out a handful of small change, he may tell you that this is money. However, he won't yet be able to tell you names of the coins.

Child Skill: Draws more competently.
What To Do: Demonstrate how to draw a horizontal line from one side of the paper to the other, using a chunky pencil that he is able to grip easily. He can copy you, though not as neatly.

Child Skill: Doesn't want your help when using stairs.
What To Do: At this age, the child probably pushes your helping hand away when he's faced with a flight of stairs. Suggest that he holds on to the banisters or on to a fixed handrail.

Child Skill: Asks lots of questions.
What To Do: He has discovered a new way of expanding his knowledge; instead of touching and exploring, he can ask you a question. Answer his questions when you can.

Child Skill: Becomes more sociable.
What To Do: He likes to play alongside other children his own age but he doesn't actually play with them yet. Don't push him – he'll get more involved in time.

Testing Child Development at Three Years

Child Skill: Jumps more confidently.
What To Do: Show the child how you can jump off the ground with your legs and feet tight together on take off and landing. You may find that he can jump this way.

Child Skill: Uses more words and more complex sentences.
What To Do: Whereas before he generally used only nouns (eg "table", "bed") and verbs (eg "went", "eat"), he now starts to use adjectives as well (eg "big", "good").

Child Skill: Enjoys playing imaginatively.
What To Do: The child and his friends play a variety of games, but they particularly like pretending to be other people, such as their parents or a television character. Encourage these games.

Child Skill: Knows the difference between "big" and "small".
What To Do: When it is snack time, offer him two bits of fruit that are of different sizes. Suggest that he eats the small piece first, then the big one – he understands what you say.

Child Skill: Recognises several different colours.
What To Do: Pile blocks in front of the child (eg five red blocks and five blue blocks). Then hand him a blue block and ask him to find one the same in the pile.

Child Skill: Draws more neatly.
What To Do: His copying skills have improved and he should be able to draw a circle shape reasonably accurately (assuming there is a circle already drawn on the page for him to copy).

Child Skill: Is independent with most aspects of undressing.
What To Do: By now, the child is probably able to undress without

your help, with the exceptions of small buttons, fine zips, shoe laces and other difficult fastenings.

Child Skill: Cuts paper with scissors.
What To Do: Place a pair of child-scissors (which have round ends and bigger handles) in his hand and let him try to cut a sheet of paper. He might manage this successfully.

Child Skill: Needs no help when going upstairs.
What To Do: When you walk upstairs, you look ahead and keep your foot on the first step while moving your other foot to the next step, and so on. This is how the child now climbs stairs.

Child Skill: Plays with small jigsaws.
What To Do: You may be surprised to find that he plays happily with a child-sized jigsaw, as long as there are only a few pieces that make up the full picture.

Child Skill: Draws an image that represents a person.
What To Do: When drawing or painting a picture of someone he knows, his finished work is definitely recognisable as that of a human figure, with perhaps the head and limbs clearly showing.

Child Skill: Questions become more detailed.
What To Do: Three-year olds have an unquenchable thirst for asking questions. Some are straightforward (eg "What's that?") but others are not (eg "Why can't I?").

How to Enhance a Child's Progress from Two-Three Years

There is lots that can be done to help a child progress when he is this age. However, he is probably more volatile than before. He isn't so responsive to requests not to do this or that because he still wants to do things his way, and he is fully prepared to pit his strength of character against anyone when he is determined to break the rules. Don't give in to the child. He needs firm management, despite the fact he challenges it. So if you don't like what he is doing, and he has a tantrum when you stop him, follow your plan of action through anyway.

Now he's old enough to understand explanations underlying the standards you set. Give him very basic reasons that he can relate to. For instance, tell him "If you eat all the sweets, there will be none left for your friends and that will make them upset."

Most children like the company of others their own age. This is the early stage of co-operative play, as children begin to realise that there are terrific benefits from joining in activities along with others. He likes drawing and painting and takes pleasure from showing these off to everyone. To him, the painting might be a magnificent representation of a king's castle, while to you this image might seem totally unrecognisable - but he's delighted with his efforts.

He becomes very easily frustrated during play activities. The moment he can't, say, complete a jigsaw puzzle or colour in a picture the way he would like to, you will see his tears start to flow. Help him relax when you see this building up. Instead of angrily removing the cause of his frustration, suggest ways that he can solve the problem without losing his temper.

Q & A

Q. *Is it true that boys take longer to gain bowel and bladder control than girls?*

A. Statistics suggest that girls are fully toilet-trained at an earlier age than boys. This applies to night training as well. However, this is only an overall trend and doesn't mean that every girl acquires toilet control before every boy of the same age. A lot depends on the child's maturity, understanding and the method of toilet training used. Toilet-training – with a boy or girl – requires patience, understanding and plenty of reassurance for the child when "accidents" occur.

Q. *What should I do with a three-year-old who clearly knows what the rules are and yet who regularly breaks them?*

A. He's not the only child this age to behave like that. The typical three-year-old is smart enough to know what is expected in your home, but lacks the maturity to grasp that these rules apply to him as much as to any other child. He's not being naughty; he simply fails to see the connection between himself and your standards of expected behaviour. He'll change over the next year, but in the meantime, keep explaining the rules to him.

Q. *No matter how often I reprimand my child for misbehaving or for annoying his brother or sister, he keeps on doing it What am I doing wrong?*

A. Perhaps he misbehaves solely for the purpose of gaining attention from you. Perhaps he has learned that behaving badly is a more effective way of getting your attention than behaving well. If this is the case, then you could try ignoring minor misdemeanours wherever possible. In addition, make a big fuss of him when you notice that he has been behaving well for a while.

5

Child Development: Three-Five Years

'I have noticed that children often become much more sociable at this stage in their lives. They genuinely seem to want to play with each other, although fights still break out every so often."

During this period, a child's social development continues to progress. Other children become very important to her and she says she is lonely if she doesn't have a chance to play with others for a day or so. Although she still has some difficulty sharing her toys, doing exactly what her friends want her to do, waiting her turn to play in a game, and listening to others, she does make an effort to build up these essential social skills. Friends matter, although one day she'll be best friends with a particular child then the next day her friendship will be with someone completely different. The instability of friendships at this age is normal and is a sign of social immaturity – it is only later that friendships are more enduring.

The early pre-school educational skills emerge, often spontaneously without any specific instruction. For instance, she develops shape and colour recognition, she may be able to count up to two or three, and she may be able to recognise her own name when it's written down. The child begins to show a thirst for knowledge as her powers of thought extend rapidly. She still asks lots of questions and her concentration improves. She is interested in a much wider range of games, toys and other activities. The learning skills that the child acquires during this phase of her life can have a significant effect on how she copes with the first infant class.

Moral development gets underway too. Young children consider the seriousness of an action solely in terms of the direct practical effect that it has (for instance, a two-year-old may think that accidentally spilling a huge can of paint on the carpet is naughtier than deliberately splashing a dab of paint on it).

However, by the time she's four or five, that same child now realises that the intention behind the act is something she must also consider (for instance, she now thinks that deliberately putting a drop of paint on the carpet is naughtier than accidentally spilling a huge pot of paint). A child's attitude towards matters like this is heavily influenced by the attitudes of the adults around her and by the examples they set – and there is every likelihood that she will copy aspects of their behaviour. This process of identification helps shape her behaviour.

Much of her previous puppy fat disappears now; her tummy slims down, as do her arms and thighs. Muscles grow stronger, and bones grow harder. Her annual rate of growth in this phase is approximately three inches (7.5 cm) and approximately six pounds (2.7 kg). The second set of teeth are waiting to come through, and her jaw broadens in preparation for this. Neurological development, in terms of brain and spinal cord growth, decelerates; when she is seven years old, a child's brain will nearly be the full adult size. Her physical maturation continues throughout this period in her life.

Testing Child Development at Four Years

Child Skill: Makes good use of large outdoor toys.
What To Do: She thoroughly enjoys outings to her local park so that she can clamber enthusiastically all over the swings, see-saws, roundabouts and any other toys that let her use physical skills.

Child Skill: Makes more mature drawings of people.
What To Do: Study her paintings and drawings that contain people. You'll see that she puts in many more details, including the nose, ears, hands and fingers.

Child Skill: Likes a good laugh.
What To Do: Her humour advances. Sometimes she laughs just for the sake of it. She also enjoys making up silly names for her friends and "custard-pie", slapstick antics.

Child Skill: Plays more maturely with others.
What To Do: Co-operative play, with sharing, turn-taking and rules, becomes part of her life now. Her desire to play with others encourages her sociability.

Child Skill: Uses scissors more effectively.
What To Do: She can cut paper in a more controlled way. Give her a small sheet of paper to cut into two pieces; she'll manage this even though she doesn't halve the sheet perfectly.

Child Skill: Shows the first signs of counting.
What To Do: The child may be able to count accurately a row of, say, three or four toys cars. However, you will need to make sure she touches each car as she counts it.

Child Skill: Recalls personal information.
What To Do: It is worthwhile teaching a child this age her first and last name and her address (and even her phone number), although perhaps she can tell you this information already.

Child Skill: Makes more varied comparisons.
What To Do: She begins to understand the concept of "different", including fat/thin, high/low, on/off, in/out, up/down, tall/small, happy/sad, and so on.

Child Skill: Confidently names two or three primary colours.
What To Do: Instead of just matching two colours that are the same, she now tells you that an object is "yellow" or "red". It is a big jump forward in her understanding.

Child Skill: Her speech is more mature and sensible.
What To Do: She is able to use words to describe her ideas and feelings, if she is given enough time to express herself. Her vocabulary contains literally hundreds of different words.

Child Skill: Likes to help with basic chores.
What To Do: Involve her when you can, even though it isn't always convenient. She can help you set the table, or clear books away, or tidy up the paint corner.

Child Skill: She is relatively agile.
What To Do: She enjoys challenges involving co-ordination and balance, such as running fast then stopping, hopping, climbing, and she may even try skipping.

Testing Child Development at Five Years

Pre-School Skill: Is interested in singing and music.
What To Do: She likes singing along to tunes played on a tape recorder or on the television. And she might even be happy to give a musical performance in front of other children.

Pre-school Skill: Has mature drawing skills.
What To Do: Ask the child to paint a picture of a house. The finished sketch will include the outline of the house and some minor details such as the door, chimney and so on.

Pre-School Skill: Increasingly manages without adult help.
What To Do: She is fully independent with toileting during the day, and

is able to wash her hands afterwards. Sometimes you might need to prompt her a little.

Pre-School Skill: Knows her daily routine follows a sequence.
What To Do: The child knows that she goes to nursery in the morning, she has juice and biscuits in the middle of the afternoon, and so on, but she can't tell the time from a clock face yet.

Pre-School Skill: Cares about others who are more vulnerable.
What To Do: She now understands that she has a responsibility to think about other people; if she sees a younger child crying, she will try to cheer him up rather than just ignore him.

Pre-School Skill: Obeys a two-part command.
What To Do: Ask her to do something that involves one action after the other (eg "Please lift the doll from the floor and put it in the toy cupboard next door").

Pre-School Skill: Has better co-ordination, agility and stamina.
What To Do: The child can probably do any physical exercise that you can do (eg running, kicking, throwing, catching), although her performance obviously won't match yours.

Pre-School Skill: Has coin recognition.
What To Do: Although she isn't aware of the specific value of particular coins, she may be able to tell you the names of one or two of them when asked. This ability steadily improves.

Pre-School Skill: Leaves mum and dad without making a fuss.
What To Do: The child isn't tearful when she says goodbye to her parents when she is left with her baby-sitter or with other children at her best friend's party.

Pre-School Skill: Develops early writing skills.
What To Do: She can probably write the first letter of her name. The chances are that it won't be very neat at this stage, but it will be legible and recognisable.

Pre-School Skill: Prefers harder jigsaws.
What To Do: With your encouragement and guidance, she's prepared to make an effort to complete a puzzle of perhaps 15-20 large pieces. Remind her to take her time at this task.

Pre-School Skill: Mixes well with other children her age.

What To Do: Arguments with friends are less common when they play together. Increased social maturity means that they know how to get on with each other.

How to Enhance a Child's Progress from Three-Five Years

There is lots to do to help a child's progress when she is this age, but boosting her self-confidence is especially important. Her belief in herself is easily affected, and you may have to work hard in order to make her feel self-assured. One way to do this is by allowing her to make some decisions about what she does and doesn't do when she is with you. For instance, she can choose which biscuit to eat, what to make with her construction set, and so on. Allowing her this degree of individual responsibility – under adult supervision, of course – gives her a feeling of control and confidence.

As well as this, the child may start to compare herself with her friends and she may feel dissatisfied with herself as a result. Young children can be very self-critical. Reassure her when she complains that she is the slowest runner amongst her friends, or that she's the worst singer. Remind her of all her strong points, and emphasise that these are more important than the skills she is not so good at. Your reassurance will help her.

If it turns out that a child has problems mixing with other children, for instance because she seems to be in fights constantly, or even that because she appears to have no friends at all, take the matter seriously. Obviously, you shouldn't make fun of her or chastise her about this, but likewise you shouldn't ignore it as she probably needs your help in order to change. Consider her social behaviour. It may be that she still has difficulty sharing her toys, or with accepting that others can go ahead of her when she is in a queue. Then give her advice about changing. You might want to role-play social situations in order to teach her new ways of relating to others.

Finally, school is approaching very soon. And it will be helpful if she has a positive attitude towards this. She should be looking forward to it with excitement and enthusiasm. You can get her used to looking at books by reading to her, and by taking her to the local library to choose books for herself. These pre-reading activities whet her appetite for later learning experiences.

Q & A

Q. *If a child has a squint, is that a cause for concern?*

A. Certainly her parents should be aware of it. But there is probably nothing to worry about – in many instances, what appears to be a squint is simply a fold of skin at the side of the eye closest to the nose, giving the appearance of a squint. The treatment for squints varies, depending on the severity. Sometimes nothing need be done; however, the child's doctor may suggest the simple strategy of covering the good eye temporarily as this will encourage the muscles of the squinting eye to work more efficiently.

Q. *Should a child be able to read by the time she starts infant school?*

A. Many children have very basic reading skills by the age of five years, skills which they have acquired spontaneously without any teaching, while other children are not so advanced. Research findings suggest that certain pre-literacy skills are important during the pre-school years, eg knowing the names of individual letters, being able to recognise when two words have the same ending-sounds, knowing that books have to be read in a certain direction, and learning nursery rhymes. These can be incorporated informally into your daily routine.

Q. *Is it better for twins to attend separate classes at school?*

A. There may be no choice in the matter if the infant school only has one reception class. Assuming there is more than one class, then the parents have to consider the options seriously. Separation at school is usually only selected in instances where the twins appear to be too dependent on each other, to the point that their development is being stifled, or when the parents feel that one twin dominates the other. What matters isn't so much whether or not they attend separate classes, but whether or not adults and children treat them as separate individuals – that's a much more effective way of enhancing their development.

Q. *What is the best way to help a four-year-old girl who can't concentrate on anything for very long?*

A. First, make sure distractions are at a minimum when she focuses on a particular activity (eg switch the television off). Second, establish how long she is able to concentrate on a particular activity before turning to something else (eg two minutes), and then the next time encourage her to concentrate for an additional 15 seconds. Continue adding a few seconds each time until you find that her concentration has increased. You could also limit the number of toys she plays with, perhaps allowing her only one toy at a time.

6

Understanding Normal Behaviour

"There have been times when I've been worried about a child's behaviour, about whether or not there really is a problem with him. It's so hard to know if something he does is just a passing phase that every normal child goes through."

Like most people concerned about children, you probably worry about a child you know, sometimes about minor things and other times about more serious matters. For instance when your nephew cried every day because he couldn't bear to leave his parents on the threshold of his childminder's doorstep, and you were worried that he might never settle down. This may have dominated your thoughts until he calmed down and you realised it wasn't a problem after all. Another child's tantrums may have frightened you into thinking that he would never grow out of them – but, of course, he did. Or perhaps you worried about a child you know because he seemed very unpopular with other children his own age, and yet he began to make friends with them after a couple of weeks.

What's interesting – and reassuring – is that you're not alone in worrying like this. You would be hard pushed to find anyone professionally involved with children who hasn't worried about a young child at some stage in their life. Yet to you, other people's worries might seem silly! Problems about child development are often subjective, and what may be a monumental crisis about a child's progress as far as one person is concerned might be a routine event to another.

What Is "Normal"?

Here are some reasons why it is often very difficult to know when a child's behaviour is normal:

- **every child is different.** There are many milestones of development that everyone agrees with. For example, there is real cause for concern when a five-year-old still talks in single words and cannot combine two words together to make a phrase or short sentence; that's not normal. Similarly, worry is justified when a child has reached the age of 18 months and still can't sit up on his own without support. But pinning down a reliable description of normal behaviour during the pre-school years is much harder.

- **every family has different values.** Children are heavily influenced in their outlook by the values their parents and other adults hold. For instance, if a child's parents are very aggressive and firmly believe that using force (either verbal or physical) is the best way to achieve their target, then he will soon behave that way too when he is with his friends. Most professionals would agree that a child imitates the examples set by the adults in his world (particularly by his parents, but also by his carers).
- **every family has different standards.** Just as children vary in their characteristics and behaviour, so do families. There will be times when you are surprised to discover that a child you know is allowed to do something, say something or perhaps eat something that you would normally frown upon. Parents set their own rules about the way their children should behave. Two families living side by side with each other can have totally different rules and limits regarding the children's behaviour.
- **your ideas on normality are affected by your upbringing.** This doesn't mean, however, that you automatically think children should be brought up the way you were brought up. On the contrary, if you had a thoroughly miserable childhood which was tainted by aggression and lack of love, then you will probably be determined that the way you relate to children should not be like this. But if you recall your childhood as a time of warmth, love and happiness, you'll probably try to create the same atmosphere in your own house.

Ask Yourself.......

Why do I think children should be brought up this way, and not another way?
Aside from the influence of your own childhood, and your own experiences as a parent, you may also be influenced through discussions with others, or through something you have read, or by watching a television programme, or even by an anecdote that someone told you. You'll have a better understanding of yourself when you have clearer ideas about the sources of your beliefs.

What are my goals for children?
For you, having good manners might be important and so you'll start to encourage the children to behave politely whenever they are with you. Or perhaps you regard having lots of friends as the top priority for children. The goals that you set for children will affect the way you relate to them, and the experiences you provide for them – and this influences their behaviour and attitudes.

How do I expect them to achieve these goals?
You may consider pre-literacy skills to be extremely important, in which case you'll think it is normal for children to work at pre-reading and pre-writing activities. Or perhaps you think the top priority is for children to be independent as soon as possible. In that case, you'll think it is normal to start potty-training very early and think it reasonable to expect toddlers to be fully dry by the time they are barely 18 months old.

How flexible am I prepared to be?
Without a doubt, you need to have clear and structured ideas about the way children should be managed, otherwise confusion will reign! Yet there are times when flexibility is appropriate, because aside from a few obvious rules (eg giving care and attention to every child, never using physical or verbal violence against them, and so on) there's no one "right" or "wrong" way to manage young children.

How easily swayed am I?
Have confidence in your own child-care skills. Just because your friend disagrees with you, say, about when a four-year-old should be expected to tidy away toys without help, you don't have to follow her point of view. Listen to other people's views on matters concerning child development if you have the opportunity, but don't change your standards without justification.

Bear in mind that there are very few behavioural or emotional problems in childhood that require specialist professional help. Despite your worst fears, there is a high probability that the cause of your anxiety is only a temporary passing phase and that it can be resolved. Every child:

- has good days and bad days.
- is naughty at times.
- needs to be loved by the adults in his world.
- has the capacity to love other people.
- experiences times when things go wrong.
- becomes frightened when rejected by his friends.
- can behave in a babyish manner under pressure.

When Things Go Wrong

There are lots of reasons why a child begins to behave in a way that is worrying. And psychologists offer different explanations, depending on their theoretical standpoint.

Those who take **a psychoanalytic view** (based on the ideas espoused by Freud) will tell you that the reason a child misbehaves is because he has a hidden, deep-seated emotion which drives his actions. For instance, a child who is annoyed with his friend may start to become irritable with other children, even if they are totally innocent. The reason for this, says the psychoanalyst, is that although the child has repressed into the unconscious his feelings of anger towards his friends, they break through, forcing him to behave aggressively towards his peers. The only way to change this sort of behaviour is to look at the child's deeper, hidden feelings, through sensitive discussion with him.

This view contrasts with the **behaviourist explanation** of a child's disturbed behaviour, which claims that a child behaves in a particular way because he learns to behave that way. In other words, he sees others doing this, copies them, and then realises that the consequences of behaving this way are quite good. For instance, he might constantly misbehave because he discovers this is a wonderful way to get attention from you. The behaviourist perspective suggests that if you want to change a child's behaviour, first you have to identify what benefits the misbehaviour brings him, and second, how you could behave differently towards him so that he in turn will behave differently.

The **humanistic perspective** takes the view that a child develops all the time, and constantly changes and grows day by day. He needs to feel valued by others, he needs to feel accepted by them, and he needs to feel trusted by them. This leads to the explanation that a child's behaviour is heavily affected by the way these emotional needs are met. Things go wrong when he doesn't feel loved, or when he feels under-valued, or even when he feels he is forced to behave in a way that feels uncomfortable. He reacts against these pressures by misbehaving. The situation will only change when his relationships with others change.

The **situationist explanation** of a child's difficult and disruptive behaviour is that he simply reacts to what happens around him at that time. For instance, he becomes aggressive when playing with aggressive children because that becomes the standard of behaviour expected of him. And he commits an act of minor theft (eg taking a sweet without permission when he has been told not to) if he is placed in a situation where the temptation is too great for him to resist. According to this perspective, you will have to look at the child's specific difficult behaviour – and the specific circumstances in which it occurs – in order to understand him fully.

The real explanation probably involves all of these theories, and more. Sometimes a child is difficult because he has an unconscious anxiety, sometimes because he gets more satisfaction from misbehaving than from behaving, sometimes because he feels under-valued, and sometimes because he reacts against his immediate surroundings. These theories have some points in common:

- **the responsibility for changing a child's behaviour rests with the adults in his world, not with the child.** He needs adult help;

he's unlikely to be able to change on his own.

- **change may be difficult to achieve.** Encouraging him to be less shy, for instance, isn't a simple task, despite the fact everyone thinks that would be a great idea.
- **there's always more than one way to help a child improve.** Try one strategy, then try something else if that doesn't work, and keep trying until you succeed.

Normal or Abnormal?

Make a list of every type of child behaviour that would seriously worry you. Take a few minutes to do this. Your list might include such characteristics as:

- shyness when in the company of others
- aggressiveness with his peers
- wetting himself when he is expected to be dry
- crying loudly whenever a cat approaches
- refusing to go anywhere unless he holds his cuddly toy
- waking up during the night with bad dreams
- sleeplessness even though he leads a busy life
- loss of appetite
- jealousy whenever his sister gets a new jumper
- a quick temper that is easily triggered

All of these are indeed troubling. But there's hardly a child that doesn't show some of these characteristics at some stage. In other words, every piece of disturbed behaviour is found in normal children as well (though not to the same extent, of course). That's one reason why you need to look further than the child's behaviour to determine whether or not it is abnormal – you need to look at all aspects of his life before you can reach such a decision.

Another reason why it is difficult to say whether or not behaviour is disturbed is that there may be a normal reason for a child to behave abnormally. Sounds confusing, but it often happens. For example, suppose you are told that a five-year-old regularly snatches food from the plates of other children during lunch at school. Compared to his peers that age, this type of behaviour is abnormal. Yet when you also are told that he is sent to school every day without having had any breakfast at all, then you will probably regard his behaviour as normal, given the background circumstances. That's why it is important for you to look at a child's actions in the broader context of his family and social background instead of considering behaviour in isolation, otherwise you will gain only a very narrow picture of his life.

Upsets Pass

Psychological research confirms that only a small percentage of children have problems that require professional help. Emotional and behavioural difficulties are much less frequent than is commonly supposed, and often the solution lies in the hands of the adults close to the child. Let's look at the following example:

The Problem: Three-year-old Ed wouldn't talk to any of the other children in his nursery. Every day, without fail, he would sit on his own as soon as his mother left him there. While shyness isn't unusual at the start, in most instances it fades within a few days once the shy child gets to know the other children. But with Ed, however, the shyness became worse; he resisted all efforts to draw him into conversation or into playing with the other pre-schoolers.

The Facts: Ed's parents are very shy, and he is an only child. Both his mum and dad have desk jobs, which means they don't have to speak to people for most of the working day, and this suits them very nicely. They have a very small circle of friends, preferring to sit at home than to go out socialising. When Ed was born, his mum and dad weren't very good at talking to other parents in the maternity hospital, and so they don't know other people who have children their son's age. This meant that the boy didn't have much opportunity to learn how to be sociable.

The Analysis: Given the way Ed has been brought up by his mum and dad before starting at nursery, his behaviour can reasonably be regarded as normal. It is less likely that his shyness is an innate personality characteristic which is resistant to change and more likely that it is due to the personalities of his mum and dad. There is plenty that could be done to help Ed become less shy.

The Solution: Ed needs some advice and support, otherwise his shyness will become even more entrenched. He has three hurdles to overcome. First, he literally does not know what to say to other children when he is with them. Second, he lacks self-confidence. Third, his parents expect him to be shy and accept this behaviour as normal. If Ed is to develop a more outgoing personality, he must be shown simple social skills (such as saying "How are you?"). He also requires reassurance that he will be safe talking to people, and he should be encouraged to make eye contact when playing.

Understanding Normality

Here are some dimensions for assessing whether or not a child's behaviour is normal. However, you won't get hard-and-fast answers, just ideas to explore further.

- **Variety.** Genuinely disturbed behaviour usually appears in a cluster, eg there's nothing serious about a child disagreeing with his friend, but it is serious when he also sleeps badly, soils himself and fights a lot with others.
- **Age.** Behaviour that is suitable for a child at one age is usually not suitable when he is older, eg you won't be bothered when a two-year-old wets himself during the day, but you will be worried if he does this when he is five.
- **Trigger.** You may be able to relate the child's troubled behaviour to something specific, eg the prospect of starting school may be sufficient to cause him to wet himself, even though he has been dry for many months or even years.
- **Persistence.** Most emotional or behavioural difficulties in childhood have a short-lifespan, eg refusal to eat food at mealtimes is common in pre-school children but it becomes more worrying if this lasts for several days.
- **Time.** The frequency of a child's behaviour matters, and it may not be as often as you think, eg don't worry if he cries every few days, but you are right to be concerned if he cries several times every day no matter what goes on around him.
- **Severity.** Sometimes a child's behaviour is mild while at other times it can be extreme, eg there's nothing wrong in his wanting to hold your hand, but it is worrying if he insists on holding your hand whatever he does.
- **Self-perspective.** The child may not see that his behaviour is unacceptable, eg his behaviour, such as lying or stealing, is much more worrying for you if he thinks he has done nothing wrong and if he fails to understand why you are so concerned.
- **Effect.** You can judge the normality of his behaviour by its impact on his life, eg dislike of dirt is normal, but it isn't normal for a child to hate dirt so much that he washes his hands several times a day.
- **Surprise.** Sudden change in behaviour can be very concerning, eg a withdrawn child is expected to be quiet in company, whereas an ebullient child who unpredictably becomes very withdrawn may have an emotional difficulty.
- **Resistance.** Normal behaviour is less resistant to change than abnormal behaviour, eg you should be more concerned about a child's aggression if you have made a lot of effort to change him and found his aggression to be quite resistant.

Q & A

Q. *Is it normal for a two-year-old to want his mum with him all the time?*
A. All young children are insecure, depending on the circumstances.

Even when a child seems quite confident and independent, this may change if, for example, he sees a total stranger – in that situation, he'll turn to his parents for support. So clinging to mum or dad is perfectly normal in a child aged two years. You'll find that his need to be with them all the time diminishes as he grows older and more self-confident; but in the meantime, his clinging behaviour is typical for this age.

Q. *Why is it that other children always seem so well-behaved, compared to my own four-year-old?*
A. Isn't it amazing how other people's children seem to behave much better than yours? Most parents feel like this at one time or another, largely because they only see other children who are on their best behaviour. It is very easy to focus on only one aspect of a child's behaviour (ie when he annoys you) and to forget that he's not like this all the time. But when you think about it, you'll soon realise that there are lots of times he behaves very well.

Q. *Is it true that behaviour is inherited?*
A. Of course there are similarities in behaviour between parents and their child. You have probably seen plenty of examples of this. Although that could mean some aspects of personality are inherited, a more likely explanation is that as a child becomes closely attached to mum and dad, he begins to "model" some of their personal characteristics. Through this process he gradually absorbs their attitudes and behaviour. So the fact that a child behaves like his parents is more to do with "modelling" than with any inherited behaviour.

Q. *Is it normal for a three-year-old boy to enjoy playing with dolls?*
A. There is absolutely no reason why a boy shouldn't play with so-called "girls' toys" and vice-versa. It's simply a matter of tradition, more than anything else. Bear in mind that only Western cultures tend to suppress the nurturing side of the male character. So don't make a fuss about this; let him play with dolls. If you deny him access – and perhaps even tell him it's wrong – then you'll create a problem where one did not exist before.

Section 2: Personal Development

This section examines personal development during childhood, focusing on specific topics that are important for all children. Chapter 7 concentrates on the vexing problem of the child who won't eat, and looks at methods to resolve this difficulty, whereas Chapter 8 considers sleep problems through the preschool years. Every child experiences potty training at some point, but it does not always go according to plan; Chapter 9 takes you through potty training step by step, offering solutions to common difficulties. And the issue of independence is discussed fully in Chapter 10.

7

Fussy Eaters

"My friend's child has never been a good eater. At the age of four months, she was so slow at feeding that one feed seemed to run on to the next. Even now, she's three years old and still takes ages to finish her lunch no matter how little is put on her plate."

Babies are rarely fussy eaters – the typical young infant gulps down her milk as though she is afraid someone else is going come along and steal it from her before she has finished! The first hint that a baby might be a fussy eater usually only begins at the weaning stage, when solids are initially introduced into her diet (medical opinion holds this should be between the ages of three and four months).

The best chance of avoiding fussy eating habits at this early stage is to give new foods in small amounts, one at a time. This strategy gives the baby a chance to adapt slowly to the changes in her food intake. She needs to adjust to the broader range of textures and tastes. Give her a drink of milk first, followed by mashed or liquidised solid food. Fortunately, she will probably adapt very quickly, although she will still enjoy the taste of milk to accompany solids (and milk remains her main source of nourishment until she is at least one year old).

Once She Is a Toddler

No matter how good an eater she has been during the first year, no matter how easily she moved from liquids to solids, her eating habits may change in the next couple of years.

It's in the toddler stage that things often become more difficult. For instance, you may be infuriated when you put a plate of food in front of a young child, only to find that she pushes it away untouched or that she spends the next ten minutes rearranging the contents of the plate without actually bringing it near her mouth.

Past the age of twelve months – and perhaps even before that – she exercises choice over what she eats, whether you like it or not. And this fussiness can persist throughout the remaining pre-school years. In fact, the most difficult age for picky eating habits is around three or four years; that seems to apply to the majority of children, though this doesn't mean the children you know will follow the same pattern.

A Proper Diet

You want a child to eat a balanced diet, one that provides her with all the essential nutrients, and you become concerned when her appetite drops or when you think she isn't eating enough of the "right" sort of food. That's why it is important for you to know the main types of food substances.

Meat, fish, eggs and dairy produce are good sources of **protein**, which is essential for satisfactory growth of a child's body tissue. Protein is also found in cereals, nuts, pulses and root vegetables. **Carbohydrates** (eg sugar, starch and cellulose) give her energy. However, if she eats too many sugary foods such as cakes, sweets, biscuits, and chocolate, or too many starchy foods such as bread, potatoes and rice, she may put on too much weight. The human body converts excessive carbohydrates into flabbiness, rather like storing fuel for later. (Too many sweets and fizzy drinks will also fill a child's stomach and prevent her from eating healthier foods.) The same applies when she eats too much **animal and vegetable fat**, which also gives her energy. These substances are present in meat, fish oil and some vegetables, butter, lard, margarine, crisps and fried foods.

In recent years, greater attention has been given to **fibre** because it aids digestion, keeps bowel movements regular, and has been linked to a reduction in cholesterol. A child gets fibre from fruit, vegetables, wholemeal bread, nuts and oats. Although **vitamins** are absolutely essential for her satisfactory physical development, her body has no way of producing these naturally. So it is vital that you ensure she eats food containing these, such as fish, cheese, eggs, butter, chicken, fresh vegetables, citrus fruits, liver, nuts, pulses and whole grain cereals. A child gets **calcium**, which strengthens her bones and teeth, from dairy products and green vegetables; and she gets **iron,** which builds her red blood cells, from red meat, eggs, bread, cereals, and green vegetables.

Salt occurs naturally in many foods so you don't have to worry about that, although you should be aware of how much salt a child puts on her food. Many adults pour an excessive amount of salt on their food before they even taste it, and you may find that children pick up this habit very quickly. If she develops a taste for very salty food at this age, it may have a long-term detrimental effect on her health – too much salt has been linked to heart disease during adulthood. If possible, prepare food with very little salt, and keep the salt cellar off the table and out of sight during the meal.

You probably have your own collection of child-centred menus. In addition, your local health centre will have lots of leaflets about the typical food intake that's suitable for a young child and these will also contain sample menus. Have a look at them, and speak to the practice nurse if you want further information or discussion. You should also listen to ideas from other people. Far better to have a range of menus to serve a child, than to plod away serving the same meal time after time.

Allergies & Additives

There is evidence that some food additives (the E numbers that are listed in the contents label) are linked to hyperactivity in childhood, though this is not definite in every case. However if you are concerned that a child's behaviour may be adversely affected by a particular additive - or that she may be allergic to a particular food product – then try leaving this item out of her meals for a couple of weeks (though don't alert her that you are doing this). Note whether or not any change has occurred during this time. Then re-introduce the food substance back into her diet and note any changes in her behaviour.

Some professionals are convinced of the link between food additives and a child's behaviour, while others find that an additive-free diet has no impact whatsoever. You may want to try for yourself anyway. Get advice from a health visitor or doctor before you start, in order to ensure that the child still receives a balanced food intake.

Natural Tendencies

One of the surprising findings from psychological research is that worry about a child's food intake is often unnecessary. In a classic research project, lasting several weeks and involving hundreds of young children and tens of thousands of meals, the young eaters were allowed to eat whatever they wanted, whenever they wanted. The only restriction on their choice was that sweets, crisps and other high fat-content foods were not on the menu. Other than that, a child could spend weeks only eating cheese if she wanted, or only eating eggs. Nobody told her what to take, or made any suggestions at all. Members of the research team and the children's parents recorded everything that was consumed during the experimental period.

You might reasonably expect that the results were disastrous, that the children's diets were chaotic and unbalanced, that they ate lots of one food and nothing of the others. But that didn't happen. In fact, the opposite occurred. Most children ventured a taste of every single food that was on offer; rarely did a child eat too much of anything. And there were no complaints of loss of appetite or sore tummies during this time. Perhaps the most surprising result of all was that qualified dieticians involved in the project agreed at the end that the food eaten by the children represented a balanced diet.

It seems as though a child instinctively knows what to eat and what not to eat. Of course, that doesn't stop her from wanting to guzzle sweets, crisps and fizzy drinks, but hopefully you feel reassured that her innate tendencies push her towards sensible eating practices. To ease any worries you may have about a child's food intake, make a record of everything she eats over, say, a fortnight. Divide the food into substance categories (eg protein, calcium, vitamins, etc.) and see what pattern emerges. You may discover her diet is more balanced than you originally thought.

Remember, however, that every child is different and that the amount of food necessary depends on her individual body size, height, age, daily routine and metabolism. And there will be times during childhood when she has a temporary surge in growth, resulting in a temporary increase in her appetite. So it's wise not to expect a child's food intake to be static and predictable; it will change from time to time.

Mealtimes

Meals are easily spoilt by a fussy eater, and tempers can fly when the response to the meal is "I don't want anything" or "I'm not hungry" especially if you know that this same child (who is pleading lack of appetite) would happily munch away at a plate of chocolate bars right now.

When parents have a child who repeatedly behaves like this, the parents may be tempted into abandoning family meals altogether. After all, serving the fussy eater on her own either before or after everyone else in the family, can reduce tension and make mealtime more enjoyable for all the others. But this is not an effective long-term strategy. Here are some reasons why parents should do their best to keep the routine of family meals, if possible:

- **communication.** Modern family life with young children is hectic, with lots of rushing around. Both parents probably work at some stage each day, and the children too have their own very busy schedules. This doesn't leave much time for everyone to talk to each other. It's worrying how little amount of time everyone in a family spends together, talking to one another. A family meal – whether it's one course or four courses – is a great chance for them all to speak to each other and to share their ideas and feelings.
- **attention-seeking.** One of the reasons why a child is so fussy about her food can be that she realises this is a good way to get attention from the adults around her. Perhaps if she sits quietly during mealtime, all the others get an opportunity to say what they want to say but she can't get a word in because she's the youngest. Perhaps she's also discovered that slopping her food all over the plate without actually putting any of it to her lips gives her centre-stage position. Separating her from the others simply feeds her desire for attention.

- **normalises.** There is no doubt that everyone wants a fussy eater to change her habits, and that faddiness during mealtime is disliked by everyone. However, if that child is then isolated and given her own meal separately, all that will do is 'normalise' her faddy behaviour instead of trying to alter it. In other words, her eating habits will become established as an agreed part of her daily routine, and the longer it goes on, the more her eating habits will be resistant to any attempts to change.
- **example.** One of the factors that will influence a change in a fussy eater's attitude to food will be the example set to her by others. Although she isn't imitating any adult pattern of behaviour at mealtimes at the moment, or the behaviour of her siblings, she may do so eventually. Serving her food when the family meal is over means that she has nobody on whom she can model her eating habits to make them more positive. This reduces the likelihood of any modification in her behaviour regarding food.
- **regularity.** Routine is very important with all children, and routine with a faddy eater is particularly important. Knowing that she has to sit with the others reinforces the regularity of mealtimes and emphasises that it is an integral part of family life, something that she has to participate in. It also provides a focal point for her food intake, and helps regulate the amount of between-meal snacks; for instance, you can tell her "You can't eat crisps now, because we are going to have lunch very soon."

Changing Her Eating Habits

Although concern about children's eating habits is common, very often change can be effected reasonably quickly if the situation is looked at objectively. Let's consider the following example:

The Problem: Azra is three years old and drives her parents to distraction with her eating habits. On most days, no matter what is served to her – even though it may be something she ate comfortably on a previous occasion – Azra picks up the fork and spends the next ten minutes rearranging the order of the food on the plate. Eventually her parents' frustration at her poor appetite spills over and they have a blazing argument with her. Later, when everyone has calmed down, her mum and dad cuddle her, sit beside her stroking her hair, and spend the next ten or twenty minutes persuading her to eat (which she does eventually).

The Facts: Aside from Azra's mum and dad, there are two older children in the family, aged five and eight. Azra attends nursery during the day, as her parents have full-time jobs. Her siblings attend an after-school club once they finish school in the afternoon. Dad collects Azra

and her siblings around 5:30pm, and when they get home 15 minutes later, they have a quick wash then sit down right away for dinner. At least three times a week, one of the older children, or one of Azra's parents, has an evening activity which forces the meal to gallop along at a hectic pace. It's not difficult, therefore, to understand why her parents' temper is ignited when they see her playing around with her food.
The Analysis: Azra has good fun at nursery, where she takes part in a busy and stimulating day. Her excitement in anticipation of seeing mum and dad builds up. And the girl is also delighted when she sees her older siblings after school. But she is frustrated because everything's so rushed after that. She barely has time to sit down at the dinner table before a huge plate of steaming food is plonked down in front of her. She's not relaxed and is desperate to tell mum and dad what happened that day. But nobody bothers with her. So Azra loses her appetite and unintentionally slops her food all over the plate.
The Solution: There are two factors contributing to Azra's fussy eating habits. First, she is too rushed. She needs more time to "come to" after being collected from nursery and being brought home. Second, she needs attention from her parents during the meal. She wants them to talk to her, to ask her what she has done that day, rather than to listen to everyone else before her. The implementation of these two simple strategies would have a major impact on the girl's eating behaviour.

Action Plan to Improve a Child's Eating Habits

1. **Have realistic expectations.** Children like food that is plain and basic, without spices or exotic sauces. There's no point in spending hours preparing a meal for a child – that's simply a waste of time. Of course, you would like things to be different, but you need to accept that her appetite is limited. Don't expect too much from her. And of course, try to ensure that she is hungry (by avoiding too many between-meal snacks) and that she is not too tired or too excited to eat.
2. **Make the meal attractive.** She won't eat anything that is too greasy, too spicy, too hot or if she finds the texture of the food uncomfortable to swallow. A child vomits more easily than an adult, and so it doesn't take much for her to start gagging when eating. How does the meal look from her perspective? Remember that she's a child with an unsophisticated palate. Her appetite is easily destroyed by a plate of food which is visually unattractive.
3. **Don't overload her plate.** A fussy eater will become even more picky if her plate contains an amount of food which she regards as too much. She'll feel pressurised and anxious, two emotions which depress her appetite very quickly. Mealtimes will be more successful if she is given smaller portions (and told that she will be given less than

everyone else) and if these small portions are placed on a large plate (which gives the impression the amount of food is small).

4. **Ensure she is comfortable.** Posture, seating arrangements and cutlery all have a direct impact on any eating experience. For instance, a two-year-old is hardly likely to scoff the lot from her plate if she can't even hold the cutlery steady, or if she is sitting so low down that she has to stretch all her stomach muscles to reach the plate, or if she has to twist and turn constantly in order to maintain a proper seating position. She needs to feel comfortable at the table or she won't eat.
5. **Give her choice.** A child will be interested in eating when she thinks she has been allowed some choice in what she eats. It's worthwhile, therefore, to let her pick from a limited range of meal options. This strategy isn't guaranteed to work every time, but it can be successful. A young child loves having control in her life. Give her two or three choices if possible, and remind her before the meal is served that she picked it herself.
6. **Try to relax at mealtimes.** Tension is infectious. All it takes is for one person to be upset at the dinner table and before you know it, everyone has lost their appetite. And the more the adults get annoyed because a child doesn't eat properly, then the worse the situation becomes. So everyone should try to relax before they sit down for dinner. Even if they feel terrible and tense, they should make an effort not to let these feelings show right now.
7. **Avoid threats.** There are few adults who can honestly say that they have never threatened a child with some ghastly punishment, as a result of her poor eating behaviour. But threats rarely work, for two reasons. First, they simply escalate matters into a head-to-head confrontation, a battle of wills; this is a no-win scenario since nobody can force a child to eat no matter how hard they try. Second, threats increase tension which in turn reduces appetite.
8. **Don't use food rewards.** By all means, tell a child that if she behaves well at mealtime tonight she'll be rewarded with an extra ten minutes of television before bedtime or extra time to play. There's no harm at all in offering her an added incentive like one of these. But don't use food (eg sweets after the meal) as the added incentive, since that focuses her attention away from the food in front of her, and may make it even less attractive.
9. **Set a good example yourself.** When eating with a child, she will watch you and everyone else. If she sees you have left some broccoli on your plate, then that provides her with justification to do the same. Of course, you can argue that you have already eaten a huge amount and that she hasn't touched hers yet, but that won't persuade her. So reflect on your own eating habits; maybe part of her behaviour at the table is an imitation of some of your actions.

10. **If possible, involve her in the preparation.** A four-year-old child can't cook a full meal, but she can help prepare it. For instance, she can pour milk into the mixture. She can also pass you items which you need to use during cooking, and she can help set out the cutlery and dishes on the table. Her help won't make mealtime preparation any faster. However, she will have a bigger interest in eating what is served if she helped make it.

Q & A

Q. *The problem with healthy eating is that there never seems to be enough time to prepare anything. How can I get round this?*

A. There are plenty of healthy snacks which are ready-made and available from shops, but these do tend to be expensive, particularly if the child has friends over to the house to play. You could try to have a stack of ready-peeled vegetables, such as carrot sticks or pieces of celery, kept in the fridge in a sealed container – that will keep them fresh and crispy for a few days at least. As well as that, have fresh fruit available, which the child can peel or wash herself. However, beware of pre-prepared health-foods that contain a lot of sugar; check the contents section of the wrapper very carefully.

Q. *How can I stop a two-year-old from being annoying during mealtimes - she makes a mess of her food and watches to see how I'll react?*

A. The best strategy is to ignore her, if you can. She has obviously learned that messing her food on the plate is a good way of getting your attention. So avoid over-reacting. In addition to ignoring her when she plays with her meal, you could try to distract her from that particular habit, perhaps by talking to her about something you know she is interested in or showing her an interesting toy – this way you will be giving her attention not just when she misbehaves at the table. And remember to give her lots of praise when she doesn't mess up her food.

Q. *I tend to be overweight and therefore diet a lot. I also talk about dieting a lot. Could this affect my four-year-old child?*

A. Yes, it could. While you may fully understand the pros and cons of dieting, she will not. She may simply copy you and your eating habits. So be careful how you present your own food management to her. Although the media tends to make a strong link between constant dieting and a satisfactory body shape, don't reinforce that with your own behaviour. Far better to encourage your child to eat a balanced diet, taking lots of exercise – and set a good example yourself.

Q. *What is the best way to get a defiant child to eat green vegetables? She hates all of them.*

A. This is always difficult and there is no foolproof plan. However, you have to help her develop a taste for them. The next time you make her a meal, take a small amount of the vegetables, mash them up and mix them through the main course. But don't tell her they are there. Then gradually build up the amount of vegetables over a period of weeks. When she has developed a taste for them, you can start to serve a very small amount separately on her plate. Some parents play pretend games with their child to encourage her to eat food (eg the train going into the tunnel), but she may soon insist that she'll only eat if you play this game with her.

8

Sleep Difficulties

'When he was about three, we had terrible difficulties getting him to go to bed at night. He wanted to stay up with us or with his older siblings the whole time no matter how tired he was. It was really hard work."

All babies cry. That's their main means of communication. After all, a baby can't use words to tell you that he is hungry, or that he is fed up, or that he would like you to change his nappy. But his piercing cry certainly ensures that you give him your full attention. Crying, therefore, is normal and is a sign of healthy development in a young baby. You would be worried if he remained silent all the time and didn't utter a sound because that could mean he had a serious problem. However, a crying baby who resists sleep at all costs can be draining. Looking after a baby like this can take up all your energy.

Facts About a Baby's Crying

Studies of infant crying have found that babies cry most frequently when they are six or seven weeks old, and that the peak period for crying is in the first three months of life.

Most babies do the bulk of their daily quota of crying (almost 40% of it) during the hours of the early evening, just when the family are trying to settle down and relax after a hard day; this can make the atmosphere at home very strained Other facts about crying to emerge from research include:

- almost 25% of babies cry persistently without any obvious reason for their tears, despite being comforted.
- during the first three months, a baby cries about two hours in total every day (though not all at once).
- between the ages of four and 12 months, his crying falls to about one hour each day or less.
- by six months, his crying is spread more evenly throughout the entire day, without that early evening peak.
- boys cry as much as girls when they are babies, and it doesn't matter whether they are only children or not.
- approximately 75% of babies only cry for 30 minutes at most before stopping.

Be reassured, however. If you are caring for a baby who cries a lot in the early months and who doesn't like to sleep, he will grow out of it eventually. This phase will soon be over. Once the three-month peak passes, there is a gradual decline in the amount of crying, both during the day and at night. For instance, only 7% of one-year-olds cry for more than three hours a day, compared to 25% of babies aged three months.

Soothing a Crying Baby

Here is a list of practical tips to lull a crying baby to sleep, though you've probably got your own favourite techniques that you found worked with your own children or your friend's children. They don't all work with every baby – it's a matter of trial and error. Keep trying until you find the ones that are right for the baby you look after:

- **move him.** Try rocking him gently, driving with him securely restrained in the car, or changing his position.
- **give physical contact.** Try cuddling him, carrying him, massaging him gently, or swaddling him in a blanket.
- **feed him.** Try giving an extra feed, giving a bottle of water, or changing his milk.
- **give background stimulation.** Try a steady noise (eg a vacuum cleaner), singing, or playing quietly with him.
- **give him a pacifier.** Try giving him a dummy, offering him a comforter, or putting him in a warm bath.
- **react to him.** Try distracting his attention, reassuring him, or just holding him calmly.

When He Won't Stop Crying

Despite all your best efforts, the baby might be one of those infants who seems to cry all day, every day, without sleeping. These never-ending wails can be enough to break the patience of the most determined parent and carer.

The most frequent reason given for persistent baby crying – especially for regular evening crying in babies around the age of three months – is "colic", even though there is no universally agreed definition of this condition. The term "colic" derives from the Greek word *kolokos*, meaning "to do with the colon", suggesting it is a gastric problem. Doctors use the term to describe a pain in the stomach that is assumed to be caused by a spasm in the tummy muscles. However, some crying at this age has nothing at all to do with pain (eg when it is due to boredom, or to a soiled nappy), and some crying is due to pain in other areas of the body (eg when the baby is uncomfortable due to teething, or has an ear infection).

In addition, the existence of colic is difficult – indeed, impossible – to verify. You know the scene in which a baby cries constantly and cannot be comforted. Then, when patted on the back, he eventually releases an enormous belch. "That's what has been making him cry," someone will say confidently to you. "Wind" is the explanation offered.

Yet continuous crying forces a baby to gulp down vast quantities of air quite quickly, without giving him a chance to release any of it gradually. So it is just as likely that the baby's loud expulsion of wind is the result of his crying, not the cause of it!

Even so, many childcare professionals maintain colic does exist, although nobody knows why some babies are affected by it and yet others are not, nor why the peak period of colicky crying is in the early evening, nor why it only occurs in the first few months of life. And there is no magic cure for the condition. You should try the list of practical tips given earlier. A baby who cries persistently and refuses to sleep – whether or not he has colic – could be one of the most difficult problems facing you as a parent. In many instances, it's as though the phase of evening crying has to run its natural course despite all your efforts to sort it out. Remember that his crying is not your fault, nor is it his. Resist any temptation to blame yourself for what's going on.

Children Often Have Disturbed Sleep

Parents also need techniques for encouraging their young child to have a nap during the day – it's not just young babies who can have sleep problems. Statistics reveal that at least 15% of children aged 18 months or older still wake up suddenly in the middle of a nap. So be reassured that he's not the only one to fight sleep. The chances are that his sleeping habits will improve over the next few years. Here are other points about children's sleeping patterns:

- babies who are breast-fed tend to wake up during the night more frequently than bottle-fed babies.
- first-born children are more prone to sleeping difficulties, compared to second born and youngest children.
- a child is more likely to wake up unexpectedly from a nap if he sleeps in a room with other children.
- an infant who transfers to solids later than normal is more likely to wake up during the night.
- girls are just as likely as boys to cause problems with their poor sleeping patterns.
- children who have had difficulties at birth are more prone to sleep problems during the pre-school years.
- a child is more likely to be an unsettled sleeper if his mother was depressed after his birth.

- there is a link between frequent, severe tantrums during the day and difficulties with sleeping.
- in many instances a child who is a poor sleeper also has other behavioural difficulties (eg lack of co-operation).

Action Plan to Help a Child Have Untroubled Sleep

1. **Make sure that he isn't upset.** No child will be able to sleep if he is tense and anxious. When he's troubled by something – no matter how trivial it seems to you – the worry will keep him awake. Try to discover what concerns him, then relax him and reassure him that a solution to his predicament can be found.
2. **Make sure that he's well fed.** A good sleep in childhood can be closely associated with food. If a young child is hungry, then the sensations in his tummy will keep him awake, or will even wake him up if he has already fallen asleep; and if he has eaten too much, the feelings of discomfort may keep him awake.
3. **Make sure he is comfortable.** You won't sleep very well if the blankets fall off, if the mattress is lumpy, if the temperature in the room is far too high or if your pillow falls on the floor and you can't retrieve it – and neither will a child. Check the room in which he sleeps provides a sleep-inducing environment that suits him.
4. **Make sure that he is healthy.** There is a clear link between health and behaviour in young children. A child who is incubating an illness may begin to have a disrupted sleeping pattern days before the first visible signs of the illness emerge. Always consider this possibility if he suddenly becomes a troubled sleeper.
5. **Make sure that he doesn't fall asleep at irregular times.** A child who nods off whenever he wants during the day will not have a predictable sleeping pattern. Of course, a child who is very tired in the morning can be very difficult to be with, but it's worth trying to postpone sleep until the time for his normal afternoon nap arrives.
6. **Make sure that he follows a routine.** The psychological benefit of a pre-sleep routine is that the child begins to adjust to the idea of sleep as soon as the routine begins, and the physical benefit of a routine is that his body begins to adjust and slow down as the routine gets underway. This makes him more likely to sleep.
7. **Make sure that there isn't unnecessary noise.** You don't need to tiptoe about the house when a child is trying to get to sleep - but having the television blaring loudly won't help. Although he'll sleep through most noises, you should try to stop loud, episodic sounds, such as other children shouting at each other, or doors banging.
8. **Make sure that he likes the room he sleeps in.** A child should associate his bedroom with pleasant feelings. It should be pleasant

from a child's point of view, and have plenty of toys, books and games for him to play with when he wakes. Decorations and furnishings should also be suitable for a child.

9. **Make sure he stays in that room.** A child is more likely to wake up regularly when he should be asleep if he knows, for instance, that he can come back into the room where you are – being in with you is more attractive than having a nap on his own. If he wakes, comfort him in his room until he settles.
10. **Make sure he feels relaxed.** Some children enjoy looking at a book or turning the pages of a comic before sleeping, because that helps them relax. Many young children prefer to have a story read to them by an adult or older sibling before they close their eyes. These calming pre-sleep activities make a child receptive to sleep.

An Alternative Approach

A child's poor sleeping pattern at night can disrupt the entire family, leaving them all exhausted. Let's consider the following example:

The Problem: Gary is five years old, and has started school this year. He thoroughly enjoys being there, has made plenty of friends and is learning a lot. Yet each night he refuses to go to bed at the agreed time. His parents have suggested a bedtime of 7:30pm, which they feel is reasonable. Gary knows that his friends also go to bed at that time, but this makes no difference to him. There are battles every night as he insists on staying up later. If he is physically put to bed by his parents, he screams until the neighbours start to complain. He finally falls asleep around ten o'clock, some three hours after the whole process began.

The Facts: He is a very capable and independent child, who is coping well at school. Even when he was a toddler, he would challenge rules set down by mum and dad, and he would be prepared to persist in challenging them until he got his own way. Gary's parents are quite firm with him, but they don't like seeing him upset. They become anxious when they hear him cry and they aren't prepared to leave him in his bedroom knowing that he's in a distressed state. They prefer to use negotiation when trying to win co-operation from their son.

The Analysis: Gary is a bright child who likes to have some involvement in decisions about his life. And he is more co-operative when he feels that his opinion has been taken into consideration. In addition, Gary's parents prefer to discuss things with him, rather than to take an authoritative role when it comes to setting rules. They won't be able to implement any strategy that involves them in a confrontation with their child, as this goes against their own natures.

The Solution: Since Gary's parents know that he fights against going to bed, and that he likes to feel he is in control of things, then they could try telling him that for the next few nights he doesn't need to go to bed until eleven o'clock at night, which is long after he is usually asleep. They should also mention that he will go to bed slightly earlier the following week. Almost certainly, Gary will go along with this suggestion because it suits him – and this means the pattern of fights over bedtime stops immediately. When Gary does go to bed at the agreed time – though he may fall asleep earlier – his parents should tell him how pleased they are that he went to bed without a fuss. This entire process should be repeated each night, except that every subsequent week Gary's bedtime should be fifteen or twenty minutes earlier. This method often results in an argument-free bedtime (close to, or the same as, the original bedtime that all the fights were about) within six to eight weeks.

Nightmares

A young child mostly has pleasant dreams, but he may occasionally have some dreams which disturb him. Nearly every child has a nightmare at some stage, a dream that is so frightening he wakes up crying, shivering and distressed. There is no need to be unduly concerned if a child has a nightmare infrequently, eg once every six months. Infrequent nightmares seems to be part of normal development.

Nightmares can be triggered by different factors. For instance, some children are more likely to have a nightmare if they eat cheese in their evening meal. Others have disturbing dreams if they watch a horror movie (or simply an adult-orientated television programme) just before bedtime. Nightmares can also be stimulated by the onset of an illness, or by something the child is worried about. These are the most common causes, and therefore if a child is prone to bad dreams, look closely at what happens in the hour or two prior to bedtime. You may find a link between his pre-bedtime behaviour and the onset of nightmares, which could lead to a simple solution such as changing his evening diet, or modifying his viewing habits.

Action Plan for Helping a Child with Nightmares

1. **Don't try to shake him out of it.** A child who has a nightmare may not be fully awake when he cries out – he could still be in the middle of the disturbing dream. His parents may be tempted to shake him as though that would bring him out of the nightmare sequence, but it could upset him even more, especially if he perceives this as part of the dream. Sharp, jerky physical movements should be avoided.
2. **Provide reassurance.** Whether he is awake or asleep, once they realise he is having a nightmare they should speak to him gently in a

soothing, reassuring voice. Stroking his forehead gently, or his cheek, will also help. Even if he is asleep, he'll be sensitive to these loving physical contacts. They should tell him quietly – but repeatedly – that he is fine, that everything's all right, and that he is safe.

3. **Try to stay calm.** Watching a child have a troubling dream is very upsetting for his parents, and they may start to become afraid. They must try to keep calm, bearing in mind that nothing dreadful will happen to him as a result of this nightmare. At worst, he'll tremble, and at best he may forget all about the experience by the time he wakes up the next morning. He needs them to be in control.
4. **If he does not wake up, let him stay asleep.** They may be alerted to his discomfort when he shouts out during the night, but he might do this in his sleep. It is perfectly common for a young child to sleep right through a stressful nightmare without waking up even once; this is perhaps the best possible outcome. They should do what they can to calm him in a way that lets him stay asleep.
5. **Listen to what he says, even though he may be incoherent.** A child who wakes up from a nightmare often has trouble distinguishing his dream from reality at that precise moment, and he may talk as though he is still in the dream. Instead of trying to make sense of his comments, his parents could simply respond by reassuring him that he has nothing to worry about, making him feel safe and secure.
6. **Take him out of bed.** Assuming his nightmare is over and he is awake, he might prefer to leave the bedroom for a few moments – this can be sufficient to bring about a change of mood. He could go to the toilet, or go with his parents for a glass of milk and a biscuit. This change of scenery will probably make him feel better because it introduces familiarity and normality into his waking state.
7. **Once he is settled again, put him back to bed.** It's better not to keep him up too long, because he may lose his tiredness altogether and then lie awake for hours. His parents should take him back to bed, and emphasise that he won't have another bad dream that night (children seldom have more than one bad dream each night), as he may be worried about having the same upsetting dream again.
8. **Consider staying with him until he's fast asleep again.** The child may want mum or dad to remain beside him in his bedroom until he falls asleep – that would be helpful for him, especially if he is still afraid. They may be concerned that this could become a habit for him every night, but such worries have no foundation. Staying with him on this single occasion won't do him harm.
9. **Ask him about his nightmare the following morning.** He might not remember a thing about what happened during the night, or even recall being upset or that his parents gave him a cuddle. This is a natural defence mechanism, and is his mind's way of protecting him

from anxiety. On the other hand, if he does remember, they might want to talk to him about what he dreamt, and about how he felt.

10. **Try to discover if there is anything troubling him.** Young children are easily upset by things that may seem unimportant to adults, such as not being the best singer amongst his friends, or even not being able to kick a ball when all his friends are able to. Mum and dad could talk to him about the key areas in his life – they may identify a trouble spot that could be responsible for the nightmare.

Night Terrors

In very rare instances, a child experiences a night terror (known as *pavor nocturnis*). This is like a very extreme nightmare, but much more frightening. The child looks as though he is living through a terrifying encounter, rather than just dreaming about it. He might yell out, or even stare with his eyes fully open. The whole episode seems very vivid, and occurs at a time when he is deeply asleep. Fortunately, he will probably remember nothing about it the next morning.

Psychologists do not know why some children have night terrors while others have nightmares. However, research shows that these dreadful dream experiences are less common amongst girls than boys. An occasional night terror is not a cause for alarm, but when they are frequent then the child might be worried about something in his life.

Q & A

Q. *Should I worry about a young boy who regularly has bad dreams whenever he sleeps during the day?*

A. You should be concerned. Although most children have a nightmare now and again, repeated bad dreams (at the frequency this boy is experiencing at the moment) are usually a sign that the child has a deeper anxiety. Think about what is going on in his life at the moment, as he could be worrying about something that he regards as serious. Maybe he has fallen out with one of his friends. Or maybe he is worried because he has overheard his parents arguing a lot. Try to establish the root cause of his nightmares.

Q. *Are sedatives good for young children who don't sleep well?*

A. There is no right or wrong answer to this question – it is a matter of preference. Some professionals totally abhor the whole idea of giving drugs to children unless they are unwell, while others wouldn't think twice about giving a child some medicine in order to make him sleep. The child's doctor is the best person to advise you on this. Children can be extremely resistant to concoctions aimed at inducing sleep;

just because a drug is a sedative for children doesn't mean that it will definitely work with every child, and also there may be side-effects to think about.

Q. *What should parents do when their four-year-old falls asleep in the car on the way to nursery each afternoon? He is really irritable on waking up.*

A. It seems as though the combined effects of tiredness and the warm atmosphere of the car are too powerful for him to resist. However, his parents could try talking to him and asking him questions about his experiences that day. Or he might enjoy singing songs with them in the car. Leaving the car window open as they drive to the nursery could also be effective. They'll probably discover, anyway, that he grows out of this habit once he is a few months older.

Q. *Is there anything wrong in parents letting an 18-month-old toddler sleep in bed beside them? They say that they enjoy his company.*

A. As with many questions of childcare, this is a matter of individual choice. There is no research evidence to suggest that there could be any harmful psychological effects from having a "family bed" like this, and if his mum and dad are comfortable with the idea, then it's up to them. There are two potential drawbacks to this, however. First, the presence of a toddler in bed reduces their privacy and restricts their sexual relationship. Second, there will be a time when they do want their child to sleep in his own bed, and at that point he may be determined not to change.

9

Toilet Training

"Potty training with Barbara didn't go as smoothly as expected. When my other children were her age they learned quickly, but it seemed to take her months. At times I found this very frustrating and we did have a couple of rows about it."

Potty training is one of these areas of child development which can go very smoothly or else be extremely problematical. There's nothing like the experience of toilet training your own child for learning the essential techniques. No matter when you start potty training with a child, you need to have a positive frame of mind in order to achieve success. So before you even begin, consider the following background points:

- **co-operation.** Potty training will only work if the child co-operates with you. You can't bully her into using the potty properly no matter how hard you might try – in fact, the more she feels pressure from you to "perform", then the less she'll respond. Encourage co-operation from her, not resistance.
- **relaxation.** Once a child has the potential for bowel and bladder control, she can use it helpfully (by using her potty appropriately) or unhelpfully (by refusing to use it, then wetting herself deliberately). You should aim to create a relaxed atmosphere when potty training so that confrontations are avoided.
- **reasons.** A child may need to be convinced that potty training is worthwhile – she may not see the need for it. After all, wearing a nappy is very comforting for most children. So give her reasons for gaining toilet control, eg because she'll be like "a big girl". This can provide an added incentive.
- **words.** Everybody has their own words for urine and faeces – you may remember the words that your parents used with you. The actual words you use don't matter (of course, they shouldn't be ridiculous because the child will also use them in the company of others) as long as you aren't awkward using them.
- **non-violence.** At times, you may feel very frustrated with a child when your attempts at toilet training don't achieve the success you hoped for. There is nothing wrong in feeling angry about this. But never transform that anger into a smack – her co-operation will cease entirely if you hit her.

- **position.** Girls always use a seated position with the potty, but boys have a choice – they can sit or stand. Neither method appears to help a child achieve potty training sooner than the other. It's entirely up to you. In the early stages of potty training, seating him may be easier to manage.

Picking the Right Time

You might be tempted to rush into toilet training as soon as you can, possibly before the child is ready for it, for a number of reasons. First, other people you know may expect you to start the process now, and you don't want them to think badly of you. Try not to be too influenced by these pressures, however. You have to pick a time for potty training that is right for the child. Every child is different – they all get there in the end, whether one begins training a few months later than another.

A second reason for starting potty training is that not having nappies to change and dispose of makes life easier. You don't need to stock a supply of spare nappies, along with changing creams, baby wipes, etc. Once a child is potty trained, chores related to nappy-changing vanish. Thirdly, the child will be pleased too, because potty training helps her become more independent. Most children want to be able to cope without needing support from an adult all the time, and having full bowel and bladder control is part of becoming independent.

And lastly, the child will almost certainly receive encouragement from other children and adults. Most people regard potty training as a significant step in development, marking the fact that she is no longer a baby any more, that she has entered the world of childhood proper. She will be given lots of praise and support from members of her family, who will encourage her by saying "You're using the potty like a big girl" or "You're a clever girl being able to use the potty like that." These comments help reinforce her desire to continue progressing.

Despite these advantages of potty training for the adults and the child, there is no point in starting the process until she is ready, usually around 20 months. However, some parents proudly announce that their six-month-old child is completely potty trained because when she sits on the potty, she empties her bladder and bowels into it. But that's not potty training, that's simply keeping the child seated on the potty because she can't get off it. In other words, the parents are controlling the child until she uses the potty; the child isn't controlling herself.

These parents will find that within a few months, when their child can toddle about independently, she won't want to sit on the potty. All their efforts at what they thought was toilet training will have been a waste of time – it could even work against them, if their disappointment adversely affects the relationship they have with their child.

Potty training doesn't work much before the age of 20 months (and in some instances, until several months after that) because until then:

- **a child doesn't have sufficient muscle control.** You automatically retain the contents of your bladder, without any conscious effort at all, even when it's half full, and you can retain the content when it's nearly full if you make a conscious effort to do so. This is because of your mature neurological and muscle systems. A child who is much younger than 20 months simply doesn't have this control – she's not neurologically mature enough at that stage.
- **a child doesn't realise her nappy is wet or soiled.** She will not grasp the need for potty training until she understands there is an important difference between a clean nappy and a dirty nappy. True, a younger child might cry when she has been sitting in a soiled nappy for a while as it eventually makes her feel very uncomfortable, but that is quite different from a more mature toddler telling you that she would like her nappy changed because she wet it a few seconds ago.

She's only ready to begin toilet training when she's old enough to understand what you are asking of her (eg when she realises that her older sibling doesn't wear a nappy like her), when you see signs that she has a more mature muscle system (eg when you find that she has not wet her nappy all day, or even for a few hours), and when she can show you that she needs to have her nappy changed (eg she tells you that she has a dirty nappy). These indicators of readiness usually don't appear until the child is between the age of 18 and 21 months.

Ages & Stages

Statistics show that girls are usually potty-trained before boys, and the ability to gain bowel and bladder control tends to develop as outlined in the list below.

12 months: Co-operates when nappy is changed. She doesn't have any bowel and bladder control at all. Yet she takes more of an interest when her nappy is changed, perhaps by bringing a clean nappy over to you, or by helping you to remove her trousers when you change her. The child enjoys the pleasant sensation of wearing a clean nappy, and is in a brighter mood as a result.

15 months: Toddles after you – or her brothers and sisters – when they use the toilet. She follows you to the toilet and takes a very keen interest in what you do there. At this age, she has no embarrassment when it comes to breaches of privacy, and so she will stare unashamedly at you in the toilet. She may do the same to her siblings, although they might not like this.

18 months: Knows when her nappy is wet or soiled. She may insist that you change her nappy immediately because she feels uncomfortable in it. Even when she doesn't let you know her nappy should be changed, if you ask her then she'll give an appropriate response. Some children are extremely proud to be able to strut up to their parent, announcing that they need another nappy.

21 months: Has some success with potty training. The child now realises that she has control and that she can achieve what you want. And the more she succeeds, the more she wants to succeed. However, there will still be the occasional accident, in which she wets or soils herself. She is very pleased with herself when she wets or soils appropriately in the potty.

Two years: Has reliable control throughout the day. Nappies for daytime wear are probably things of the past. She's well used to trainer pants, and co-operates fully in toilet-training with you. You will find she insists on getting the potty herself, then places it in a comfortable position – some children plonk it down in front of the television! The child sits on the potty until she has used it.

30 months: Is extremely confident with the potty. In almost every instance, she tells you when she wants to use the potty; she no longer relies on you to remind her. Her confidence with bowel and bladder control is high. And if you do suggest to her that she might want to sit on it, she may become furious with you. Nevertheless, if she becomes too excited or forgetful, then she may wet herself by mistake.

Three years: Is fully toilet trained during the day. You can go out with her in the knowledge that she can attend to her own toilet needs without any help. (However, you might want to take spare pants and clothes, just in case she has an accident.) She may also be dry and clean during the night, though this skill is generally acquired only after a child has established control throughout the day.

Four years: Consolidates her potty training and increases in confidence. Now you don't need to have any worries about taking her out shopping with you or for a day trip, because you know she is reliable when needing the toilet. Aside from being able to tell you, she can hold on for some time before she begins to feel uncomfortable. If she does have an accident, she will be very upset.

Five years and older: Has bowel and bladder control day and night. Most (but not all) children this age no longer wear a nappy at night. She can probably last through the night without waking to go to the toilet, or if she does wake up, she is able to go by herself. She feels confident enough to cope independently with the toilet at school. If unwell, though, her control may temporarily weaken.

Potty Training Begins

Once you are confident that the child is ready physically and psychologically to begin potty training, then take her through the following step-by-step training programme. Let her proceed at a steady pace.

Step 1: **Think positively.** Put all pessimistic thoughts about potty training out of your mind so that you have a positive attitude. Instead of focusing on the potential problems, such as wet carpets, fights with the toddler, and feelings of frustration, think about the pleasant feelings you will have as she makes progress. She'll detect your emotions and respond accordingly.

Step 2: **Help her think positively.** Take her out with you when you buy her a potty (if you use the potty of an older child, wrap it up as a present for her). This increases her attraction to it. Don't worry if the first thing she does is put it on her head – let her play with it in whatever way she wants. After a while, tell her what the potty is for and how she should use it.

Step 3: **Encourage her to sit on the potty.** This is a crucial step, because it establishes in her mind exactly what the potty is for. The child could feel insecure with her nappy off so be patient with her. If she resists, encourage her gently until her bottom rests on the potty itself. Once she is used to the idea, have her sit on it several times each day; the longer she sits, the better.

Step 4: **Reassure her if she's upset, praise her if she's not.** Some children become very distressed when they discover what they have done in the potty – they could feel disgusted. That's a normal reaction. If she is upset, smile beamingly at her, telling her how pleased you are with her for using the potty properly – and do the same if she is delighted with her performance.

Step 5: **Introduce trainer pants.** At first, you'll simply remove her nappy, sit her on the potty until she uses it, then put a nappy back on again. However, after while, think about giving her trainer pants. She'll feel good about this because she associates pants with older children, and may not be too concerned about leaving her day nappy behind.

Step 6: **Continue to build up her confidence.** Once she has begun to gain control over her bowels and bladder, potty training gains momentum. But she still has a long way to go. So keep encouraging her each time she uses the potty and keep reminding her how pleased you are with her. Her confidence in the toilet will increase steadily until she is fully independent.

Step 7: **Encourage her to take responsibility.** As potty training progresses, you should gradually hand over responsibility to her.

> For instance, she should get the potty out herself, she should pull her own trainer pants down if she can, and she should also begin to wipe her own bottom. Your final aim is for her to go to the toilet herself without involving you at all.

One of the most important things to remember as you progress through these stages is that a child won't learn unless there is a peaceful, relaxed atmosphere. If you get tense, she'll get tense; and if she gets tense, her muscle control is affected. So try not to become agitated with her. She's not deliberately setting out to upset you. Learning any new skill takes time; potty training is no different in this respect.

There's nothing wrong in a toddler wanting you to read a story to her while she's sitting on the potty, or wanting to play with a toy. Let her – activities like that encourage her to associate pleasant feelings with sitting on the potty, and that can only help. Likewise, she might become rather boring with her insistence on a lap of honour every time she uses the potty, but your positive response always increases her motivation.

Potty Training - Common Difficulties

Potty training rarely goes smoothly. Tempers get heated, despite the best of intentions, and at times you may feel as though she is going backwards instead of forwards. This often happens. But for every problem with potty training, there is a solution. Here is a list of the most common difficulties reported by parents and professionals, and suitable solutions which you may find helpful.

Problem: Regular fights over toilet-training.
Cause: Trying to achieve too much, too soon.
Strategy: Calm down, and take a less intense approach with her. You need to take the tension out of the situation. Have a short break from potty training if you think that would help. If you don't change, the situation will get worse.

Problem: Child sits on the potty quite happily but doesn't use it.
Cause: She doesn't understand what the potty is for.
Strategy: You can do one of two things at this point. You could keep going anyway, since she is quite willing to sit when you ask her to. Or you could stop for the time being until she's a little bit older. It's entirely up to you at this point.

Problem: When the child goes outside, she has a toilet accident.
Cause: She didn't use the potty before she got ready.
Strategy: Give her plenty of time to prepare for a trip to the shops. Re-

mind her that you want her to use the potty beforehand, and reassure her that she can go to the toilet even when she's not at home. She probably just needs to build up her confidence.

Problem: Doesn't use the toilet in other people's houses.
Cause: Lack of confidence, and insecurity in unfamiliar toilets.
Strategy: Ask her why she prefers not to use the bathroom in someone else's house. It may be that she is unsure how to lock the door behind her, or that she feels the toilet seat is too large for her. If she has a particular worry, try to solve it for her.

Problem: No bladder control, after months of potty training.
Cause: A physical difficulty.
Strategy: There are minor physical problems that can affect the rate at which a child gains bowel and bladder control, although these are not very common. For instance, her urethra may be blocked. The family doctor is the best person to investigate this possibility.

Problem: Slow progress with potty-training.
Cause: The child takes longer to learn.
Strategy: Give her time. Each child learns toilet training at her own pace. Some children are very quick and pick up the essential skills within a few weeks, while others can take several months. These differences are all within the range of normal development.

Problem: Fully toilet trained, but suddenly loses bladder control.
Cause: The child is worried about something.
Strategy: Identify the main stresses in her life, whether she is troubled by something at home, or at nursery with other children her own age. Let her express her feelings, and offer reassurance, comfort and practical advice (if you can).

Problem: Won't sit on the toilet, although happily uses her potty.
Cause: She is afraid of falling into the toilet bowl.
Strategy: Buy a child-sized toilet seat that will fit inside the existing adult-sized toilet seat, enabling her to sit securely on it. This will make her feel steadier and safer. Without this piece of equipment, she may be terrified when sitting on the toilet.

Becoming Dry at Night

Typically, a child will almost certainly gain day control before she gains night control. Almost 90% of children are dry at night by the age of five or six years, while the remainder can take another couple of years before achieving a dry bed each night. The chances are that a child shows signs of readiness for night training by the time she is three years old (eg her parents discover her nappy isn't wet in the morning even though she has been wearing it all night). For many children, night control happens spontaneously without much training, while others do need positive encouragement and adult input.

Once you are confident that a child is ready to begin night training, take her through the step-by-step training programme below:

Step 1: **Explain what is required.** Tell her that you now want her to go through the night without wearing her nappy. She'll probably have expected this anyway, but there's no harm in spelling it out to her. You can emphasise that you hope her bed will be dry in the morning, and add that she should not become upset if it is wet – she'll just have to try harder the next time.

Step 2: **Make adequate preparations.** Buy a waterproof cover for the mattress in case the child wets during the night – this is bound to happen at least once or twice, especially at the beginning. Second, make sure she knows how to find her way from her bedroom to the toilet on her own, or place the potty in her room. She may like you to leave the hall light on.

Step 3: **Let her get on with it.** If you find that she is wet in the morning, you should try not to get annoyed – she needs reassurance that tomorrow the bed will be dry when she wakes up. This boosts her confidence. If you find that she is dry in the morning, then it's time for a celebration!

Not Always Easy

Night training is often less troublesome than day training because the child understands what toilet training is all about. However, problems can occur. Let's consider the following example:

The Problem: Alice is four years old and is fully potty trained during the day. She was slow to attain full control but has been consistently dry from morning until night for over a year now. Night-training has not been successful, however. Her parents have tried everything they can think of to motivate her, without success. She wakes up in the morning thoroughly soaked and appears to be unconcerned about this.

The Facts: The girl has always needed prompting to move from one developmental stage to the next; she sees no benefit to be gained by behaving more maturely. A similar pattern was seen with potty training during the day, which took several months. Alice is one of those children who tends to be passive, and who needs encouragement to become more independent. She certainly is capable of gaining night control, but is completely unconcerned if she doesn't. This is why she doesn't make a fuss if the bed is wet each morning.

The Analysis: Progress won't be made until Alice is positively motivated for change. As long as she remains uninterested in gaining bowel and bladder control at night, she is unlikely to reach that stage. Her parents have tried shouting at her, though this does not motivate her at all. Now is the time to consider a strategy which uses positive reinforcement for success, instead of punishment for failure. The adults in her life need to improve her motivation to have a dry bed through the night.

The Solution: Alice's parents could try using a star chart, which is a simple sheet of paper with a square on it for each night of the week. They'll explain to her that whenever her bed is dry in the morning, they will give her a gold star to stick on the square for that day. The aim is for her to get as many stars on the chart as she can, each week. A surprisingly simple technique, the implementation of a star chart can arouse the child's enthusiasm. Maybe it is the added attention that the chart brings her. Whatever the reason for the chart's appeal, it often works. Alice's parents could use this method with her for around three or four weeks.

Q & A

Q. *What is a bell-and pad?*

A. This is a small buzzer device which wakes a child as soon as she starts to wet – her urine flow completes a circuit which then sets off an alarm. Psychologists would not usually recommend a bed-wetting alarm like this until a child is six years or older because she needs to understand what she is supposed to do when she is woken by it. These alarms can be effective, but often everyone in the house is woken up by the buzzer…except the child herself.

Q. *What equipment will I need for potty training?*

A. The major potty training equipment that you'll probably need includes a regular potty with splash guard or a potty-chair, terry-towelling trainer pants or disposable paper trainer pants, a toilet seat with a safety-lock to keep it firmly attached to the adult toilet seat, a toddler step to help the young child reach the toilet seat, and a waterproof PVC mattress cover.

Q. *Should I keep a special set of books and toys for a child to play with when she is sitting on the potty?*

A. You may find this technique helpful, especially in the early stages when you are trying to encourage her to sit on the potty for more than just a moment. The set of "special" toys and books may be a sufficient incentive. However, you need to be careful that she doesn't forget the purpose of sitting on the potty – namely, to empty her bladder and bowels – and that instead she thinks it is simply another play situation. You have to strike a balance or potty training won't progress effectively.

Q. *Why does a two-year-old go off into a corner while soiling her nappy, instead of asking me for the potty?*

A. Some children develop this habit because they are still uncomfortable using a potty. The child is clearly not fully confident about toilet training yet. She is used to soiling her nappy – after all, she has been doing this since she was a baby – and she prefers to continue with this practice. But she also knows you don't want her to do this, and hence she tries to conceal herself in a corner of the room or behind the sofa. Stay calm and give her lots of reassurance. She will use the potty eventually.

10

Achieving Independence

"I always encourage my child's independence. For instance, although I don't rush toilet training we don't leave it to chance. The same applies to learning how to dress themselves and so on. I think it is important for a child to learn to do things for himself."

It's natural to want children to be able to do more for themselves, yet you may not always know what to expect of them, and when to expect it. For instance, do you agree that the average age a child should be able to:

- walk independently without any support is 15 months?
- sleep in a bed instead of a cot is two years?
- leave you without crying hysterically is three years?
- sit on the floor, without toppling, is six months?
- brush his teeth without help is four years?
- cross the road safely is five years?
- know that hot things can burn is 18 months?
- tie his own shoelaces is around four years?
- tell the time from a clock face is five years?
- hold a spoon for feeding is two years?

Maybe you agree with eight of these statements, or six of them, or perhaps you even agree with just two. Maybe your friend thinks that your choices are entirely wrong. Yet you'll almost certainly be right in whatever you choose because the fact is that many milestones of independence during childhood are attained by different children at different ages, and these individual differences are rarely cause for concern.

Attitudes

There are three main views that parents and professionals have towards independence in childhood:

- **rigorous.** These parents are determined that a child will become independent as quickly as possible. They are not particularly comfortable meeting the dependency needs of a growing child, and don't like basic child-related chores such as washing, feeding, dressing, and so on. They would much rather that he grew up a little so that he could do more for himself. So they try to move him on from "babyish" behaviour to "big boy" behaviour. Independence is rewarded with praise, dependence is punished with irritation.

- **realistic.** These parents don't have an axe to grind either way. They are not especially keen to be bogged down by practical child-care tasks but they recognise that independence has to be a gradual process. They take the view that a child has to see the point of becoming independent or else he won't be very keen to co-operate with them. Expectations are reasonable, being neither too demanding nor too lenient. There is recognition that there are other children his age who can do more for themselves, but they aren't bothered by this.
- **casual.** These parents believe that a child should be allowed to develop at his own pace, without any undue pressure placed upon him. There is no harm at all in staying at the same developmental stage for a little longer than normally expected, as far as they are concerned, because the chances are that the child will always catch up eventually. For them, childhood should be a time of happiness, not a time of training, a time of being fussed over, not a time for carrying out chores. They won't push a child into independence.

These perspectives represent three points on the continuum from high expectations (rigorous) to low expectations (casual). As you might expect, the most effective attitude is the "realistic" perspective – children usually dislike extremes, and the other two attitudes push the child to be either too independent or too dependent.

You should also take account of a child's emotional needs when trying to influence his level of independence. For instance, a young child who is insecure may become even more afraid if he feels his parents expect too much of him, whereas that same approach might suit a child who is very confident, adventurous and single-minded. A lot depends on his personality. Similarly, a child who is challenging and rebellious may react disruptively to parents whose demands for independence are too rigorous, while a more passive child might welcome that type of structure and planning.

Independence Develops Gradually

The list below provides you with guidelines about the main stages of independence from birth to five years. Remember, however, that these are guidelines only. Every child is different.

Three months: Sleeps for a few hours without adult attention.
How To Help: As long as you are sure that the baby isn't hungry, dirty or uncomfortable, try not to rush over to him instantly when he wakes up crying. Instead, wait a moment or two before responding to him.

Six months: Reaches out for toys in front of him.
How To Help: Sit him comfortably on the floor, surrounded by cushions if necessary. Place a couple of small toys just outside his reach so that he is encouraged to reach out and grasp hold of them.

12 months: Wants to help you dress him.
How To Help: Dress him slowly, and make a big fuss of him when, for instance, he stretches out his arms while you put on his jumper. Let him try to manoeuvre his arms into the sleeves himself, as far as he can.

18 months: Tries to drink out of a cup without spilling any.
How To Help: Let him try to hold the cup as it is brought to his mouth, even though he can't hold it all by himself. He wants to make an effort. This is the first stage of being able to feed himself without help.

21 months: Wants to climb a flight of steps.
How To Help: Let him crawl up the stairs if he wants, but be with him all the time. You might even want to hold his body while he tries to climb them. He may prefer to come down on his bottom.

Two years: Has bowel and bladder control during the day.
How To Help: Have a structured plan for toilet training, and implement it when he shows signs of readiness for this phase of development. He'll gradually progress and achieve full control.

30 months: Opens and closes doors.
How To Help: Show him clearly how a door handle operates. He may not be able to turn a circular door knob but he should be able to work a pull-down handle by himself. This is a difficult task, but he will master it.

Three years: Separates from parents.
How To Help: Reassure him that he'll be fine without you, that the other adults will look after him and that he'll have fun. Don't get upset if he shows signs of anxiety at first – he will learn to cope on his own.

Four years: Plays safely in the garden.
How To Help: Tell the child he can play in the garden on his own, but that he mustn't stray beyond the fence or gate. Then watch what he's doing without letting him see you. Praise him when he stays in the area.

Five years: Pours a glass of juice from an open-topped jug.
How To Help: Give him a jug of orange juice and a cup, and show him how to hold the jug in both hands, then gently tilt it towards the glass until it starts to fill. Then leave him to get on with the task himself.

Later Childhood & Adolescence

The development of independence takes on a different meaning as the child grows beyond the pre-school years. Now, it's not simply a matter of managing without adult help – independence also means freedom of choice and being able to make decisions for himself. In most families, battles over independence occur over issues like choice of friends and out-of-house activities. The growing child wants to choose what to do, when to do it and the company that he keeps.

This intensified desire for independence may affect his relationship with his parents. For instance, he may begin to resent them for reminding him to do his homework – "I know what I've to do" is the familiar cry of the older child. Or he may resent being given any advice at all because he believes he is old enough and capable enough to manage on his own. You may hear him argue that "I don't need anyone to tell me what to do."

Encouraging independence at this stage in a child's life is a very demanding challenge. Always listen to his request for independence (eg when he asks not to do his homework till later) and treat him seriously. Of course you don't have to agree with him, nor do you have to give in to his demand. But at least discuss the issue with him. He wants to be treated with respect, even if you have a different perspective from him and would prefer him to listen to your advice.

Barriers to Independence

In most instances, a child has a natural instinct to become independent, to be able to do things on his own without help, although he often needs support to achieve that target. However, there can be emotional barriers to independence. In other words, there may be psychological reasons why a child has difficulty shedding his dependency on adults during these formative years.

Illness: Jim is two years old and suffers constantly from coughs and colds. Mum and dad feel sorry for their toddler, and try to avoid any activities that might be too taxing for him; when he is unwell, they keep him in bed, ply him with endless hot drinks and snacks, and do as much as they can for him. Jim, of course, is having a wonderful time. He is the centre of attention, and has parents who do everything they can for him, especially when he is ill but also when he is well. At times, they do ask Jim to do something but now he flatly refuses. He is so used to being dependent that the prospect of change is too difficult for him.

Encouraging Independence Despite Illness

His parents feel sad to see a child tucked up in bed, feeling and looking miserable. Yet if he thinks that they are worried, this will make him worried too. Of course, they should be sympathetic when he feels ill, but that doesn't mean he has to regress to a state of total dependence. As soon as he is on the mend, he can start to do more for himself, otherwise being ill will become a more attractive state than being well.

Hazards: Five-year-old David is not allowed to play outside his house – even in the garden – without strict supervision. He and his parents live in a quiet cul-de-sac, but they are very conscious that accidents can happen. As a result, David does not feel very safe unless his parents are with him. He has been given so many warnings about the terrible things that might befall him that he perceives the world as dangerous and frightening. For this young child, everything can end up in disaster. By now, his parents don't need to supervise him so closely when he is in the garden because he wouldn't dream of leaving this apparent safety zone.

Encouraging Independence Despite Hazards

They are quite right to point out to their child that he faces danger in some situations if he is not careful. But the fact is that many children do get through childhood without breaking a limb, burning themselves or giving themselves an electric shock. It is better to teach a child how to avoid unnecessary risks (eg by not touching sharp knives, by not running quickly into a busy road) than simply to tell him that such risks exist.

Learning Difficulties: As three-year-old Colin has learning difficulties, his parents don't expect a great deal from him. Professionals involved with Colin have indicated that he has a problem learning new skills and this is likely to be a pattern that will continue into the future. Ever since recognising that he has this difficulty, his mum and dad have taken a very gentle, unchallenging approach with him, in the hope that he will develop at his own pace and in his own time. Colin could achieve more, but his parents' assumptions about his future slow progress mean that they don't try to motivate him to become more independent.

Encouraging Independence Despite Learning Difficulties

It's not that children with learning difficulties can't become independent, just that they will achieve this at a slower rate. That's why it is important to have expectations, though these should match the child's stage of development, not his age. Targets for independence should be less ambitious, and should be less challenging than for a child who is developing normally, but there still have to be targets all the same.

Spoiling: Daniel has no brothers or sisters. He is now five, and his parents decided from the moment he was born that they wouldn't have any other children in their family. They spoil him, and his grandparents spoil him too. For Daniel, total dependence on mum and dad is a way of life.

He doesn't resist the idea of independence – it simply never occurs to him. His parents are only now beginning to realise that he may have difficulty adjusting to the demands of the infant school when he starts there in a few months. A recent visit to the school confirmed that the class teacher expects children to be independent.

Encouraging Independence Despite Spoiling

By all means, shower a child with love and affection – that's every child's right. Yet this does not mean that his parents have to wait on him hand and foot. They can spoil a child and have expectations of his independence at the same time. A child benefits from being able to do things for himself, from being able to manage on his own. This still leaves them plenty of opportunity to spoil him if that's what they want.

How to Help a Child Become More Independent

There is no magic needed for helping a child become more independent. You just need to make sure that you and the child work together. Gaining independence requires him to take a leap in the dark, as it were, to take a risk of trying to achieve something that he can't already do. That's why he needs your support every step of the way.

He may be afraid of failure, or may simply be afraid that he won't be as capable as his friends or his siblings. So give him lots of reassurance that he can succeed at whatever he aims for. If he thinks you are taking a genuine interest in him, then his motivation will be higher.

Some children aren't very keen to become independent because they don't see any point in it. You need to tell him the benefits of being less dependent. Spell it out to him clearly. For instance, "If you learn how to pour yourself a glass of lemonade, then you don't need to wait for me to do it for you" or "If you tidy the toys away quickly, you'll have a few more minutes to watch television." A child will understand practical examples like these, which will add further incentive for him.

It's also important not to expect too much too soon. What may seem a simple task to you (eg pulling his socks off) may seem monumental to a poorly co-ordinated toddler. He'll need time to master each task properly before he can move on to the next stage. And just because one child found it easy, say, to learn how to brush his teeth, this doesn't mean the next child will learn to be independent at the same speed. Expect gradual and steady progress – this pattern will give the child the confidence that he needs.

Try not to be over-protective, however, or the child may have no belief in his ability to cope on his own, he may have poor self-esteem and little self-confidence, and he might be very shy in the company of other children his own age. In addition, a child who is over-protected often cries easily as soon as things go wrong, and has difficulty making friends.

Stranger Danger

By the time a child is four or five years old (possibly sooner and certainly no later) he needs to be told that not all adults are friendly, that some may be dangerous. Of course, his parents need to strike a balance between making him aware of "stranger danger" and making him so frightened that he doesn't want to venture out on his own.

Make the rules clear and simple (eg "Don't talk to a grown-up you don't know," "Don't take sweets from a grown-up you don't know") so that he is not in any doubt, but tell him in a way that reassures him instead of frightening him. Explain also that if he gets separated from his parents in the supermarket – which is very easily done – he should speak to someone wearing the store uniform (show him what that is). If he has a choice, he should speak to a woman rather than a man.

Sadly, some children experience abuse that is physical, emotional or sexual. Even though the child may not tell anyone about the abuse, it may show in his behaviour. Signs that a child is being abused include irritability, poor sleeping patterns, overt and inappropriate sexual behaviour, aggressiveness to others, fear of strangers, nervousness with adults, withdrawn behaviour, and tearfulness. The list is endless.

However, it is not possible to conclude with any certainty that a child is being abused simply on the basis of these characteristics (since they are also seen in children who are troubled but who aren't abused). If you think that you may have justifiable concerns about possible abuse then speak to your local Social Services, who are specially trained to deal with these matters.

Letting Go

One of the joys of raising a child is watching him grow and mature, as his full potential unfolds. But that can be painful too – there's something very special about having a young child who becomes attached to you and who needs you every step of the way – and this can interfere with the process of establishing independence. Let's consider the following example.

The Problem: Four-year-old Amul will not leave his mum's side. Wherever she goes, he has to go or else he has a screaming tantrum. Even the thought of being left in during the evening with a babysitter is enough to send him into hysterics. Sometimes, his reluctance to be away from mum is so strong that he begs her to take him with her when she goes to the toilet. And the same thing happened when she tried to leave him at nursery. His reaction at her departure was so distressing that the nursery staff reluctantly agreed he was not mature enough to stay there.

The Facts: Amul is an intelligent, likeable child who has a very close attachment to his parents, and to his mother in particular. Like most families, they enjoy spending time together. Indeed, his mum has liked this so much that she postponed her return to work (she had originally planned to go back part-time when Amul was around three years old), preferring to be with her son – and she postponed his start to nursery for the same reason. She takes him everywhere with her, and he is always well behaved in the circumstances, doing exactly what she asks.

The Analysis: The mother-child emotional bond is strong, and that's very positive; Amul's self-confidence will become stronger as a result of this relationship. But it has also become stifling for the four-year-old. He has become so dependent on his mother that he can't manage without her. This suits his mum because she enjoys being needed in this way. Everything is fine, until the prospect of having to cope on his own looms up, and then he goes to pieces. Other children his age have long passed this phase of dependency, and are able to stay with at nursery without any difficulty.

The Solution: Amul needs to learn how to become less dependent on his mother. However, this will be most effectively achieved if done gradually, with support and encouragement. For instance, mum could take him to the nursery and stay with him the entire time during his first day. After a couple of days, she could say that she's going out for a few minutes and that she'll be right back. This period out of Amul's sight can increase by five or ten minutes each subsequent day. With this approach, the need for mother and son to be together all the time will lessen, and they'll both benefit from his new level of independence.

Q & A

Q. *I look after a three-year-old who doesn't know when to draw the line. How do I teach him that there is a limit to his independence?*

A. Once a young child has gained enthusiasm for doing things by himself, there are times when he does go too far, perhaps by trying to make a cup of coffee or by attempting to bake a cake. That's perfectly normal – and it is up to you to make the limits clear to him. When he does go too far, explain that to him. Tell him that you will decide what he can and cannot do by himself in your house, and that you will guide him in this. Suggest that he asks you if he is unsure, before going ahead single-handedly on a particular activity.

Q. *How do you motivate a child to become independent, when he is quite happy for me to do everything for him?*

A. One reason for his lack of motivation may be that he perceives the challenge of independence as being too difficult for him. Perhaps he needs each task – whether it is putting his jumper on or washing his face – to be broken down into small, manageable stages. In addition, you should consider your own actions. Are you giving him sufficient encouragement or do you do everything for him anyway? Be prepared to persist with your encouragement, whether or not he responds positively. He will eventually show interest.

Q. *I'm worried because my toddler has no sense of danger. If I take my eyes off him for a moment, he often ends up with a minor injury.*

A. All children like to explore, even though they don't yet know which objects are dangerous and which are safe. So you are quite right to be worried about this toddler. But simply restricting his movements and explorations isn't sufficient by itself – after all, he'll never learn about his environment that way. By all means offer a good level of supervision when he wanders about – and keep a close watch so that you can prevent any harm coming to him – but do allow him some limited freedom to establish his independence.

Q. *How can I be patient when my child takes ages to get ready when we are going out? He makes me so late.*

A. There are three strategies you can adopt to help reduce the tension. First, start getting ready ten minutes earlier than normal, so that he has more time available to tidy up and get his shoes and jacket on himself. Second, break down the task of tidying up dressing into small stages so that he can cope more easily. And third, pick a time when you are less rushed, and use that as the time to practise getting ready. He is much more likely to achieve independence with these strategies than with the current situation.

Section 3: Emotional Development

This section is devoted entirely to emotional development in early childhood. Parents and carers have to establish discipline with children, and Chapter 11 considers various alternatives for achieving that goal. Chapter 12 looks at temper tantrums – that normal but frustrating aspect of the pre-school years – and suggests strategies for dealing with tantrums effectively. Chapter 13 gives valuable advice for dealing with a child who misbehaves. Other potential emotional concerns – the use of comforters, and childhood fears – are examined in Chapters 14 and 15 respectively.

11

Discipline

"I didn't think much about discipline until Sarah was two or three. I began to see then that I needed to be quite firm or else she'd just do what she wanted. I wasn't too happy at laying down rules and regulations but I knew I had to do this for her sake."

You would probably agree with other people who suggest that all children need discipline, but you may not agree with their definition of discipline. For one person, it might be a harsh system of rules, while for another there might be greater flexibility. When considering discipline with a child, always remember that:

- the origin of the word "discipline" comes from the Latin word which means "learning" – in other words, a child should learn through discipline. Try to create a system that is most effective for her to learn rules, rather than a system of coercion.
- learning is not only the acquisition of knowledge. A child who learns a rule by rote may only be able to apply that rule in a specific situation. However, if she fully understands a rule (ie she learns it properly) then she will apply it to all situations.
- discipline is not simply about a child's behaviour towards you, but is also about your behaviour towards her. All actions are two-way. What she does affects you, and vice versa. So when setting out rules, think about your behaviour too.
- every child is caring and loving by nature. There are plenty of children who have been brought up without much discipline at home, and yet they are still sociable and sensitive. There is an inherent tendency to be kind to others.

Ideas

Here are some varied ideas about discipline. Think about them in relation to the children that you know, and decide which, if any, you feel most comfortable with:

Rules: "Discipline is essential for all children, otherwise they would run wild. A screaming baby would grow up to be a screaming toddler, who in turn would grow up to be a screaming pre-schooler. Children have no innate self-discipline at all; they need proper guidance by adults in the early years or they will remain selfish and insensitive. Rules need to be explicitly set out, and all children must follow them."

Punishment: "There can't be discipline for young children unless there is a system of punishment that can be carried out instantly. Discipline involves learning rules, and what better way to learn rules quickly than by punishment for breaking them? A child who knows she will be punished for not doing what she is told, will make sure she follows the rules laid down at home and when she is with others."

Love: "A child who is severely disciplined will grow up thinking the adults in her world don't love her. The problem with discipline is that it is only about what adults want (ie good behaviour, peace and quiet) and has nothing to do with what a child wants (ie the right to be recognised as an individual who also has feelings). A child needs love instead of discipline – that's a more effective way of encouraging good behaviour."

Freedom: "Adults often hide behind discipline because they don't know how to cope with giving a child freedom. Yet this stifles the child's creativity and imagination. It is better to let a child do what she wants when she is young. She'll learn by her own mistakes; there is plenty of time to teach her how to conform later on. Discipline represses a child's natural energy and enthusiasm, and as a result is destructive."

Change: "Discipline should change as a child changes. Part of maturing involves learning how to cope with change, so there is no point having the same set of rules for behaviour day after day, month after month. What is suitable behaviour for a two-year-old isn't always suitable for a five-year-old, for instance. Adults need to be flexible all the time, ready to review their discipline on a daily basis."

Sensitivity: "Discipline should always be responsive to a child's feelings, and should be adapted accordingly. Before rules are established, she should be given an opportunity to discuss them, to give her opinion on them and then for the final decision about rules to be made jointly. Always listen to a child's views, and be prepared to be flexible when she complains about something. This links discipline with growing up."

None of these ideas is satisfactory as it stands at present. Each presents an extreme view of one aspect of discipline only, whereas a balance is required. However, they all contain elements of the essential ingredients for effective discipline. Let's look at each of the key points again, this time taking a more balanced view:

Rules: They establish in the child's mind what you expect her to do, and how you expect her to behave. But she doesn't need rules for everything. Give her some space to make decisions for herself. If you have rules to govern everything, then she'll not learn to think for herself.
Example: The rule "Never speak back to an adult under any circumstances" sets out clearly that you expect her to stay silent whenever you tell her off for something. True, this will get her blind obedience, but little else. However, the rule "Don't be cheeky to an adult under any circumstances, but don't be afraid to voice your opinion" achieves respect while also encourages her to have an opinion.

Punishment: The prospect of a punishment serves to remind a child that her actions have a consequence, and this can be useful as long as she knows the punishments before she breaks the rules. However, discipline should also contain a system of rewards for good behaviour.
Example: She is more likely to respond to the rule "Don't smack another child on the face when he annoys you" if she realises that she will be severely reprimanded and sent to bed early for breaking that rule. Yet you will also achieve the same positive behaviour from her if you make a point of giving her a special reward (eg an extra cuddle, an ice-cream) when she behaves in a caring way towards others.

Love: Discipline without love is cold, horrible and pointless. That sort of discipline will achieve blind obedience from a child, but this will stem from the fear of rejection, not from any positive emotion. Love and discipline are perfectly compatible – they are not mutually exclusive.
Example: Rules can be positive and negative. For instance, negative rules usually always start with the word "Don't" (eg don't spill water on the floor when playing, don't run up the stairs noisily). Positive rules show what is expected (eg keep water in the water tray when playing, try to walk quietly when going upstairs). A child feels more loved and secure when the majority of rules are positively framed.

Freedom: A child needs to have some freedom in her life – even if she is only 18 months old – or she will not learn to become independent. She will be too dependent on others. Lack of freedom results in lack of initiative. But too much freedom can overwhelm a young child.
Example: If you say to a child "I don't mind if you put the toys away, it's entirely up to you, I'll let you do whatever you want," then it's a fair bet she'll leave them and go on to something else. You can still give her limited freedom while ensuring that the task is completed, for instance "I would like you to tidy your toys and then help me put these clothes away. You can choose which one to do first."

Change: Rules should always have flexibility and adaptability, as a child grows older, otherwise, for instance, she would have the same bedtime at age five as she had at age two. Too much change, though, leaves her not knowing what you expect from one day to the next.
Example: There is no point in applying the rule "Finish your meal or you won't be allowed to have any sweets" for a couple of days, then not applying it, then suddenly deciding to apply it again. Yet there is every justification for being flexible about this rule, for instance, when you know she is particularly excited about going to a party that afternoon and that this has depressed her appetite.

Sensitivity: The child's feelings are important. She is an individual in her own right, with her own emotions and ideas, and these should be considered. But don't bend over backwards about it, otherwise she'll continue to think everything must revolve around her.
Example: She may feel hurt when you punish her for shouting at her brother even though he deliberately smashed her jigsaw puzzle. She should be allowed to say "That's not fair, he was horrible to me and I'm very angry at him," and you should listen. In response, you could say "I realise that you are annoyed, and I'll speak to your brother in a moment, but what you did was still wrong and I don't like it."

Discipline By Age

Professionals disagree over when discipline should begin. Some argue that **a baby** is so small that she cannot possibly be expected to understand a system of rules because she doesn't understand what is going on around her - these professionals claim that a baby, therefore, should be picked up whenever she cries. Others argue that discipline should begin at birth, and that an undisciplined baby will grow into an undisciplined child. They claim that a baby should be expected to follow a routine and that she shouldn't be picked up every time she cries. There's no "right" answer to this debate.

However, there is no doubt that discipline should begin once a child understands the meaning of the word "no", which is usually between the ages of **nine months and one year**. Now, she is old enough to understand the meaning of the words "yes" and "no", and also to understand when you are displeased with her for misbehaviour. The fact that she has this understanding doesn't mean that she'll always do what you say. At around the age of **18 months**, her resistance to discipline can be very strong. Expect her to become confrontational at times when you stand in her way – this is a normal reaction from an angry toddler who wants to be more powerful than adults.

By the time she is **two years old**, the situation has probably worsened! Unfortunately, the additional six months of age only bring increased vigour, increased determination and increased temper. You might expect that her maturity would make her more responsive, but at this stage in her life things work the other way round. A two-year-old can be utterly disagreeable, often at the times you least expect. She hasn't yet acquired the quality of patience, and she's not prepared to wait for anything. Surroundings don't matter – she's just as likely to make a scene in a crowded city-centre shopping mall as she is in the privacy of her own home. A two-year-old reacts impulsively in direct response to what she wants, without considering anyone else.

The next year sees maturation and the awareness that discipline is a reciprocal process. When she is **three years old**, the child now realises that she isn't the only one who is expected to behave appropriately and caringly towards others – other children also live according to the same expectations. This gives her a sense of comfort, a feeling of well-being, and she makes more of an effort to conform to discipline. She is especially keen to have adult approval for good behaviour (because at this age she desperately wants to please) and may become very huffy when you reprimand her for something.

At the age of **four years**, she starts to show signs of becoming a disciplinarian herself. For instance she won't hesitate to tell you off for breaking a rule that you expect her to follow (eg when you put your feet on the table, or eat a sandwich without having a plate underneath to catch the crumbs). Take these rebukes in the spirit they are intended – she is simply testing out what it's like to be at the other end of discipline. She will also be quick to remind her peers about their behaviour. In this way, a child demonstrates her maturity. Of course, she will continue to challenge rules when it suits her, but now she recognises that discipline is not just something that applies to her. At this age, you can also explain to her that it is not sufficient for her simply to say "sorry" when she does something wrong, and that she has to feel genuinely sorry and to try not to repeat the behaviour.

The typical **five-year-old** has internalised many of the standards of behaviour that she has already experienced at home, and therefore she is able to discipline herself when she is on her own. She is no longer totally reliant on an adult to tell her how to behave. For instance, she knows that it's not right to barge to the front of a queue, and that she should share her sweets when she is with others instead of munching them selfishly on her own.

This acknowledgement of rules also makes her ready for the demands of infant school. Teachers expect pupils to do what is asked of them, without putting up a fight every time they are asked to do something and without complaining too much. And starting school will be so much better if she has become used to discipline during the pre-school years.

A school-aged child wants to **play a more active part in discipline**, because she has her own ideas about rules. You may find that she challenges some of the standards of behaviour that she previously accepted. She does not do this out of malice, nor does she do this from lack of respect for you. It's just that she considers herself old enough to have her own view and she wants you to hear what she has to say.

Smacking

Don't be fooled by the popular saying "Spare the rod and spoil the child". The fact is that violence against children can never be justified, even if it is an apparently harmless smack. Violence encourages violence, and if you get into the habit of smacking a child when she torments you, then you'll soon smack without even thinking about it. Find other ways of disciplining a child. Let's consider the following example:

The Problem: Three-year-old Lorna constantly touches objects that she isn't supposed to, no matter where she is. At home, she is forever pulling things off shelves and fingering anything she can get her hands on. No matter how often her parents tell her not to touch, Lorna keeps touching. They find this habit annoying and almost every day Lorna ends up with a smack on the bottom from either mum or dad.

The Facts: Lorna is a very determined child, and doesn't respond to reprimands or even physical punishment. Her parents smack her for misbehaviour but it doesn't appear to have any effect. They are very frustrated by the girl's behaviour, but can't think of any alternative.

The Analysis: The girl probably persists with her irritating habit of touching everything at home for three reasons. First, this satisfies her curiosity. Second, she's bored a lot of the time and this keeps her occupied. And third, she knows it irritates the adults and that at some point it will force them to give her more attention. Smacking obviously is not a successful way of dealing with Lorna's misbehaviour – if it were, then she would have stopped fingering objects at home a long time ago. There is no point in persisting with a strategy for discipline that isn't working. Indeed, the chances are that the parents' use of smacking actually encourages the behaviour it is supposed to stop because it rewards the child with attention (negative attention, but attention all the same).

The Solution: Lorna's parents could find alternative non-physical strategies for maintaining discipline. They could consider distracting the girl when she touches things (instead of reprimanding her), which would focus her attention on to another activity. Or they could tell Lorna that she will be rewarded if she can go for a time without touching anything on the shelves. Or they could try to ignore some of the irritating behaviour. Any (or all) of these non-violent techniques – in addition to non-physical punishment for misbehaviour – could encourage Lorna to behave more positively.

Everyday Crises

Everybody finds children difficult to manage sometimes. Here are suggestions for what you should do if:

….. **a child doesn't do what she is told.** Keep telling her, while explaining why you want her to do this. Don't give up when she resists your discipline. Console yourself with the thought that her behaviour will become easier as she grows older and more mature.

…..**you start to lose your temper with a child.** Walk away into another room. Sometimes the pressures of being with an argumentative pre-school child can drive you to distraction and it is reasonable for you to take a break from her for a couple of minutes.

…..**you find yourself nagging at her when she's with you.** Try to concentrate on her positive aspects. Remind yourself that she's not terrible all the time, that she's only difficult some of the time. Constantly nagging at a child only increases negative feelings.

…..**she flies into a rage when you don't let her do what she wants.** Don't give in to her, otherwise she will learn that this behaviour helps her achieve her goals. A screaming child can be hard to resist, but you should make a solid effort not to give in to her.

…..**you feel terrible after arguing with a child.** Try to forget about it – she certainly will. Conflict between you and her is inevitable sometimes. It doesn't mean that you are a bad person or that she is a naughty child, so avoid dwelling on your disagreements with her.

…..**you know a child misbehaves in a specific situation.** Avoid the situation if at all possible. Suppose, for instance, she always misbehaves in the afternoon because she is so tired; you could encourage her to have a short nap after lunch.

Spoiling

No child was ever born spoiled. It's something that happens to her as a result of other people's behaviour towards her. So if you suddenly find yourself thinking about a child "You're behaving like a spoilt brat the way you are asking for all these things," don't blame the child. It's not her fault.

A child who is spoilt construes the world as entirely revolving around her, because every experience she has confirms that view. For instance, her parents let her do what she wants when she wants, they buy her whatever she wants, and they are never prepared to say "no" to her about anything. She needs to maintain this position of control over her parents by making ever-increasing demands – the fulfilment of these demands makes her feel in control, continuing the cycle of spoiling.

If you do find yourself with a spoilt child, then be ready to say "no" at times. Nothing terrible will happen to a child if you refuse to give her what she wants. Talk to her about your reasons for this decision. She may be in a bad mood with you because she hasn't got what she wanted, but she will calm down eventually and will probably listen to what you say (even though she might disagree with you).

Q & A

Q. *I know people who say that they were smacked as children and that it never did them any harm. Surely that's evidence that it works?*

A. There are more people who have fearful memories of being smacked in childhood than there are those with fond memories of a beating. Although there are individuals who don't perceive smacking as a negative form of control, evidence suggests that smacking doesn't work and that there are better ways to discipline a child. Any child can be bullied into behaving properly by a more powerful adult, but that's not what raising children is about. They need love, not fear.

Q. *I want to be firm with the three-year-old I look after, but I always give in to her when she makes a scene in a shop. What should I do?*

A. It is never easy to be firm with a child when there are onlookers, each of whom is keen to give you advice about what you should do. But you are responsible for her and you have to decide what to do. Warn her in advance that you'll take her out of the shop if she misbehaves; then if she does carry on in the shop, pick her up and go – leave your shopping behind if you have to. Once the child realises you will carry out your promises, she may behave more reasonably.

Q. *Why is it that one child does what she is told, while her younger sister challenges me virtually all of the time?*

A. Every child is a unique individual, with her own strengths and weakness and her own personality characteristics. There are so many factors that could contribute to this contrast in their attitudes to discipline, such as jealousy between them, or varying levels of self-confidence. You will probably never know why they are both so different, so stop worrying about it. Just accept that there are individual differences between the two children, and do your best to keep your rules anyway.

Q. *At what age does a child start to be self-disciplined so that she doesn't have to be told how to behave?*

A. Much depends on the child herself. However, she is unlikely to achieve a reasonable level of self-discipline before the age of four or five, and it may take longer. She really has to be quite mature before she no longer needs an adult to provide clear guidelines. As well as that, she needs plenty of experience of playing with other children, without supervision. Children who attend playgroup or nursery usually achieve self-discipline sooner than children who don't have these opportunities.

12

Temper Tantrums

"Eric was so good-natured when he was a baby. But he changed when he was about two. Suddenly he had a short fuse and would explode as soon as he couldn't get his own way. His temper was ferocious."

You probably won't have many problems with discipline when a child is much younger than a year, but from then on things may change. At this point, he may start to challenge the rules, and you'll probably start to see his temper emerge in the form of tantrums. A typical tantrum at this age involves the child crying, yelling inconsolably with rage, throwing things around and even hitting you; he might lie flat on the floor screaming, or bang his head against the wall.

There are several reasons why tantrums are common at this age:

- a two-year-old enjoys becoming independent. Now, the child becomes aware that he is an individual with feelings of his own and with his own opinions that may clash with other people's views. His likes and your likes are often different.
- he still sees the world only from his point of view. Toddlers are naturally egocentric and expect the world to revolve around them. In time, he'll grow out of this but at the moment the growing child expects to be firmly in the driving seat.
- he hasn't learned ways of controlling his temper. Everybody has a temper – even you! Part of growing up involves gaining control over angry feelings so that others are not hurt by them. A toddler has still to learn this.
- the child is easily frustrated. Toddlers have little patience, and become frustrated very easily over minor events that don't go according to plan. So a simple crisis, like not being able to grab hold of his toy when he reaches for it, can trigger a raging tantrum.
- he wants to get his own way. At this stage of his life, he is determined to do what he wants, no matter how much it might inconvenience others, no matter who tries to stand in his way. When he can't get his own way his anger quickly spills through.
- he believes he is very powerful. A toddler who is told "no" keeps asking anyway. He doesn't do this to be naughty; rather he believes he is powerful enough to make things happen just by wanting them to happen, and so he persists until he achieves his desired result.

No wonder many parents and carers find this a stressful and emotionally-draining period in the child's life. Toddlers are so self-possessed, so unaware that other people have feelings too. Lots of adults find that the constant battle of wills between themselves and the toddler is exhausting, as each becomes more and more determined to gain control over the other. And it can go on and on.

Avoiding Tantrums

Tantrums can be avoided at times; all it takes is effort and some careful planning. And it is certainly worthwhile – an afternoon punctuated by frequent tantrums is no fun for anybody. The list below highlights some typical incidents with toddlers that frequently result in tantrums, and suggests ways that these could potentially be avoided before the explosion point is reached.

These strategies are not guaranteed to work every time with every child, but they may be effective sometimes. Remember that the best way of managing tantrums is to prevent them happening in the first place, if at all possible.

Flashpoint: The child regularly pulls the tape out of the cassette player; when you try to stop him, he has a tantrum.
Avoidance Strategy – Distraction: Instead of waiting until he touches the cassette, try to distract his attention – with a game, or a book – as soon as he begins to wander over towards it.

Flashpoint: He loves to play with ornaments that are within his reach; when you try to stop him, he has a tantrum.
Avoidance Strategy – Removal: Although not always possible, try to avoid placing objects that are easily within his reach; there is no point in putting temptation directly in his path.

Flashpoint: He often becomes fractious and irritable towards the end of the day; his temper is easily triggered.
Avoidance Strategy – Calming: Try to maintain a calm and relaxed atmosphere; make a specific point of slowing the pace down so that neither you nor the child is rushed.

Flashpoint: While waiting in the checkout, the toddler is furious with you because you won't let him have a bar of chocolate.
Avoidance Strategy – Alternatives: Try to find another checkout that doesn't display sweets, or shop at a time when queues are unlikely. There usually are alternatives.

Flashpoint: When he tries to complete an inset-board puzzle, he gets very angry if he is unable to find the solution straight away.
Avoidance Strategy – Grading: Try to find a puzzle that is easier than the one that upsets him; mastery at an easier level will help develop his confidence and reduce his frustration.

Flashpoint: The child always loses his temper when another child wants to choose the activity or game for them to play next.
Avoidance Strategy – Warning: If you know a toddler is prone to tantrums in a situation that he has to face, then remind him in advance that he must try not to become angry.

Staying In Control

Tantrums are probably inevitable when a child is around two or three years of age, no matter how hard you try to stop them from occurring. It's simply a fact of life at this stage in his development. However, the way a tantrum develops once it has started, and the way it finishes, depends on you as well as on the child.

Before deciding how to deal with him, you need to decide about your own behaviour during one of his tantrums. You can be certain that if you lose your temper in response to his loss of temper, then that will inflame the situation. You have to stay in control of your own anger when he is in a rage. One of you needs to be calm, and as you are the adult the responsibility for keeping a level head rests with you. Here are some reasons why you have to take charge of your emotions (and the child's emotions) when he has a tantrum:

- **he may have no control at all.** While there are times when a child loses his temper in a controlled and manipulative way in order to wear down your resolve, most times he has lost control completely. He needs you to settle him; he may not manage on his own.
- **he may be very frightened.** Young children can become terrified at the ferocity of their own temper. As his tantrum builds up, the loss of control coupled with the intensity of his feelings, may totally disorientate him – he may become afraid of his own rage.
- **your calmness will spread to him.** When the child is in a tantrum, he will be reassured to see you relaxed, and this reduces his own tension. If he sees that you are calm, then he may become less agitated. But if he sees you raging too, this may increase his own anger.
- **he copies your behaviour.** How you behave in front of a child influences his behaviour, since a lot of what he does is straightforward imitation of your own actions. So staying calm even though he is behaving abominably towards you provides a good model of behaviour.

Use whatever technique you can in order to stay in control of your feelings. Some adults keep calm during a child's tantrum by simply ignoring it altogether, while getting on with another task – though the danger is that the adult does this only for so long, then suddenly screams uncontrollably at the child.

Some stay in control by leaving the child raging in one room while they themselves go into another room until he has calmed down; this can work but runs the risk that the child may cause considerable damage or even hurt himself in temper. And others keep reminding themselves quietly that remaining calm is good for the child when he has a tantrum. Use whatever method you are most comfortable with, but do your best not to match the child's screams with screams of your own.

Don't Give In

There is nothing pleasant about watching a child have a tantrum. You feel terrible for him (because he is so upset, because you know that he's well-behaved most of the time, because you know he'll be sorry afterwards) and you feel terrible for yourself (because you don't like having rows with him, because you think you might have been able to avoid it, because you just want a peaceful and relaxing day). For all these reasons, giving in to a toddler may seem the best and quickest way of ending his tantrum. But you will create more problems than you will solve with that strategy. Let's consider the following example:

The Problem: Sharon has a baby, Lisa, aged nine months, and a toddler Kevin, aged two years,. As soon as she starts to change Lisa's nappy, the two-year-old starts whining. Before the nappy has been changed, Kevin has progressed from moaning to leaning heavily into his mother, as though deliberately coming between her and the baby. When Sharon gently pushes him away with a warning that she needs to finish changing her baby, he gets very angry. Nine times out of ten Kevin starts crying and yelling at at this point. Both end up annoyed with each other. The same pattern can be repeated two or three times each day.
The Facts: Kevin is a typical toddler who likes as much attention from his mother as he can get. He is not too pleased with the fact that he has a younger sister; he feels jealous and threatened by her presence. Watching his mum in such close physical contact with the young baby makes him seethe with envy every time. In a matter of seconds this envy has been transformed into a temper tantrum which is focused on his mother and the baby. He can't help himself.
The Analysis: The toddler's tantrums have three main aims. First, he wants to stop his mother from doing something that he doesn't like (ie bathing the baby). The tantrum disrupts the process. Second, he needs to

vent his jealous feelings that are troubling him greatly. He doesn't have any other way to express these negative emotions. And third, he wants to turn his mum's attention away from her baby on to himself. Kevin's outrageous tantrum means that Sharon has no choice but to focus on him more than on his younger sister. And so his tantrum is successful, as far as he is concerned.

The Solution: Sharon might have more peaceful nappy-changing experiences if she tackles Kevin's misbehaviour directly instead of leaving it all to chance. For instance, she could talk to him about his feelings towards the baby, explaining to him that he needn't feel jealous of her. Although Kevin might show no reaction to these comments, he will feel reassured by them. Sharon could also try to meet his demand for her attention, without giving in to his attempts to interrupt her. She could, for example, ask him to help her with changing Lisa's nappy. These basic strategies would reduce the frequency of his tantrums.

Tantrum Tips

Once in a tantrum, a child may be unable to get out of it himself. A young child can easily become locked into a particular mood state because he hasn't yet got the maturity, social skills or personal control to initiate change on his own. He needs your help to calm down. Here are some tips for resolving a tantrum, though much depends on the individual child. You may need to experiment before achieving success:

- **stay calm and relaxed.** You may be tempted to get annoyed at the child in the hope of shouting him down – or perhaps because you are so frustrated and angry yourself – but this will only escalate the tension. Instead, act as though you are calm.
- **cuddle him.** A young child can be afraid of his own temper, and a tantrum may be very frightening for him. Put your arm round him, even though he may shirk away from you at first, because this caring physical contact reduces his anxiety.
- **keep him safe.** During a tantrum, he might accidentally or deliberately injure himself, perhaps by bumping into something or by banging his head against the wall in temper. Make sure that he does not hurt himself if you can avoid it.
- **reassure him.** Tell him that everything's going to be fine, that he has no need to get himself so upset, and that you'll be able to sort something out with him once he calms down. React to his unreasonable behaviour with reassurance.
- **explain to him.** The child always retains hope that his tantrum will force you to change your mind. So don't leave him in any doubt – explain to him that his tantrum won't get him what he wants. Repeat this several times no matter how often he loses his temper.

- **change location.** You may find that taking him away from the scene where the tantrum started is sufficient to decrease the severity of his temper, eg take him out of the shop, or move him from the playroom to the kitchen.
- **ignore him.** A child who launches into a tantrum for the sole purpose of gaining attention may calm down eventually if his outrageous behaviour is ignored. This is not always possible to do because of the chaos that he causes, but it certainly is worth a try.
- **remove him.** He may gain control over his temper if you take him into another room and leave him alone for a minute or two (at most). Tell him you'll see him very soon once he stops shouting – this may be enough to help him regain control.
- **remove the frustration.** Sometimes a tantrum is linked to a specific object, such as a toy that frustrates him or a vase that he wants to play with. Removing the object from his sight may reduce the intensity of his temper, although he will take time to calm down.
- **distract him.** Act as though he isn't having a tantrum. Chat to him in a friendly way and give him something that might catch his interest, such as his favourite toy. This strategy can bring a child out of a tantrum very quickly.
- **follow your normal routine.** Get on with another task or activity while he stomps about in his fiery mood. That might be reading a book, cooking a meal, or whatever. Just continue with your normal routine, despite his temper outburst.

Once the temper tantrum has passed, both you and the child will feel exhausted. He might even want to go to sleep. Use that post-tantrum time to get close to him again, to talk about what has happened. Don't reprimand him angrily for his misbehaviour, no matter how tense you feel at that time. Instead, tell him how sad you were to see him so upset, remind him gently but firmly that having a tantrum definitely won't make you give in to his demands, and suggest that he makes more of an effort the next time to control his temper. He may not be very talkative at this moment, often because he feels guilty and embarrassed about what he has done. Keep talking to him anyway, as your message will get through eventually.

When He Is Older

Many of these tips for managing a child's tantrum become inappropriate when he is much beyond the age of two or three years, simply because his temper is more ferocious and his physical strength is much greater. For instance, removing a screaming seven-year-old from one room to another may be physically impossible for you. That's why your approach to managing tantrums when a child is beyond four or five years has to alter to take account of his changing developmental skills.

The main difference in your approach lies in the source of control. When a child is younger, you must take charge when he loses his temper because he has neither the understanding nor the maturity to cope himself – if you left a toddler alone indefinitely while he had a tantrum, you would probably find that he was still in an angry mood hours later. He depends on you to provide the control for him. However, the ownership of this control can pass to the child when he is school age – he is mature enough now to realise that tantrums are unacceptable, that they upset everybody and that he could avoid them if he really tried. With your support and guidance, he'll begin to grasp that the onus for management of his temper rests with him.

Your approach at this age, therefore, should contain the following elements:

- **explanation.** Be open with him, telling him that now he's older he must stop behaving like a younger child. Explain that you get very upset when he loses his temper and that you expect him to try hard to control it the next time.
- **advice.** Give him suggestions for controlling his temper himself. For instance, he could come to tell you he is beginning to feel angry, he could walk away from the troubling situation, or he could watch his favourite video tape.
- **reminders.** If you see him about to have a tantrum despite all your previous warnings, remind him of the "cooling-off" strategies which you suggested to him – this may motivate him to use these techniques now. Tell him what to do to keep control.
- **praise.** Show how happy you are with him when you see that he effectively brings a potential outburst under control. He'll be as delighted as you. Point out that you are sure he'll do the same the next time he feels his anger stirring.
- **monitoring.** Every few days, check how he is getting on with his temper control. Hopefully there have been no tantrums, but ask him about any times that he nearly lost his temper yet managed to stop himself from exploding with rage.

Q & A

Q. *I look after a four-year-old who is so apologetic after a tantrum, and promises not to do it again. So why does he then have another tantrum a few minutes later?*

A. The child's sorrow and guilt following a tantrum are genuine. However, the fact that he feels bad about what he has done does not mean he is able to stop himself from behaving the same way the next time. Adults have enough difficulty with controlling their emotions during a bout of temper, never mind a young child. When he says he is sorry after a tantrum, believe him and accept what he says to you at face value. Cuddle him, reassure him that you still care for him even though he was bad-tempered, and ask him to try harder not to lose his temper when the situation arises again.

Q. *What should I do about breath-holding tantrums? My 21-month-old toddler holds his breath in temper until he passes out.*

A. Breath-holding tantrums are very frightening. They occur when a child is so angry that he sucks his breath in, blocking the back of his throat with his tongue. But he can't do himself any harm because as soon as he starts to faint, his tongue relaxes and air begins to flow into his lungs again. Some adults find that blowing towards the back of the child's throat stops a breath-holding attack; others hook the child's tongue forward using their index finger. He'll grow out of this habit in the next couple of years, at the latest.

Q. *When I put him into another room during a tantrum, he tears the place apart and I have to intervene. What should I do?*

A. Although this strategy works with many children, clearly it doesn't work with this child and so you should stop using it. There is no point in persisting with a technique that only makes matter worse, even though you wish it would work. You may find it helpful to try other ways of dealing with his temper tantrums, such as distracting him onto something new or cuddling him until he calms down – it's a case of trial and error until you find a method that works with him for a while.

Q. *Isn't it wrong to isolate a child when he's having a tantrum because this could make him very frightened?*

A. That's a possibility, which is why he should only be on his own during a tantrum for a very short time (ie one or two minutes). Before putting him out the room, tell him you are going to do this if he doesn't calm down. When he persists with his tantrum, put him out the room, but explain to him that you are doing this for a moment until he calms down. After a couple of minutes have passed, bring him back in again whether or not he has settled and then repeat this process if necessary.

13

Moral Behaviour

"I know straight away when she's done something she shouldn't have because her face goes bright red just above her cheekbones. And she knows that I know. Mind you, that doesn't stop her from being naughty the next time."

There will be occasions – and perhaps lots of them – when you describe a child's actions as "naughty" because she has behaved in a way that breaks the rules, and has annoyed or upset you. But the accusation of naughtiness towards a child's behaviour makes three assumptions. First, that she wilfully and deliberately tried to break your rules, that her behaviour was no accident. Second, that she has full control of what she did, and could have made a choice not to behave that way. And third, that she isn't bothered about what she has done because she doesn't care about right and wrong.

Looked at this way, it doesn't make sense to call a baby or young infant naughty, because she simply has not got that sort of mature understanding; she has not yet reached that level of intellectual maturity. And much of the so-called naughty behaviour during childhood has other explanations.

Right and Wrong

Psychological research confirms that a young child's understanding of right and wrong usually develops in a series of stages, along the following approximate lines:

Stage 1: Me, I, Myself. From birth until around 18 months, a child probably doesn't understand the concept of right and wrong. She still sees life in terms of her own needs, and so she thinks any action to satisfy these needs is justified. She acts without thinking about the consequences or implications for herself and for others. That's why it is usually inappropriate to describe a very young child as naughty.

Stage 2: I'm Listening. From around the age of two years onwards, the situation changes. She is still determined to place her feelings ahead of yours, but at least now she is able to listen to you. Most times she'll do what she wants anyway, even though she fully understands your opinion. She listens to your rules, and often remembers them, but gets carried away with the strength of her own feelings.

Stage 3: "More" Is Naughtier. A three-year-old has a much clearer understanding of right and wrong. However, in her mind, quantity matters more than quality. For instance, she can't understand why you are angrier with her for deliberately pulling a button off her coat than you are with her for falling accidentally and tearing her jacket badly. She assesses naughtiness by the effect of her behaviour, not the intention.

Stage 4: I Didn't Mean It. When a child has reached the age of four or five years, she knows that intention matters; she knows that deliberate misbehaviour is much more serious than accidental misbehaviour. When confronted by you for apparently naughty actions, her defence will be that she didn't mean to do it. The use of this argument is proof that her sense of right and wrong is at a more mature level.

Stage 5: You Could Do Better. The typical five-year-old thinks it is her job to police the moral behaviour of everyone else. So she points out that her friend shouldn't leave the toys in such a mess because it makes life harder for everyone else, or that you shouldn't take a snack between meals because that could stop you from eating a full meal later. She will develop a more flexible attitude within a few years.

Stage 6: It's Not Clear Cut. From the age of seven years, the child has a clearer sense of right and wrong and she knows what she should and should not do. However, she may begin to challenge some moral standards because she recognises that the circumstances surrounding behaviour are also important. For instance, she we will argue emphatically that she was entitled to hit another child who was about to hit her.

Lying

Nobody likes it when a child tells lies. No wonder; the act of lying is dishonest and deceitful. But the reasons why children tell lies are often different from the reasons adults tell lies – adult lies are generally for the purpose of concealment.

Reason For Lying: She might tell a lie because she wants to change the recent past. A child may genuinely believe that if she says something didn't happen then it might mean that it really didn't happen. That's why she will deny drawing on her white blouse with a pen even though you caught her at it. If she is only two or three years old she will genuinely believe that constant denial of the action will make her previous behaviour disappear completely.

What To Do

1. Don't get too angry with her. Naturally, you will be furious to hear a denial from a toddler when you saw her misbehaviour with your own eyes, but remember that she is still very young and sees the world differently from you.

2. Avoid trying to get her to tell you the truth. The chances are that by now she can't actually remember what really happened – she has probably distorted her memory of the incident so that she now believes her own version of events.
3. Encourage her to deal with the consequences of her behaviour, even though she may not admit responsibility. For instance, if she denies spilling sugar on the floor, ask her to help you clear it up anyway as that helps her understand the consequences of her actions.

Reason For Lying: She may lie to protect herself from punishment. Again, this is very common in children of all ages. If someone challenges you, your instinctive reaction is to protect yourself. This is a child's reaction too. So she instinctively denies her naughty behaviour when challenged because she knows that denial may get her out of a tight corner. As she grows older she recognises this strategy only gets her deeper and deeper into trouble.

What To Do

1. Accept this is normal behaviour from a child in the face of danger. This doesn't mean that you should consider her denial to be acceptable, just that you should realise it stems from self-preservation, not deliberate malice.
2. Make your punishments fair, not extreme. If the consequence of admitting her guilt is an outrageous punishment that is well in excess of her minor misdemeanour then she will lie twice as hard in order to save herself the next time.
3. Reassure her that you still care for her even though she has told you a lie. A child who fears her parents will love her less because she has behaved wrongly will instinctively lie to prevent this situation from occurring.

Reason For Lying: A child may lie to you for the sake of making her life more interesting. For instance, she might insist that she is able to jump over the garden fence, despite the ridiculous nature of such a claim – she wishes she had such ability. If she is only two or three, the line between fantasy and reality is so blurred that she may think these exaggerated claims are true, whereas by the time she is a few years older she knows that they are made up.

What To Do

1. Avoid the temptation of confronting her with reality. To do so is a pointless venture. After all, you can't be one hundred per cent certain that she didn't jump the fence! As long as these claims are infrequent, they are harmless.
2. Show an interest in her tales, without passing any comment which might show you disbelieve her. Listen attentively and nod at the right

moments so that she knows you are listening. She may have told the story to gain your attention in this way.
3. Tell her that you love her the way she is, and that you wouldn't want her to be different. She may look at you strangely when you say this in the middle of her insistence that she is the fastest runner, but she'll like hearing you say it.

Stealing

Next on the list of naughty behaviour comes stealing, which is a very anti-social action because it involves deliberately taking another's possessions without permission – the thief benefits at the victim's expense. So a child can't steal unless she fully understands the concept of "personal possession", and she won't fully grasp this concept until she is three or four years old. Of course, even a toddler knows when someone takes her toys and she creates a fuss when that happens; yet she'll forget about the toy once it has been out of her sight for a while. And if she has taken a toy from her friend, she'll soon think it was hers to start with.

By the time a child reaches school age she knows exactly what stealing is and why such behaviour is wrong. She may try to justify minor thefts, say, from her sibling's pencil case because she has been a victim of his petty thefts of her possessions, but at that age she will admit her behaviour is improper when you confront her.

Reason For Stealing: A child might steal something from you or from a friend because she thinks stealing is thrilling. Some children have a daredevil streak in them; they may be tempted by risk and danger. So the attraction of theft from a child's point of view is that it is unusual, it is challenging and it is exciting. She may not even see it as theft, more as a test of her personal skills. And when caught she might say " But I only did it for fun."

What To Do

1. Explain the impact of her stealing. She probably only sees the action in terms of the excitement it brings her, so make sure she realises the victim doesn't find it exciting. Remind her that the victim is upset by her behaviour.
2. Suggest other ways that she can have fun. Let her know that you are happy for her to enjoy herself, as long as it isn't at someone else's expense. Tell her the next time she wants to enjoy herself she should play with her own toys, not steal.
3. Give her a strong reprimand. The best way to discourage this type of stealing in the future is to ensure she finds it totally unenjoyable – and receiving a severe telling-off from you will certainly reduce the pleasure derived from the theft.

Reason For Stealing: The most common reason for theft at any age is that stealing satisfies the child's basic greed, the desire to have something quickly without having to pay for it. For instance, a child might steal a sweet from her friend because she is hungry and she hasn't got any sweets of her own – the theft brings immediate gratification. This also applies when she steals a toy from a shop. Most acts of stealing by older children fall into this category.

What To Do

1. Show your disapproval. She must understand that this type of behaviour is not acceptable under any circumstances. Be prepared to punish her (reasonably) when you discover the theft, and express your extreme displeasure.
2. Make her return the stolen goods. The child may be able to do this while avoiding a face-to-face confrontation (eg she leaves the item on her friend's desk when she is the only one there), but if not she must return the stolen objects anyway.
3. Suggest ways of achieving the same goal without stealing. For instance, she could ask her friend to let her play with the toy for a while, or she could ask her brother for a sweet. This allows her to access the items in an acceptable manner.

Reason For Stealing: When a child is older, the influence of her peer group starts to have a much more significant effect. She wants to be liked by them and will be prepared to do what they ask in order to stay accepted by them. In some instances, stealing is due to pressure from friends. Often a child who steals under these circumstances suddenly finds herself alone when her action is discovered – her friends are nowhere to be seen.

What To Do

1. Do not accept this explanation from the child as a reasonable excuse for her theft. While she may be partly justified in apportioning some of the blame to her friends, she should realise that the full responsibility for the action rests with her.
2. Remind her that she is older now and has to make decisions herself. Explain that she should not do what other people tell her simply because she wants to be liked by them; she needs enough self-confidence to make independent decisions.
3. Look closely at her group of friends at the moment. Every child may succumb to the temptation to steal, but if you find the child seems to be getting into bother regularly, then it may be time to encourage new friendships to replace her existing pals.

Swearing

From the first few moments of life, a child begins to develop her language skills. And by the time she is two or three years old she uses a wide range of words, phrases and sentences to express her feelings and ideas to you. Language is such a powerful tool of communication when used positively in this way by a growing child. And it is also powerful when it is used negatively, for instance, when she swears. This type of language is certainly unusual in a child under the age of three or four, but it can happen occasionally.

Reason For Swearing: If a child swears when she is only two or three, then there is every likelihood that she is simply copying another older child or adult whom she has heard using the same words. At this age she doesn't even know the true meanings of the words, just that she feels like a "big girl" when she uses them. She does not use these words in the normal adult sense (eg to express her anger, to emphasise the full strength of her feelings).

What To Do

1. Try not to laugh. There is something amusing about a young child's innocence when she swears, because she does not understand the implications of these words. But if you laugh at her she'll take this as encouragement.
2. Think about your own use of language and about the way other adults in her life speak. Two-year-olds don't mix with many people who are likely to swear, so it's worth thinking about the language used in the child's environment.
3. Emphasise that swearing is not pleasant, that you do not approve of her use of these words. This may come as a total surprise to her (because she heard adults use the words in the first place) but make this point plain to her.

Reason For Swearing: An older child may learn to use swearing in order to express her disapproval or anger. She is mature enough now to understand the difference between words that are acceptable and words that you disapprove of, even though she might not understand the actual meaning of a swearword. By the time she is four or five, she recognises swearing is used by people when they are angry, and she uses these words in the same way.

What To Do

1. Show your disapproval instantly. If you are satisfied that she genuinely understands that she is swearing and that these are "naughty" words, then reprimand her immediately, telling her that using these words is naughty.

2. Encourage her to use other words to express her negative feelings. She is entitled to be angry, and she is entitled to express this verbally – but only using her normal vocabulary. She is not entitled to swear to express her feelings.
3. Explain that other people will react badly when they hear her swear. For instance, if she swears in her class, her teacher will be furious with her and her friends' parents won't want their children to play with her.

Persistent Misbehaviour

Some children are naughtier than others, and a child who persistently misbehaves is very hard to handle. A constant run of minor incidents throughout the day is enough to wear down even the most resolute parent. But the pattern of misbehaviour has to be halted at some stage. Let's consider the following example:

The Problem: Adrienne is five years old. Hardly a day goes past at the moment without an incident involving misbehaviour (which she always denies outright) at home, or an annoying act of minor theft (such as removing crayons from her brother's school bag). Adrienne's mum finds this situation very draining. She does not know whether or not to believe her daughter, and distrust has crept steadily into their relationship; she does not particularly enjoy Adrienne's company any more. The girl attends school each day, and her behaviour there is also challenging.

The Facts: Adrienne has always been a difficult and challenging child. Even as a baby, she was slow at feeding and slept irregularly. Her parents have struggled to develop a more stable pattern of behaviour with her but they have not succeeded. Since the age of three, Adrienne has increasingly used lying and stealing in the house; although these actions are minor, they worry her parents greatly. Her mum and dad do their best to discourage their daughter from being naughty. However, nothing seems to work. They had hoped that she would be more settled when she started school but this has not happened.

The Analysis: Naughty behaviour has become an established part of Adrienne's life at home. And feeling helpless and negative about that behaviour has become an established part of her parents' reaction. Both child and adults have become stuck in a cycle of naughtiness – they all perceive her as a naughty child, they expect her to behave that way, and they feel powerless to effect change. Now her parents only react after the event; they have given up all attempts at preventative measures. Her class teacher, however, has a more positive outlook. She wants to work in conjunction with Adrienne's parents in order to positively change their daughter's actions.

The Solution: Mum and dad should try to regain control of the situation. Positive strategies are required. The parents and teacher could try a number of techniques, for instance, they could focus on the times she does not behave in a naughty manner and praise these instances of good behaviour; they could be less negative when reprimanding her (eg instead of saying "You're naughty for telling lies" they could say "I'm upset that you've lied because you are such a lovely child and I know that you can tell the truth"); they could ignore some lesser incidents of misbehaviour instead of reacting to everything that she does; and they could acknowledge that her behaviour might stem from dissatisfaction and discuss this with her (eg "I think you misbehave at home because you are angry with us about something. Let's talk about it"). These strategies are more likely to lead to a resolution of the behaviour than simply continuing along the rut they are in already, especially when there is a joint approach between home and school.

Q & A

Q. *My three-year-old has started copying an older child who has a habit of telling lies, and now she tells lies. How can I discourage her from this?*

A. You need to be very direct with her. She probably thinks that telling lies is the sort of thing "big children" do and that if she tells lies, then she'll be more grown up like the older child. So make it clear to her that you disapprove of her telling lies and also that you strongly disapprove of the other child telling lies. As long as you take firm action early, you'll find that she soon regards lying as less attractive than she does now.

Q. *What should parents do when they are convinced their child didn't start swearing until she went to school?*

A. They may be correct in their observation. It may be that their child has started to pick up these speech habits from some of the other children in her class, and hence her use of these words at home. The best strategy is for the parents simply to discourage her from speaking that way when she is with them (giving her an explanation of why you would prefer her not to use these words). They should tell their child that even if she hears some other children swear she should not copy them. This should be repeated regularly to her.

Q. *Why does a five-year-old steal toys from the cot of her six-month-old brother? She can't possibly want to play with the toys.*

A. It looks as though the older child is jealous of the baby, and her stealing is a sign of this jealousy. Rather than challenging her about the stealing – which is simply an expression of her insecurity and jealousy that you are giving your attention to the baby – spend some time talking to her about this. Encourage her to express her feelings, and listen to what she says. Reassure her that she is cared for as much as the baby. This reassurance, coupled with the fact that you acknowledge her concerns, should be sufficient to greatly reduce her temporary need to steal.

Q. *Since I reprimanded my child for telling a lie – and not a very big one at that – she appears obsessed with right and wrong, ready to chastise anyone who she thinks may not be telling the truth. Why?*

A. Your initial reprimand has focused her attention on to the whole issue of telling lies, and has made her very conscious of it. She's also discovered that other people tell lies too, and her innate sense of justice tells her that if she gets into trouble for it then everyone else should. Don't make a fuss about this apparent obsession; she'll pass through this phase within the next few months.

14

Comforters

"He had to have his grubby old teddy with him wherever he went, and that habit lasted until he started school. I wasn't bothered, except for that time when he lost it for a couple of days - he was distraught until teddy reappeared."

In most instances, a child has a favourite cuddly toy that he loves snuggling against – and it is probably one that he's had since he was a baby. Or maybe he cuddles a remnant from his old cot blanket. Research indicates that at least half of all children under the age of five years have an object like this. Psychologists use the term "comforter" to describe this sort of cuddly toy because cuddling it brings a child a feeling of comfort and well-being. Comforters can vary depending on the child's age and stage of development. The list below identifies the most common comfort objects during the early years:

three months: Even at this stage in his young life, a baby is often able to sleep better when he is surrounded by a blanket that he has used before or when he snuggles up to a cuddly soft toy. You may find that when he is given a new blanket for his cot – or when his old blanket is returned after being washed – he is unsettled and restless.
one year: The typical one-year-old does not yet have a specific comforter, but he does show a fondness for objects that he used to play with. Although new toys will always be welcomed by him, he will be reluctant to discard his old toys. He prefers to store the old and new together in his cupboards.
18 months: A toddler may still be extremely fond of the first cuddly toy he had when he was a baby. By now, after a year and a half of regular usage, the toy shows signs of wear and tear – but that makes no difference to the toddler. He loves it anyway, and perhaps its worn look and feel makes the toy attractive to him.
two years: Like many children of this age, a child may enjoy sucking a dummy, even though he is able to drink from an open cup and no longer requires a bottle. He'll probably not be too fussy about which dummy in particular he sucks because the attachment is to dummies in general, not to any one in particular.
three years: He left his cot some months ago, and now sleeps in his own bed. However, you may find that he still insists on having his old

cot blanket with him, spread over the covers at night. In some instances, a three-year-old will be happy to walk about the house with his old cot blanket trailed over his shoulders.

four years: By now, comforters from the child's earlier years will be in tatters, and may even be completely unrecognisable to anyone other than him. However, he still likes them when he is tired, unwell or perhaps when he watches television in the evening. He will be reluctant to agree to a replacement.

five years: A child has a more mature attitude now that he is ready to start school and he'll not want his friends to know that he has a comforter (even though they each have one too!). As a result, the comforter tends to be a newer toy, and he may prefer to carry it with him rather than to be seen snuggling up to it.

The Psychology of Comforters

To be honest, psychologists don't know why young children have an emotional need for comforters. It's not simply a case of insecure children needing a comforter more than secure children – almost every child has a comforter sometimes. In fact, the results of psychological studies have revealed that a child who has a comforter before he reaches school age has better relationships with other children once he is in school, and he is less likely to be shy, less likely to be lacking in self-confidence and even less likely to experience nightmares. It's as though having a comforter could actually be good for a child.

Here are some possible reasons why a child likes a comforter:

- **familiarity.** It's the instantly recognisable feel, smell and even taste of the comforter that makes the item so appealing to him. He knows exactly what it will be like to hold and this provides him with reassurance. Familiarity, in this case, does not breed contempt.
- **babyhood.** When a child has a comfort object from the time when he was a very young baby, its appeal for him lies in that link. Most children have fond memories of the early years and so are happy to use a comforter that is associated with that period.
- **security.** Life is more demanding for a child when he is older. He clings to his comforter for security because he doesn't always have his mum and dad right beside him. The comforter makes him feel safe and ready to face the world independently without them.
- **confidence.** Watching a three-year-old child sucking at his old cot blanket while waiting to meet new children might make you anxious and have doubts about his maturity. Yet he probably holds the comforter at that precise moment because he is slightly nervous.
- **anxiety.** You might take a good luck charm with you when you have to deal with a situation that makes you nervous (eg visit to the den-

tist). A child does this too, though in his case he prefers a comforter to a lucky mascot. The comforter helps him beat his anxiety.

- **regression.** Under pressure, he may behave in a babyish manner. This is perfectly normal. So if he is unhappy about something, he might deliberately use the comforter because he knows that is what he liked when he was younger. This behaviour makes him feel better.

Comforters - Good or Bad?

Most adults are unhappy to see a young child trailing an old cuddly toy around with him wherever he goes, but there is absolutely nothing wrong with this sort of behaviour as long as it doesn't become too extreme. He will probably grow out of his comforter by the time he's five anyway, no matter what you think.

The advantage of a comforter is that it helps a child to relax; it is virtually guaranteed to induce positive feelings and that can only be good for him. Knowing that he has his comforter clutched firmly in his hand may be sufficient for him to deal competently with any crisis. During his toddler stage, a comforter may calm him. For instance, allowing him to have his comforter on holiday means that he will be able to sleep happily in a strange bedroom. Or giving him his cuddly toy when visiting the doctor will ensure that he co-operates during the consultation. Once the child is three or four years old, he can take full control of using the comforter; he decides when to cuddle it and when to leave it. He enjoys having this element of control in his life.

On the down side, however, comforters can be a bit of a nuisance, especially if the child becomes too attached to it. You'll already be aware of this if you've ever had to deal with a child who refuses to go out the front door until he has found his comforter. It doesn't matter a jot to him that you are ready and waiting to go, that everyone else is also ready to go, and that the taxi is waiting. If he can't find his comforter, then everyone has to look for it. He'll probably be miserable during the whole outing if he has to leave it behind.

And then there's the image created by a child who has a comforter with him. A baby with a cuddly toy is cute but a five-year-old clinging desperately on to a grubby old teddy gives an entirely different impression. He may look immature and babyish; although he isn't bothered by this, you might be. Hygiene is also an important issue. Old cot blankets and old stuffed toys get dirty and harbour germs.

Part of the attraction for him is its well-worn feel, so the child won't thank anyone for cleaning it. He may be furious because washing has given the comforter a different feel, smell and taste and it's not what he is used to. He may even refuse to part with it for a day or so while it is put through the wash cycle.

The choice about comforters is a personal one. Remember that there is nothing inherently wrong with a comforter, but at some stage the child will have to learn to survive without it.

Going to Extremes

For some children, the excessive need for a comforter can be a sign that something is wrong. A child who is extremely anxious or insecure may grow to be too dependent on his favourite cuddly toy. Let's consider the following example:

The Problem: Since he was a baby, Tim's favourite cuddly toy has always been a small giraffe, made of very soft material. Now that he is four years old, the legs of the giraffe are long since gone, and there is only one ear. However, he adores this furry little animal and likes to cuddle it when falling asleep. Recently, however, his need for this item has grown. He insisted on taking the comforter with him to his nursery one day - and then made a terrible fuss when his parents initially told him he was not allowed. Since that day, he has clung tightly to the giraffe whenever he has gone to his nursery. His parents are alarmed by this behaviour, which they associate with a much younger child. Other children are beginning to laugh at him too.

The Facts: Tim is usually a very confident boy who copes with new experiences in his stride. He's rarely upset, and even when he is, he tends to sort things out by himself. He is a popular child, with lots of friends. Tim was not especially reliant on the comforter until recently. His parents have discussed this problem with the nursery staff who confirmed that he appears to be less secure at the moment. They added that a couple of new children joined Tim's group recently, and perhaps he feels a little bit isolated.

The Analysis: The sudden change in the child's dependency on the comforter is a sign that he is worrying about something. Having a comforter in childhood is normal, but an extreme need for a cuddly toy is less typical. His insistence on having the object with him at all times when he is in nursery demonstrates that he is insecure and anxious. At this stage, the most probable cause is the new children. Young children usually don't like change (in fact, few adults enjoy unpredicted change) and they can be unsettled by this. Although Tim is a popular and confident boy, he takes time to make friends. The reorganisation may have rocked his confidence and security, forcing him to fall back on his old familiar friend, the half-chewed giraffe.

The Solution: The comforter is only a symptom of Tim's anxiety, not the cause, so there is no point in making the use of the comforter the sole focus of attention. Any strategy which aims to stop Tim taking this toy with him all the time, and which doesn't look at the underlying reasons, will only make matters worse. Straightforward removal of the giraffe will increase his anxiety. The best way forward is for the adults in Tim's world to take a closer look at him, in order to identify what may be troubling him. If it is the new children in his nursery group, then she should reassure him that he will get to know the others soon, that they will like him, and that he will soon enjoy their company. Even if Tim's parents can't find out the cause of his underlying worry – and this often happens – they should continue to reassure him and to take an interest in his daily routine. Giving attention in this way may be sufficient in itself to reduce his reliance on the cuddly toy.

Comfort Habits

Children under the age of five often have comfort habits, rather than comfort toys or comfort objects. Here are some typical comfort habits in this age group, though you will find that habits and objects vary greatly from child to child:

- **hair-twiddling.** Typically, the child twiddles his hair while concentrating on either a game or a television programme. His hand reaches for his hair almost automatically without any effort, and his fingers start to twiddle a clump of hair at the side of his head. He probably twiddles the same section of hair each time; if he does this a lot, then that section will be thinner than the rest of his hair.
- **thumb-sucking.** This is an extension of sucking a dummy in earlier years, only without involving an object. The child puts his thumb (or in some instances, his index finger and his middle finger) deep into his mouth and sucks away on it. If this persists, the skin on his thumb may become rough or broken. Thumb-sucking puts pressure on the child's teeth and this could cause damage if it continues.
- **face-stroking.** It is surprising how many children, when they are deeply absorbed in an activity, begin to stroke part of their face gently and rhythmically. This might involve the child's cheek, his chin or his upper lip. You probably do this to him when trying to soothe him, and so it is likely that he continues to use it as a comfort habit himself because it is strongly associated with feelings of relaxation.
- **genital-rubbing.** Masturbation in childhood is simply another type of comfort habit. A child enjoys rubbing his genitals, not for sexual stimulation in the mature sense of the word, but because he simply enjoys the warm, soothing sensations. Psychologically, there is no difference between this comfort habit and any other. That's why it is important not to overreact with embarrassment (or disgust).
- **rocking.** When a child is upset, you might sit him on your knee, hold him snugly in your arms and gently rock him back and forth un-

til he calms down. He loves this close, caring physical contact. No wonder he tries to replicate the same feelings by gently rocking himself when he is on his own. But these movements do not mean he is upset; he rocks because it is another way to help himself relax.

- **nail-biting.** He may enjoy nibbling away at his fingernails, or even nibbling away at the skin surrounding his fingernails. There's something very purposeful about this habit, because the child studies the progress of his nail-biting very closely. Like thumb-sucking, the repetitive action of biting nails brings his fingers in direct contact with his mouth – and it is this touch which he finds enjoyable.

What To Do

In most instances, a child will grow out of his comforter or comfort habit spontaneously, whether or not you do anything to alter his behaviour at the time. However, you may want to give him a helping hand. Try the following suggestions:

- **avoid battles.** A child's comfort habit will become more entrenched if you start fighting with him about it. The more that his comforter gains in importance for you and for him, the more he will hold on to it, determined to resist all attempts at change. So try not to become annoyed with him (eg "I'm getting really angry at you with that stupid blanket"), or to make a fool of him (eg "You look silly with your fingers stuck in your mouth"), or to compare him (eg "Your younger sister doesn't want her teddy all the time").
- **consider his perspective.** As far as the child is concerned, having a comforter is good fun, that's all. He doesn't have any rational explanation for his behaviour when you question him about it (eg when you ask what he likes about his cuddly toy he'll reply "I don't know, I just like it"). But the fact is that he does enjoy having the object or the habit, and it does help him feel at ease. In addition, he won't see any reason to change things at the moment. So expect some resistance, because he gains emotional satisfaction from it.
- **take a gentle approach.** Is not easy to break a dependency habit. Your approach needs to be supportive, encouraging and steady. Don't go for the "cold turkey" strategy which involves immediate and complete withdrawal of the comforter. That's unreasonable. He cannot be expected to break his habit that quickly. Far better to suggest that he tries to avoid using the comforter for a specific amount of time (eg for an hour at first), then gradually extend this period. His ability to cope without the comforter will increase slowly.
- **note any positives**. He will only give up the comforter or comforter habit if he feels that this change in behaviour brings him some benefit. That's why you need to tell him how happy you are with his new

behaviour. Other ways of rewarding him for not using the comforter include pointing out that he looks like a "big boy" now, reminding him that his friends will not laugh at him any more, and maybe giving him a special treat because he has tried so hard. You can do this even if he stops the comfort habit for a few moments.

Q & A

Q. *What is the best way to persuade a three-year-old to let me wash his cuddly toy? He bursts into tears when I even suggest it, and the toy is filthy.*

A. He is probably worried in case you are using this as a subtle trick to get rid of his comforter altogether, and understandably he doesn't want to co-operate with you. One way round this hurdle might be to give him some control over the cleaning process. For example, you could let him wash the toy himself in soapy water (with your help and supervision), then rinse it himself, then let him place it somewhere safe to dry. By putting him in charge of the cleaning process you will reduce his anxiety about cleaning the toy.

Q. *Whenever I give attention to my older child, my younger child suddenly insists I help him find his favourite cuddly toy. Does he feel insecure?*

A. The chances are that his request for the comforter has nothing to do with feelings of insecurity – it is just his way of gaining your attention and of reducing his boredom. He doesn't like it when everyone else is busy on other activities, leaving him to make his own amusement. And so he suddenly cries for his comforter in the hope that you will stop what you are doing and focus on him for a while. One way you could try to get round this is by making sure he settles at an activity of his own before you turn away to do something else. He won't want the comforter if he is purposefully occupied.

Q. *Do you think I could stop a five-year-old from biting his nails by putting a sticking plaster over his fingertip? People have told me this works.*

A. This is a popular strategy (along the same lines as painting his nails with a ghastly-tasting solution) and it has been found to work with some children. But it can turn into a challenge and confrontation rather than a help and support. For instance, the child might try to pull the plaster off when you're not looking or he might simply start biting a different nail – and you can hardly put ten plasters on his fingers several times each day! Punitive methods like this take responsibility for change away from the child on to the adult, whereas change is more probable when the child himself is actively involved in the process.

Q. *My child is two-and-a-half, and he constantly has his hands inside his pants, playing with himself. Should I ignore this?*

A. You could ignore this behaviour if you want to – and he may stop spontaneously – but if you are troubled by this habit, then you should take action now. One way would be to try to distract him, perhaps by giving him a toy or game to play with; this may work immediately. You could also simply tell him to stop, though he may not always respond; and you can also take his hand from inside his pants, if he doesn't do as you ask. This is what you would do if you wanted to discourage him from touching anything; the same principles apply here too.

15

Children's Fears

"Tina screams hysterically whenever she sees a dog, and I have no idea why. I realise she's only two, but she has never been bitten by a dog or anything like it so I don't understand where the fear comes from."

Virtually every child is afraid of something sometimes. It may not be what you are afraid of, it may not be rational from your point of view, and it may not be what you'd expect her to be afraid of, but she has a fear all the same. And that's normal.

Her fear needn't be especially strong – indeed, most childhood fears are quite mild and for much of the time don't have any significant impact on the child unless she is actually confronted with the focus of her fear. Only occasionally are childhood fears intense enough to have a disruptive effect on a child's life.

Research has discovered the following facts about fears:

- a minimum of 90% of all children under the age of five years have a specific fear at some point.
- the typical child between the age of 12 months and five years has three fears, though some have more.
- children in this age group show evidence of being afraid on average once every four or five days.
- girls tend to have more fears than boys, and the fears of boys tend to be less intense than the fears of girls.

Children Are Susceptible

Of course adults also have fears, but their fears are usually more controlled and less irrational. For instance, you may be afraid of the dentist because previous experiences there have been unpleasant and painful – your fear may well be justified. However, children's fears are more vivid, less based on previous experience, facts or reality. The list below identifies key factors influencing the development of fears during childhood.

Unlimited imaginative ability: From the toddler stage onwards, a child's imagination develops at a very fast rate. Her vivid imagination is not restricted by a broad knowledge of the world nor by a great deal of past experience. So she can imagine anything about anyone. In her

young mind, there are no limits. She can become afraid even when there is no possible risk to her at all, because she imagines the danger.
Example: A young child runs away when she sees a cat come near her, even though the animal is passive and friendly. When she sees the cat, she sees a ferocious animal with long snarling teeth, who will snatch her up and run off with her. To you such an idea would seem silly but to her vivid imagination, such an idea is perfectly possible.

Powerlessness: Although a young child is often self-opinionated, she also knows that there are some things she cannot do by herself. For instance, she knows that she cannot run away quickly if something frightens her, and she realises that she is not as strong as people who are older than her. This generates a sense of powerlessness in the face of danger and renders her more susceptible to fear.
Example: If an older child is terrified of small animals, then she can remove herself from them by running away, or by moving to another room or by asking the animal's owner to hold it steady. A young child isn't as effective in dealing with her fear; for instance, it may not occur to her to ask for the animal to be restrained.

Fantasy: A child younger than the age of three or four years can't always tell the real world from her fantasy world. The power of her young imagination, coupled with her lack of worldly experience, results in a blurring of boundaries between what is real and what is simply the product of her own mind. Pretend-play situations can quickly turn into upsetting experiences precisely for this reason.
Example: When she wakes up during the night, especially as a result of a bad dream, she may not realise that she is awake. She may regard reality as part of her dream, and this can be very frightening for her. Similarly, she can become so absorbed in a play sequence that she forgets it is only play, that it's not as real as she believes it to be.

Symbolism: Around the time that a child reaches the age of 18 months, her ability to use symbolism develops. This means that she can visualise an object as though it is something else completely different; as far as a child is concerned, for instance, a shadow can be a monster, a cat can be a ferocious animal, a glass of milk can contain secret poison. Many fears in childhood develop in this way.
Example: If a child sees any object at all – even though it is apparently innocuous as far as you are concerned – she can use her imagination to transform it into an entirely different object. A spoon can become a secret weapon, an insect can become a wild beast that will devour her entirely. Therefore a child can develop a fear of anything at all in her mind.

Perspective: She sees the world from her point of view, using the knowledge and understanding she has already acquired. However, the world looks different when you are a child; small objects look large, and large objects look huge and overpowering; small animals look big, and larger animals look terrifying. This results in the child being aware of dangers that older children don't even think twice about.
Example: A harmless fly can totally terrify her because it seems so big from her point of view. A bath can seem enormous, terribly slippery and extremely frightening – she may feel vulnerable and insecure unless she is able to grip tightly on to a handle. She could also be afraid of having her hair washed in case the soapy water hurts her.

Types of Fears

Psychologists have researched the nature of children's fears for almost a century and the results prove that a child can be afraid of absolutely anything. For instance, there is the **fear of failure**. Virtually every child wants to succeed, it's as simple as that. She wants to achieve whatever she sets out to achieve, and it doesn't matter whether her target is to be the best reader in infant school or to be the fastest runner in secondary school. There is a basic human need to succeed, and fear of failure can be very upsetting. A child who is afraid of failure may be unwilling to try anything new in case the challenge proves too difficult for her (eg she refuses to go on the climbing frame because she is afraid she won't be able to get to the top).

Other types of fears are connected to her relationships. For instance, a child may be **afraid of loss of love.** She wants to be loved by her parents (and by her carers), and the prospect of losing that love is too awesome for her to imagine. So any action which suggests the love for her may be diminishing will make her afraid. Of course, this doesn't stop her from misbehaving but it does make her tremble when she is reprimanded. A child who is generally insecure will be particularly prone to this type of fear (eg she cries hysterically at the slightest telling-off from you).

Another relationship-based anxiety is her **fear of separation.** For instance, she clings to her parents when they take her to a friend's house or when they drop her off at nursery because she is afraid that something bad will happen either to her or to them once they are apart (she may even be afraid of death). This type of fear is more common when the child is aware that her parents argue a lot (eg she is afraid of leaving them in case they will not be there when she returns).

Fear of being hurt is very common in children under the age of five. They are less aware of the potential harm that could happen to them because they don't fully understand everyday hazards. Yet those hazards that they are aware of may make them disproportionately afraid. For instance, food that is too hot can terrify a child – the fear of being burned intensifies when she sees a steaming plateful. Often these fears of danger are illogical (eg a two-year-old clutches on to an adult when taken to the local swimming pool; she does this despite going into the shallow pool, while wearing arm-bands that will keep her afloat).

And the final common childhood terror is the **fear of small animals**. Surprisingly, small animals can be more frightening to a young child than large animals. Maybe it is the speed at which small animals scurry about, or that they remind her too much of her favourite soft toy. The child may be very distressed when she realises that a normally-caged small animal has become free (eg a hamster let out of its cage can frighten her more than a large dog). The same applies to insects, such as spiders, worms, butterflies and crickets.

The Need for Security

Fears which undermine a child's security in her relationship with her carers can be extremely damaging and are best tackled as soon as possible. A child who is afraid of losing her parents' affection will be unhappy. Let's consider the following example:

The Problem: Carolyn is five years old and is a very nervous type of child. She is on edge a lot of the time, and tends to be easily upset by change or by unexpected alterations to her daily routine. Well-behaved most of the time, Carolyn gets up to mischief occasionally. Her parents regards this as normal but still reprimand her anyway. Whenever she is told off she over-reacts, screaming in fear, pleading with them to forgive her and repeatedly stating how sorry she is. Her parents want the girl to respond positively to her reprimands but they can't understand this rather extreme reaction.
The Facts: Carolyn has an older bother who can be an absolute pest at times. He is regularly in trouble at school and his parents are frequently summoned to speak to the head teacher about him. Consequently, his parents' relationship with him is negative at the moment. They constantly criticise his behaviour (for completely justifiable reasons), and they punish him when he causes distress to others. Arguments between parents and son take place virtually every day.
The Analysis: The constant bickering within the family has unsettled Carolyn, despite the fact that she is usually uninvolved. She witnesses her parents criticising her older brother, which makes her afraid and insecure. She doesn't want to be rejected by them. At Carolyn's age, she cannot distinguish between criticism of her brother and criticism of her brother's behaviour; she assumes that when he is reprimanded her par-

ents' love for him lessens. That's why she is so upset when she is in the spotlight – the thought of losing the love of the adults in her world terrifies her, even though there is no basis to her fear.

The Solution: Carolyn requires reassurance that annoyance from her from mum and dad is not the same as outright rejection by them. They need to explain to her that they can be angry with her and yet love her at the same time. Carolyn clearly feels they have either one feeling or the other, but not both together. In addition, they have to ensure that when they do punish her for misbehaviour, the matter is over and done with. Through these strategies, this sensitive five-year-old will gain confidence in her relationship with mum and dad; she'll realise that while reprimands are not pleasant they are not the end of the world, and she won't be so afraid all the time.

Fears Change with Age

A child's fears change as she grows older during the early years. What she was afraid of last year might not bother her at all this year – and her current fear may be something that didn't trouble her at all previously. Here are the most common fears, according to age:

- **12 months.** Her natural shyness at this age means that she may develop a fear of strangers. It's not a serious problem – it just means that whenever the child sees an unfamiliar face, she will try to hide in some way, perhaps by covering her face or tucking herself behind you. She needs you to reassure her that she is safe.
- **18 months.** Fear of the toilet is very common. The attention paid to her as potty training begins forces her to think more about the toilet than ever before, and many children develop anxieties about it. She may be afraid of falling down the toilet bowl (it looks huge to her) or of something dreadful creeping out of it.
- **two years.** Fear of separation from mum and dad often develops at this age because the child experiences separation from them for the first time, at playgroup or parent-and-toddler group. On the other hand, if a child is already used to temporary breaks then her fear of separation can decrease as her confidence grows.
- **30 months.** Popular fears at this age include fear of small, fast-moving animals and also fear of darkness. This latter probably intensifies because the child has now moved into her own bed, and also because potty training is well underway; this means she is more likely to wake up in darkness during the night to use the toilet.
- **three years.** These earlier fears are often still present, although they diminish as the child's sense of security and confidence has increased over the previous year. Now, other fears show through, such as the fear of ghosts and other imaginary things, and fear of thieves. A child

is heavily influenced by her television viewing.

- **four years.** Her vivid imagination means that fears of fictitious animals and make-believe people can be strong. Fear of failure can dominate. If a child attends nursery, she probably compares herself with others; the realisation that they are in some ways more competent than she is can make her afraid that she won't succeed.
- **five years.** A child will be afraid of "scary creatures" and "bad people", though not as intensely as when she was younger. Fears are more related to her new life experiences, such as fear of going to the dentist (one reason why dental care should start very early on in childhood), and fear of not being liked by her teacher.
- **six-ten years.** Achievement at school becomes very important, and the typical child in this age group wants to gain good marks in classroom assignments. A run of low scores can seriously upset her, denting her self-confidence and increasing her anxiety. She needs to experience success or her fear of failure will intensify.
- **11 years.** From the age of around 11 years onwards, her biggest fear is of rejection by her peers. Other children the same age become extremely important to her. She shares the same views and wants to be accepted by them. Any sign that she is not part of the group can devastate her. She fears rejection.

Childhood fears are usually transient and may last for less than a year; some are more durable, however. Much depends on what started the fear in the first place and the way that this is handled. For instance, if a child is startled by a dog and cries with fright, this could develop into an established fear if her parents keep her away from dogs everywhere they go after that incident. Her parents' behaviour could keep the fear simmering and growing. In contrast, if her parents reassure her that she is safe, that the dog won't harm her, and if they encourage her to stroke the dog gently, then the chances are she'll soon forget about her fright.

Adult responses to their own fears can affect children. Suppose you are afraid of going to the dentist, but have to take a child with you on such visits when she is younger. The child will sense your fear even though you may not say anything to her about it, and she will learn this fear from you. By the time it's her turn to visit the dentist, she'll be petrified. Fears are contagious.

Preventing Fears

Some (though not all) childhood fears can be avoided if suitable preventative techniques are used when the child is young. Here are some suggestions to help stop a child developing fears (although bear in mind that she may acquire fears despite all efforts):

- **prepare her in advance.** If you know that a child has to face a stressful episode in the near future (eg a short stay in hospital) then give her notice. Tell her what to expect, and remind her that you will be with her. Answer any questions that she has about the procedure.
- **be calm yourself.** Your fear will spread to her. If you are anxious about the challenge facing the child, don't show it otherwise her fear will intensify. Have a calm and relaxed outward manner, and try to avoid indicating that she should be worried about what lies ahead.
- **teach her to cope.** You can help her develop the ability to cope with a potential fear by suggesting strategies for her to use. For instance, if she is afraid of not being good at reading when she starts school, then give her extra attention when she is learning to read.
- **avoid frightening experiences.** A child will love fairy stories and other tales which have an element of excitement in them – the appeal of these stories often lies in their ability to generate a touch of fear. Yet too many frightening childhood tales may induce fears.
- **be discreet.** Like most adults, you probably have fears. But keep them to yourself. Don't let the child hear about them, if at all possible, because the realisation that you are afraid of something may be sufficient to make her afraid of it too. She may copy you.

Action Plan for Beating Fears

If all your preventative steps have failed, and a child does have a genuine fear despite all your attempts to avoid it, then you will have to help her conquer her fear. This action plan will help you work with the child to overcome it:

1. **Treat her with respect.** Her fear may seem trivial, but it is very real to her. She's not acting this way just for fun; so don't treat her in a way which might suggest you think she is being silly. You recall what you feel like when you are afraid – her feelings are exactly the same.
2. **Reassure her.** As far as she is concerned, the object of her fear is insurmountable. She'll benefit from your reassurance that she will cope. Keep saying this over and over, in a gentle tone. She gains emotional strength from your confidence in her.
3. **Discourage avoidance.** A child won't overcome her fear if she avoids the focus of that fear; in fact, that will make matters worse because she won't develop skills for coping. She has to face her fear – with your support – and see for herself that she can manage.
4. **Help her relax.** Fear generates a physical response in the child. Her muscles tense, her teeth clench together, and her hands grip tightly. Encourage her to relax her body muscles when she feels afraid and to breathe more easily. These physical changes have a calming effect.
5. **Self-reassurance.** When you are afraid, you perhaps use the tech-

nique of telling yourself not be afraid, telling yourself that you will cope, and so on. You can suggest to the child that she says similar things to herself when she is afraid, as this boosts her confidence.

6. **Imagery.** You can use a child's imaginative skills to beat her fear. First, she can visualise herself successfully going through the frightening experience unafraid. This prepares her for the real thing. Second, she can imagine that you are safely alongside her.
7. **Persistence.** Keep working with the child, whether she's a toddler or an eight-year-old, until she has beaten her fear. Accept that some fears are harder to change than others but that they can all be changed eventually. She needs you to persist with your support.
8. **Acknowledge progress.** With your help she'll make progress eventually, though this may be in very small stages. Show your delight when you see that she is more confident and less afraid than previously – this gives her further incentive to continue with her efforts.

Q & A

Q. *My older children keep a hamster at home, and my youngest child is terrified of it. Should we get rid of the hamster?*

A. Removing the hamster would remove the cause of your youngest child's fear on this occasion, but it wouldn't help her beat it. And your other children would lose out. Rather than avoid the problem altogether (ie by removing the hamster), do what you can to reduce the child's fear. Gradually introduce her to the hamster in a series of small stages, eg at first she looks at it in the cage, then she watches you hold it, then she touches the hamster while you hold it, etc. You'll probably find that her fear soon eases.

Q. *What should I do about an 18-month-old child who has no fear of anything at all, and constantly puts herself at risk?*

A. The fear of personal injury is not as strong in a toddler as it is in an older child. That's why toddlers explore everywhere without hesitation, no matter the potential risk of hurt. Your task at the moment is to keep her safe by supervising her play and by telling her the dangers that she might face. In the next six to 12 months, her fear of personal injury will increase and she will start to avoid danger when she can, as a result.

Q. *I am afraid that my child will be lonely in the nursery and I am thinking of postponing the start. Should I?*

A. No. Part of growing up involves learning to cope without mum and dad beside her all the time; this is a very healthy process. However, it looks as though it is you who is afraid of separation in this instance, not your child. If you maintains this habit of staying with your daughter all the time, you will encourage her to be afraid of leaving you, and that will not be in the child's best interests. Make an effort, just grit your teeth and say goodbye to your child in the morning. Be reassured that your little girl will cope fine at nursery.

Q. *Do children get phobias? I know a child who is so afraid of dogs that she has stopped playing in her garden.*

A. Surveys indicate that less than 5% of young children experience a phobia, so it is unlikely that the child's fear is a genuine phobia. The main difference between a phobia and a fear is that a phobia is more extreme (ie the child's terror is extremely strong), it is more persistent (ie the child doesn't respond to help) and it has a more serious effect on the child's life (ie she worries about the focus of her phobia for much of the time). If this child's fear of dogs continues to be severe for much longer, it might actually be a phobia.

Section 4: Social Development

This section recognises that getting on with others is important in childhood. Chapter 16 focuses on social development and suggests ways you can help a growing child acquire essential social skills. Chapter 17 looks at the whole question of self-confidence, explaining why it has such an effect on a child and offering suggestions for boosting self-confidence. Shyness is the central theme of Chapter 18, which explains that children often experience temporary episodes of shyness between birth and age five, and the topic of sibling rivalry is dealt with in Chapter 19.

16

Social Development

"He has changed so much over the last couple of years. He was utterly irritable and anti-social when he was a toddler. Now that he is almost five years old, he plays well with the other children and he rarely fights."

A young child who is sociable is a sight to behold! And it doesn't matter whether he is playing happily with a couple of other children his age, or just chatting away to adults – a child who can relate well to others is a pleasure to be with. Yet it's hard to know what makes one child more sociable than another. Here are some common ideas about social development in children that you may have heard others express or that you may support yourself. Think about them in detail, about their implications for children and adults, and about whether or not you agree.

Common Idea
"A child is naturally friendly and will get on fine with others if they are left alone together. Problems start when adults interfere."
The Reality
While there is no doubt that a child has an innate need to mix with other children and adults, this does not mean that he knows how to satisfy this need. For instance, a baby has an innate need for food and milk, but he cannot possibly satisfy that need without help from his mum and dad or carer. A child needs guidance so that he can effectively satisfy his need to be sociable in a suitable way.

Common Idea
"A child is selfish and would do everything to suit himself if he was given the chance. He has to be taught to think of others."
The Reality
It is true that when a child is under the age of three or four years, he sees the world mainly from his point of view. But that is not selfishness, rather it is just that he doesn't yet fully understand the perspective of another person. As he matures emotionally and intellectually, he begins to realise that other people also have feelings and ideas. This is a natural process of maturation, although he will benefit from your guidance.

Common Idea
"All children love being the centre of attention. They thoroughly enjoy people looking at them and generally fussing over them."
The Reality
For every child who thrives on being the centre of attention, there is another child who finds such situations embarrassing and uncomfortable. As with most aspects of development in the pre-school years, every child is different when it comes to liking attention. You'll soon get to know how each child reacts when he is in the spotlight – and if he is unhappy, you'll do your best to help him avoid it in the future.

Common Idea
"A child doesn't need to play with others during the early years because he'll have enough opportunities when he starts school."
The Reality
There are young children who have little chance to play with others and yet they cope well socially once they start school. But there are also those who struggle badly in that situation. Learning to be sociable is like any other learning episode; the best way to improve is through varied and frequent practical experience. So a child is more likely to learn how to get on with others when he is able to spend more time with them.

Common Idea
"An only child has problems with other children because he gets too used to his own company and to the company of adults."
The Reality
There is little evidence to support this. Of course, an only child has less interactions with other children because there are no other children in the family, and he does spend more time with adults than with children. But most parents of only children are aware of this potential difficulty and take steps to avoid it, by taking him to activities involving other children, and by inviting other children over to the house play with him.

Common Idea
"Brothers and sisters are naturally horrible to each other. Parents just have to accept that fights at home are part of family life."
The Reality
While bickering is common at home, especially when the children are younger, there are many brothers and sisters who get on well together. A lot depends on their personalities and temperaments, and also on the way they are managed by their parents when they do disagree. Each child in the family has to feel important and valued; if that feeling is conveyed successfully to all the children, fighting will be less frequent.

Common Idea
"A grumpy, anti-social toddler will grow up into a grumpy and anti-social child, and there is nothing that anyone can do."
The Reality
There does not have to be any link between sociability at the age of 12 months and sociability at the age of five years. Remember that many infants are predictably demanding and self-interested at times; this is a normal phase they go through. It is only as they grow older that they become more responsive to other people. So there is nothing to stop an unsociable toddler developing into a highly sociable young child.

Common Idea
"A child inherits his ability to be sociable from his parents – if they are friendly and popular, then he develops that way too."
The Reality
Sociable parents do tend to have sociable children, but this is not because the quality of 'sociability' is genetically transmitted from one generation of the family to the next. The real reason for this link between parents and child is that sociable parents provide a model of sociable behaviour which their child gradually imitates. Put simply, it's a case of setting an appropriate example which their child is likely to copy.

Age & Stage

A child's social development moves steadily forward. The list below outlines the main transitional stages in his sociability.

Three months: By now, the typical growing baby has shown his first smile that is genuinely in response to an adult's smile. He clearly enjoys the company of other people and is quite happy to be the centre of attention at all times. You'll find that he watches you closely while you move around the room, as though he does not want to let you out of his sight. The more you fuss over him the better, as far as the young baby is concerned.
How to Encourage Him
1. Laugh and joke with him as often as you can. Even though he will not understand the complexity of adult humour, he will enjoy seeing you smile at him.
2. Talk to him as often as you can while holding him close to you. A young baby can focus on your face more clearly when it is reasonably close to his.
3. Let him be with other adults as often as possible. In the next few months he will probably become shy, but at this stage he even enjoys the company of people he doesn't know well.

Six months: His smiles and giggles are more consistent now, and you can predict what will cause them. He is more alert and more able to control his body movements. The typical infant of this age tries to engage others in social contact by babbling loudly in order to attract their attention. Alongside this sociability, however, there are often signs of infant shyness. He may burst out crying when a stranger approaches.

How to Encourage Him

1. Talk back to him when he babbles at you – this is the first stage in developing the art of conversation. He will think this is great fun, and will chuckle away to himself.
2. Reassure him that he is safe when he becomes upset in the presence of an unfamiliar adult. Hold his hand and comfort him, don't hurry him away.
3. If you can, sit him on the floor alongside another infant approximately the same age. They probably won't actually make any attempt to move towards each other, but they will stare.

12 months: The typical one-year-old loves all forms of social interaction, whether it is sitting on your knee while you sing to him or tell him nursery rhymes, or being in the company of others his own age. The child's natural sociability shows through but he may become very distressed when another child doesn't conform to his expectations. It is through that sort of social experience that he develops his social skills.

How to Encourage Him

1. Play lots of games with him that involve physical contact. For instance, "This little piggy" or "Incy wincy spider" will be greeted with squeals of delight.
2. Let him play alongside others his own age if possible. He needs these opportunities to mix freely with other children in his age group. He may take time to settle.
3. If he does squabble with another child because they are both trying to play with the same toy, calm him, take the toy from him and tell him he will play with it in a minute.

18 months: The toddler enjoys being with a familiar adult and becomes unhappy if separated from that person, even for a few moments. He realises that he can begin to do more for himself. However, he still expects to get his own way. The child also recognises that smiling is a useful means of getting others to react positively towards him, as well as a means of expressing his pleasure.

How to Encourage Him

1. Talk to him and laugh with him as you dress him, and show how pleased you are when he tries to help. This provides good encouragement for him.

2. Take him out with you when you go shopping (assuming his behaviour is mostly acceptable) because this makes him more aware of other people.
3. He'll like the company of other children even if he stays by your side during that type of activity. Just being in the presence of other children his age helps him grow more sociable.

Two years: The company of other children becomes increasingly important, and you may find that he becomes irritable and uncooperative when he has played on his own too long without a friend. When he is with other children, however, he may squabble with them because he hasn't yet learned how to play quietly with them. A child may try to get more of your attention, possibly by misbehaving in front of you.

How to Encourage Him

1. Play games with him when he is with you. He'll learn to tolerate frustration and to take turns, and he can use these social skills when he plays with other children.
2. Do your best to ensure that he has someone to play with most days. This may be difficult at times to organise but it's certainly worth making the effort.
3. Always try to be positive about his social behaviour, pointing out the good aspects (eg he gave his friend one of his toys to play with). Try not to focus on his misbehaviour.

Three years: He is more sociable now, a quality which shows through in all his relationships. The child may, for instance, become less upset when he isn't allowed to do what he wants because he realises that others also have feelings and that these feelings are as important as his own. He is less self-centred and this makes him easier to get on with. The child has particular friends whom he prefers more than others.

How to Encourage Him

1. Let him know how pleased you are when things go well with him. Point out that he's been friendly and pleasant that day, and that you prefer this sort of behaviour.
2. Provide him with opportunities to mix with other children his own age. You may mind other children, or perhaps you might meet up with another parent and her children.
3. Ask him to help you with basic chores, or to help other children. At the age of three, he's capable of putting wastepaper in a bin or of tidying his toys.

Four years: Playing with other children is easier for him; bickering is less frequent now. He is much more caring towards you and others, and he gets upset if he thinks you are upset. He likes to do as much as he can for himself. Due to the child's increased language skills, he talks to you about his friends, his favourite games, and what sort of activities he most enjoys. He still needs plenty of attention from you.

How to Encourage Him

1. Give him board games that must involve two or more children. They have to mix together and co-operate in order to play the game properly.
2. Let him see that you are interested in his friendships. Listen to his moans and groans about other children (if he has any) and advise him how to cope with any social difficulties.
3. Increase his social experiences, where possible. Remember, though, that four-year-olds often prefer playing with others their own age when there is adult supervision.

Five years: A child is very keen to be accepted by other children, and will be quite distressed if he thinks they are leaving him out of their games – peer group approval matters. In class, he chooses to sit beside pupils that he likes; he has a special group of friends to play with during the intervals. He'll be very excited whenever he is invited to a friend's birthday party. You'll probably find that he is generally more helpful.

How to Encourage Him

1. Suggest techniques that will help him be more sociable, such as waiting in a queue without pushing to the front and sharing his toys and sweets with his pals.
2. When he falls out with a friend, reassure him that he will be able to make new friends because he is so likeable. Cheer him up so that he is not too upset.
3. Encourage him to respect other people's feelings (eg tell him that he shouldn't point out a child's disfigurement or disability as this will embarrass the child).

Six years and older: Friendships continue to chop and change at the moment. One day he is best friends with a child and the next day they have fallen out. By the age of nine or ten, however, friendships are more stable and long-lasting. Around the age of 11 years, peer group relationships begin to dominate the child's life. He wants to dress like the others and to be in their group.

How to Encourage Him

1. Take him seriously when he tearfully tells you that the other pupils in his class are invited to a party but he has been left out. This is a serious blow to him.
2. He may lack confidence making friends. For instance, he might want to spend time with particular children but not know what to do. Suggest some activities for them.

3. Don't tease him. During adolescence, children become aware of the significance of opposite-gender friendships. This is a new and exciting phase, and teasing will reduce his confidence.

Social Play

Psychologists have studied the development of social play, and have found a steady progression, which runs along the following lines. From birth until around the age of 12-15 months an infant tends to play alone. It's not so much that he ignores other children, more that he doesn't even realise they are there. **Solitary play** at this age means that even if you put him in with a group of children his own age, he still isolates himself from them. By all means point out to him that this child is playing with a ball, and that child is playing with a shape-sorter, but don't expect him to show interest.

From around 18-21 months onwards, he starts to look more closely at other children when playing near them. However, he continues to keep himself to himself. **Onlooker play** (the second stage in social play) is more advanced than solitary play, but does not involve direct contact with others. Don't be dismayed when, for instance, he is with a group of other children and yet all he does is sit and stare. This is a normal stage that most children go through. The strange thing is that although he only looks at them when playing in the same room, he'll probably burst into tears when he realises it is time for them to go.

His continued maturity in the next six months to a year means that his play activities begin to copy those of other children. In other words, he likes to watch what they do and even to play with the same toys, but he is not yet ready to interact with them. He has almost reached the stage of readiness for proper social play.

And that stage arrives at the age of three to four years. Now, the barriers to social interaction have fallen away; the child is mature and confident to interact with others in **associative play**. This is a very interesting phase for him because he learns from other children and they learn from him. They start to share their toys with each other (an extremely important social skill) and may even try to show each other how to play with that particular item. But it falls short of full co-operation. For instance, a three-year-old and his friend may start to play a simple game, yet each plays according to a different sets of rules.

Eventually, however, the stage of **co-operative play** finally arrives, usually around the age of four or five years. The child plays with another child in the true sense of the word. He and his friend understand that they both share a common purpose and that they must co-operate or they can't achieve that goal.

Arguments, Not Play

There are occasions when a child spends more time fighting with other children than he does playing with them. He may need help to sort out the problem. Let's consider the following example.

The Problem: Whenever two-year-old Ghulam goes to his childminder, he ends up battling with the other children she minds. At first, he was quite shy and withdrawn, unwilling to go near any other child – if someone approached him, he hid behind the childminder. But this phase passed after a couple of months. As Ghulam's confidence grew, he gradually became more adventurous. Now, he is so confident and self-assured that he marches up to any of the other children and snatches the toy from their hands, without any concern for their distress. The other parents have started to complain about his aggressive behaviour during play.

The Facts: Ghulam is a typical child of this age, who thinks mainly of himself and who is unaware that his actions have consequences for others. His mum is very outgoing. She was troubled when her son seemed so shy at first, and is pleased that he is less withdrawn now; she thinks it is better that he stands up for himself when he is with his childminder than it would be for him to get pushed around by the other children. However, she is upset by the complaints from the other parents about Ghulam.

The Analysis: Through playing with other children, Ghulam has realised that he does not need to be timid and withdrawn. He has realised that he is safe with the childminder, that nothing terrible will happen to him there. With this new-found confidence, he has begun to assert himself. The difficulty is that this state of affairs is achieved at the expense of the other children – he doesn't think of them at all. His mum is so pleased with the change in his shyness that she doesn't want to say anything to him about his behaviour. She doesn't want him to become meek again.

The Solution: Although Ghulam is just a toddler and cannot fully understand the social implications of his behaviour, he has to start learning sometime. And now is as good a time as any. Along with his childminder, his mother needs to take a more active part in encouraging more appropriate social play from him. She should reprimand him whenever he grabs a toy from others without permission, she should remind him that he must wait until no other child is playing with it before he takes it, and she should give him praise when he hands a toy over to another child without making any complaint. Ghulam assumes that his mother's passive reaction when she sees him being forceful is her approval of this type of behaviour. If she continues to allow him to play in this way without doing anything to change the situation, he will have little incentive to learn how be more sociable, and the childminder will face an uphill struggle.

Q & A

Q. *How can I help a three-year-old become more popular? He doesn't seem to have many friends, and prefers to play alone.*

A. Popularity depends on many characteristics, some of which you can't alter significantly (eg physical appearance, intelligence) and some of which you can improve (eg being able to share, having a friendly facial expression, having good eating habits). Before making any changes in a child's behaviour, however, think about whether or not he is bothered by his apparent lack of popularity. He may be content to have only a few friends. Perhaps the best approach is to take no action at the moment, though keep a close eye on his progress socially; if you feel that he is rejected by his peers, then you can help improve his social skills.

Q. *Why is it that one child is sociable and makes friends easily while his sister is the exact opposite? She is quiet and withdrawn.*

A. Every child is different, and even two children in the same family, with the same parents, from the same house, can be entirely different. Temperament varies from child to child, often for no apparent reason. Try not to compare the two children with each other. The withdrawn child already knows that her sibling is more outgoing and she does not need a reminder. Comparisons may drive a wedge between them. Instead, accept their individual differences in personality, and don't be concerned about it.

Q. *My four-year-old is usually attracted to the sort of children I don't like. What should I do?*

A. You need to handle this situation very carefully. Of course, you have a right to approve (and disapprove) of your child's friends at this age. However, you can't stop your child liking them. If you make a point of keeping him separate from them, he'll want to play with them even more. There are a number of strategies you could pursue. First, accept that you cannot manipulate children's friendships in this way. Second, encourage your child's to make friends with other children, for instance by inviting them over to your house to play with him after nursery or at the weekend.

Q. *My child has fallen out with his best friend. He is only four but he is very tearful. Should I speak to the ex-friend's mother?*

A. Assuming you can approach the ex-friend's mother in a reasonable and calm manner, then it is a step worth thinking about. Before doing that, however, try to ascertain from the child the real reason for the break-up of their friendship. If it was a small incident, then they may forget about it within a day or so. If it was a major incident, then perhaps you can advise the child on what action to take to restore the friendship. Should that fail, you may want to speak to the former friend's parents, but bear in mind that they may be entirely unsympathetic. In addition, suggest to your child that there are other children he could have as friends.

17

Self-Confidence

"Barbara has a strong sense of her own identity, her own likes and dislikes, her own strengths and weaknesses. She's quite confident and always willing to try new activities when she's with me."

Before a child can mix comfortably with others, she has to have a sense of who she is as an individual. She needs to have some ideas about her own characteristics, her own capabilities and about how other children and adults see her. In other words, a child's social and emotional development depends on her understanding of herself; if she likes who she is, then she'll make friends more easily than if she dislikes herself. Her self-concept is important.

I Am An Individual

In the early months of life, a baby doesn't realise that she and her parent (or carer) are separate individuals, and that there is a world out there which functions independently of her. This may sound odd because, as an adult, you know that you are a separate person, as is your friend, and so on. But a baby doesn't see it that way. Her early experiences teach her that she and her parents are totally connected. For instance, when she cries from hunger, food suddenly arrives at her lips; when she cries from coldness, a blanket suddenly appears to warm her up; and when she cries from boredom, toys suddenly appear before her. The baby sees an instant connection between her wants and their satisfaction, and this makes her believe that she and everything else around her are one and the same.

It's not until well into the second year of life – from around the age of 12-15 months onwards – that the child develops a proper awareness of her own separate identity. Based on the techniques used in several classic psychological experiments, here are two ways you can test out a young child's sense of individuality:

Test 1: The mark method: Let a young child play with a mirror for a few minutes (the type that is plastic and is therefore childproof). Encourage her to look at her own reflection. Then take the mirror away from her and put it to one side. Play with her at any game for the next couple of minutes, and during that play time, gently put a dab of lipstick on her forehead. (You have to do this very subtly, so that the child doesn't realise what you have done; you might have to practice it several times with other people until you achieve this without being noticed). Once the mark is in place, give her the mirror to look at again.

What She'll Do: If her self-awareness is developed, then the moment she sees her mirror image she will realise that this is her face and that there is a red mark on her forehead, and she'll touch her forehead on the exact spot where the colouring is. Psychologists have found that less than 50% of children aged 18 months try to touch the mark. By the age of two years, almost three quarters of the children touch the mark, and the figure rises to virtually 100% from the age of three years onwards.

Test 2: The problem-solving method: Use a range of toys with varying complexity for this test, for instance, two inset boards with different numbers of pieces, a small jigsaw, a larger jigsaw, a shape sorter, and so on. The main point is that they should be challenging and they should be varied in their degree of difficulty. Then show the child how to complete one of the simple toys, and ask her to copy you. This should be followed by a more complex toy, which she has to copy, continuing the process until you demonstrate toys that are much too demanding for her. Watch her reaction as she works her way through these tasks.

What She'll Do: If her self-awareness is developed, then she will be content at being able to complete a task and will become troubled when the task is too demanding for her. However, if her self-awareness isn't developed, then she won't be bothered about failing because she lacks understanding that she has not got the necessary skills. Psychologists have found that the typical infant aged 15 months or younger is unconcerned, whereas a child aged two years or older is concerned.

The following suggestions will help you encourage a child's sense of individuality:

- **use her name when you speak to her.** From a very early stage, an infant realises her name refers only to her. She will also realise that although there may be other children with the same name, when you say it and look at her at the same time, then it is she you are addressing, not anybody else. By the time she is three or four years old she will be able to tell her name to any familiar adult who asks.
- **teach her names of body parts.** For example, hold her hand and tell her this is her hand, hold her foot and tell her this is her foot. She will learn this gradually. When she's around 18 months she might only be able to point to one body part when you ask her (eg her foot), but by two years she can name several, and by three and four years she points to her eyes, ears, nose, mouth, hands and feet.

- **develop her use of proper names.** Language helps a child express and identify the distinction between herself and others. From the age of 12 months onwards, she will start to refer to familiar people by their name; she is able to use these appropriately. Encourage her to name people, eg to call you by your name, and to call her siblings by their names even though she may not pronounce them properly.
- **play games that involve imitation.** She'll have great fun joining in activities that involve her imitating your behaviour, and this helps develop her self-awareness. A simple game like "Simon says" (ie you make a specific action which she then copies) forces her to concentrate first on you, then on herself. Whether she is one year or five years old, she'll enjoy copying your actions time after time.
- **encourage her to use pronouns.** Several months after a child starts to use proper names in her speech, she will begin to use pronouns too. This represents a more advanced stage in her self-development. Initially the pronouns will refer to her (eg "Me want") but by the time she is three or four years they will have extended to others (eg "He hit me"). Respond positively when she uses these words.

What Am I Like?

Once a child has begun to grasp that she is a unique individual, separate from everyone else around her, she then begins to define what sort of person she is, and what her personal qualities are. Here are some facts from psychological research about young children:

- they have a very strong (and often totally unrealistic) belief in their own abilities. For instance, the typical three-year old is completely convinced that she can run faster than anyone else, that she can draw a prettier picture than anyone else, and that she is the best singer ever. Lack of self-doubt is dominant at this stage. She ignores evidence that suggests she may not be as capable as she thinks.
- they believe that they are skilled in all areas of life. For instance, a young child's self-belief is not confined just to her artistic ability or her vocal ability or her learning ability. She considers herself to be equally competent in all these aspects. Once she starts school she'll be more aware of differences between herself and other children, but for the moment she thinks she is an expert in everything.
- they tend to define themselves in terms of their possessions, in some cases even when these possessions are very abstract. For example, a toddler will talk to you about "my teddy", emphasising that she has ownership, a three-year-old talks about "my playgroup" because she regards it as a very fundamental part of her world, and a five-year-old talks about "my teacher".

Young children use very clear-cut categories for defining themselves. Ask a child to describe herself to you. Her response will depend very much on her age and maturity. Between two and three years she will define herself in relation to very specific, observable physical characteristics, such as age, size, height, and colour of hair. For instance, she can tell you whether she is a little child or a big child. She uses these characteristics as though they are independent of each other, eg she doesn't see the connection between her age and her height. She may be able to tell you that she is a girl, not a boy, though gender identity is not fully established until a later age.

However, between four and five years she defines herself in relation to others as well as in relation to herself. For instance, instead of saying "I'm a small child" she'll now say "I'm taller than my little sister." And the child compares herself to other children the same age because it has finally dawned on her that she isn't marvellous at absolutely everything, that some children are more skilled than her at some things. Through social play, she learns about the qualities of her friends, giving her a baseline for self-evaluation.

The following suggestions will help you encourage a child's awareness of her own talents and abilities:

- **encourage her to talk about herself.** Make a special point of asking her about her personal qualities. Ask her specific questions such as "How tall are you?", "What colour is your hair?", "What are your favourite foods?", and give her time to formulate an answer – she may have to think long and hard. This focuses her attention on her personal attributes and away from her personal desires.
- **talk about her skills rather than her characteristics.** Once she appears able to describe herself in terms of observable physical characteristics, broaden the criteria to include other characteristics. You could ask new questions, such as "Are you good at running?", "Are you able to build interesting models?", or "Can you sing nicely?" This encourages her to take a broader perspective of herself.
- **teach her personal information.** By the time the child has reached the age of four or five, she is mature enough to realise that she has a unique name and that she stays in a house with a unique location - this is part of her self-identity. Try to teach her these basic bits of personal information, such as her age, her home address and perhaps even her home telephone number.
- **listen to her opinions.** A young child has plenty of strong opinions about herself, about you, and about other people she knows. Of course you may not always like what she says or agree with it, but do listen to her point of view. This reinforces her sense of self. By all means take issue with her ideas but try to do so in a way that doesn't make her afraid to talk to you in the future.

- **encourage her to talk about other children.** By the time she is ready to compare herself to others (around the age of four or five) she probably has had plenty of opportunities to be with other children; therefore she has enough information to make such comparisons. Remind her that life would be boring if everyone were the same and that differences make life interesting.

I Feel Good About Myself

Every young child needs to feel good about herself; she needs to like herself and to value herself – and if she doesn't, then she'll be thoroughly miserable and lack confidence. So it is important that she takes a positive view of the information that she learns about herself during the pre-school years.

One of the remarkable qualities of young children is that their self-confidence is staggeringly high. True, there are episodes of shyness and at times there is fear of new situations, but generally a young child is very content with herself and her own abilities. She plays comfortably, and quickly recovers from any minor irritations and upsets. In other words, her self-esteem (the value she places upon herself) is high.

The position changes, however, in the next couple of years. When she is around five years old you may find that her confidence takes a dip. And there are very good reasons why such a change in self-esteem occurs at this age.

First, this coincides with the time when she starts to compare her qualities to those of other children. The realisation that she isn't the best at everything can be a serious blow to her self-esteem. Comparisons are inevitable but they do not always prove to be favourable.

Second, her level of social play is more mature now which increases the complexity of her games. At this age children's games can be very challenging, with winners and losers – being on the losing side all the time is unlikely to raise a child's self-confidence.

And third, her intellectual abilities are put under the microscope when she starts school. Maybe she is a talented dancer and is rightly proud of this ability; yet this might suddenly pale into insignificance in school, where greater emphasis is placed on academic achievements such as learning to read and learning to count.

The combination of the child's increased self-understanding and her more varied social and educational experiences leaves her self-confidence highly vulnerable; it is easily dented by a comment or reaction from another child or adult. Put simply, she is more self-critical. In some ways this is a welcome change because it means that she is more willing to listen to reason, more willing to accept that she may not be right all the time, and that can contribute to a more peaceful atmosphere.

Yet in other ways it can be a drawback because the typical four- or five-year-old may be very prone to tears, becoming upset at what appears to you to be a very trivial incident.

Alongside this new-found self-criticism comes the concept of self-blame. One of the annoying things about a toddler is that she never accepts anything is her fault. She either denies the misbehaviour completely, insisting her innocence even when caught red-handed, or she points the finger at someone else (often her sibling or best friend) claiming that he was responsible, not her. Toddlers refuse to accept blame. Within a couple of years, though, the child becomes all too ready to accept her own failings. Whereas a three-year-old might blame the carpet for the fact that she tripped up while carrying a glass of milk and take no personal responsibility at all for the incident, a five-year-old is much more likely to admit that it was her fault.

The difficulty with this change in attitude and self-understanding is that it can lead to a severe drop in self-esteem which may be difficult to restore. A child can easily get locked into a cycle of ever-decreasing self-confidence, as her lack of achievements reduces her belief in herself, which in turn makes her less willing to try the next time. Children of this age are extremely concerned about their failures, compared to the unshakeable self-confidence of the younger child; girls are more vulnerable to this effect than boys.

The following suggestions will help you encourage a child to have a high level of self-esteem, and to feel good about herself:

- **be supportive and interested.** She wants to share her experiences with you, to tell you what happened to her that day, and to have a positive reaction from you. She also wants you to help her when she has a problem that needs to be resolved. She won't value herself unless she feels valued by you. So make time for her.
- **provide a varied range of leisure pursuits.** Young children are notoriously fickle, fascinated with an activity one day and yet bored with it the next. However, the child's self-esteem will stay high if she finds something she is skilled at, whether it is a sporting activity, dance activity or artistic activity. Every child is talented at something.
- **praise effort, not outcome.** It's easy for a child to concentrate only on what she does or doesn't achieve; in other words, to concentrate on either success or failure. Yet it is also helpful to focus on the process that led to these outcomes. A child's self-esteem will be higher when she feels you value her efforts, not just the result.
- **tell her how much you like her.** No matter what age the child is, she loves hearing that you think she is terrific – and she is. Her relationship with you has a big influence on her self-confidence, so use this to good effect. She will never tire of hearing how pleased you are with her, or of hearing you say she is a lovely child.

- **try not to compare her with others.** Her confidence will not improve by having it repeatedly pointed out, for instance, that her older brother could set the table when he was her age, or that her older sister smiles more. Comparisons with others will happen spontaneously, but try not to encourage this yourself.

I'm Not Good at This

When a child nears the end of her pre-school years, she becomes more vulnerable to learned helplessness; this means that she is easily influenced by her failures and can lack all belief in her ability to cope. Let's consider the following example.

The Problem: Lorraine is unhappy at the moment. Over the past few months she has been attempting to learn the names of the primary colours, but she finds this difficult. And her lack of success at this task has been emphasised by her awareness that other children whom she plays with can name red, yellow, blue and green without any problem. Now this four-year-old has a very low opinion of herself. She tells her mother "I can't do it, I'm stupid." Her negative attitude is spreading to other areas; her parents have noticed that she doesn't want to try anything new and that she gives up very easily.
The Facts: Lorraine always has difficulty learning new concepts, but she can succeed as long as she has plenty of practice. She does get fed up, though, when she sees other children mastering activities easily. Her parents encourage her as best they can and help her with learning tasks. They know how keen she is to learn the different colour names and have spent a lot of time with her for this purpose. Each day they give her colour identification activities. But Lorraine seems to have lost her self-esteem and regularly says that she isn't as good as her friends.
The Analysis: Like many children her age, Lorraine's confidence is fragile. Her failure to learn colour names has rocked her. She is gradually moving towards a state of learned helplessness, and soon she will take the view that there is no point in trying anything at all because success is bound to elude her. Part of the problem lies in the approach used by the adults in her world; they want to help her, but their effort is directed solely at the learning task, not at the feelings associated with it. The regular colour-naming practice supports Lorraine's own view that this is a vitally important skill at which she is failing – it makes matters worse. Part of the problem also lies in Lorraine's lack of self-acceptance; she has just discovered that some children are more capable at colour-naming than her and she construes this as a weakness in her abilities.
The Solution: Her parents and childminder should adopt a number of strategies which have three aims, namely, to help the child understand

that learning the names of colours is not the most important thing in the world, to help her understand that she has talents and skills in other areas, and to help her understand that she can be strong in some skills and weak in others. Less time should be spent on the learning of colour names; she'll master this eventually. Her parents should also talk to her about the things she is good at, and when she mentions these they should explain that this proves she is a capable girl. In addition, they should discourage her from making self-critical statements; she needs to develop a more positive attitude and should continue to try new experiences whenever an opportunity arises. Lorraine has to learn that she has nothing to fear from occasions when success proves elusive.

Q & A.

Q. *How can I change a three-year-old who is extremely territorial? She hoards her toys and sweets.*

A. She is no different from most children this age, who recognise that objects belong to people and that their own objects belong to them. In time, the child will eventually understand that when she gives another child one of her toys to play with for a while, the toy is still her possession – this is obvious to you, but not to her at this stage in her development. It's a case of learning through experience; she will be less defensive once she has had opportunities to lend her toys and see them returned. Talk to her about this, encourage her to share with her friends. Reassure her that sharing her toys is not the same as giving them away.

Q. *What can I do to stop a two-year-old's obsession with names? Every time she sees someone she says "What's name? What's name?"*

A. It looks as though the child is at that fascinating stage where she has just discovered each person is a distinct individual with his or her own name, and she wants to learn these different names. This is a natural phase. Within a few months she'll begin to focus more on the names of those children and adults in her immediate world, such as her siblings and her best friends, and less on the names of strangers. In the meantime, however, try to be patient with her and answer her inquiries as best you can. She's only trying to make sense of her world by asking you lots of questions.

Q. *Should I worry about a five-year-old boy whose favourite type of play involves dressing up in old skirts, blouses and women's shoes?*

A. The child clearly enjoys imaginative play, and the availability of old clothes helps him in this type of play. By dressing up in adult clothes he can pretend to be an adult, and then he can act out these characters through his imaginative play sequences. There is nothing for you to be concerned about. However, you can broaden the array of clothing that he has for dressing-up play so that there is a good mixture of male and female items for him to wear, This will provide him with a broader range of pretend-play options.

Q. *How can I motivate a four-year-old to try physical activities? She refuses to attempt things like jumping because she insists she is not good at these tasks.*

A. She may well be right in her anticipation of sporting failure – a child who thinks she's not good at athletic activities is usually correct. But that's not the point. Her recognition that she isn't the best is stopping her from taking part at all, and as a result she's missing out on an enjoyable part of her childhood. You need to encourage her to take part, regardless of her potential success or failure. Tell her that she'll have fun participating and that plenty of other children find these activities difficult so she is in good company. Remind her that the winner of a race is not only the child who crosses the finish line first – the winner of the race is also the child who crosses the finish line and can honestly say "I did my best."

18

Shyness

"I was very surprised by four-year-old Ben last week. He's normally such a confident child, but when his friend visited last week, he suddenly refused to speak to her at all. I had to spend ages persuading him even to say hello to her."

Shyness can be seen in many different situations, depending on the circumstances, the individual child and the relationship between the child and the other people present. Everyone knows shyness when they see it, but shyness is hard to define. However, you will be more able to help a child overcome his shyness when you understand his feelings when he shrinks from public attention or when he backs away from a crowded room. The main emotions associated with shyness are:

- **lack of self-confidence.** A shy child has little faith in his own ability to cope with meeting people. This usually happens when it is children or adults he doesn't know, but the same feeling can occur when he is surrounded by familiar faces. The child doubts his social skills, believing that he will not know what to do or to say when someone else starts to talk to him. This lack of confidence makes him shy.
- **fear of rejection.** One of the thoughts running through the mind of a shy child is that the other children will reject him, and this thought is enough to bring on a bout of shyness. The fear of rejection is often irrational; it does not have to be based on a previous unpleasant social experience. But it is very real to the shy child who would rather miss out on the occasion altogether than be laughed at by others.
- **embarrassment.** The prospect of being the centre of attention is enough to make a shy child cringe. He wishes his cheeks wouldn't go red, that his mouth wouldn't suddenly dry up and that the words would not disappear from his lips. Yet these are the effects of embarrassment. A shy child may be so worried about being embarrassed when he meets people that this worry brings on the embarrassment.
- **insecurity.** A shy child may feel disorientated when he meets other people for the first time. This is partly due to the fact that he has to cope with an unfamiliar situation (eg a party), perhaps in unfamiliar surroundings (eg someone else's house) with unfamiliar children (eg children from another area). This level of unfamiliarity makes him feel insecure and unsettled. His shyness is a natural defence.

Shyness Varies

No wonder, then, that a shy child prefers "flight" instead of "fight"; no wonder that he prefers to protect himself with a shield of shyness when he experiences these emotions. Avoidance is his instinctive reaction. Remember, though, that shyness in childhood varies in several different ways. The list below outlines some of the key characteristics of shyness that you may see in a child.

Intensity: He may be extremely shy on one particular occasion, and yet be less shy the next time these circumstances arise. Or he may be mildly shy one day and much more shy the next. The intensity of his shyness can change quickly.
Example: When a child first meets new children, he might look down at the ground for most of the session and make sure that he speaks to nobody at all, children or adults. Yet within a few weeks his level of shyness will have eased greatly.

Duration: You may find that a child's shyness lasts for only a few seconds or that it lasts for hours and hours. It is hard to predict how long his shyness will last in each instance since a lot depends on the specific situation that he is in.
Example: When you take him out shopping with you, he acts shyly when you stop to talk to someone whom you know but he doesn't. However, within a couple of minutes his shyness vanishes and he speaks to this person quite happily.

Frequency: He is only shy sometimes, often when you least expect him to be and sometimes not when you do expect him to be. You'll have an idea of when his shyness is likely but you can never be sure. Few children are shy all of the time.
Example: He hates telling nursery rhymes or singing songs in front of a group of people, even if he knows them well. Yet there will be occasions he does this confidently without batting an eyelid, even though you expected him to be shy.

Persistence: A child may be shy just during one phase of his development, and this period of shyness could last for only a month or two, or even less. With other children, however, shyness can last for much longer, perhaps for a year or more.
Example: There can be differences in levels of shyness amongst young children. One might have been shy only when he was a toddler, while another might not have shown any signs of shyness until he was almost school age.

Resistance: Like most characteristics, shyness can be changed if the child is given help. But the extent to which shyness can be overcome is very variable. You may discover that he remains shy despite your having spent hours and hours supporting him.
Example: A few basic confidence-boosting statements could be enough to help a child shed his shyness almost instantly (eg "Don't worry, the other children will like you") or it might turn out that he needs a lot more help than that.

Age Matters

There are two aspects of shyness. First, there is the emotion connected with shyness. Second, there is the behaviour associated with shyness (eg turning away, refusing to make eye contact, failure to speak, and so on). Both these aspects change as a child grows during the pre-school years.

It's easy to assume, for instance, that a child isn't shy because he doesn't act in a shy way. In fact he may be feeling extremely shy but working hard not to show it in his behaviour. So when thinking about a child and shyness, remember that he may feel shy but act confidently (eg in order that nobody will notice his shyness) and he may act shyly yet feel confident (eg he knows that shyness is a good way to get other people's attention).

How a child's shyness manifests itself does partly depend on his age. During the first year, the seeds of shyness are sown. While a newborn baby can't really tell one person from another and therefore doesn't exhibit any signs of shyness, by the time he is six months old he can distinguish familiar faces from unfamiliar ones – he may be shy when he realises a stranger is looking at him or talking to him. And by 12 months, the child may become quite clingy to you in the presence of someone he doesn't know.

The typical toddler who is 18 months old is a very ebullient character; he charges about everywhere, full of confidence and without a care in the world. Until he meets a stranger that is. In the face of an unfamiliar figure, he becomes transformed into a quivering, shy toddler who will do anything he can to avoid that person. For example, he might run around the supermarket at fever pitch, ignoring all your requests to pay attention to you, even when you raise your voice. Yet when one of the supermarket staff simply smiles at him, he scurries over to you in shyness, hiding himself behind you. This is genuine shyness.

His gradually increasing confidence in the next six months or so means that the typical two-year-old is not so easily distressed by shyness. Of course, he is still shy but the panic reaction shown when he was slightly younger is no longer in evidence. For example, when he sees relatives that he hasn't spoken to for a couple of months he may just stare blankly at them, neither talking to them nor ignoring them. He copes with shyness by giving a more neutral response than he did before (he might even turn his back on them and busy himself with another activity). This ability to respond in a less impulsive way to his feelings of shyness is a sign of his increasing maturity.

A child probably has had plenty of experience of meeting other children by the time he is three and so the shyness of a three-year-old is more controlled. He is more confident socially, and this enables him to mask any shy feelings which he might have. You'll probably find that when he meets other children he actually enjoys the experience and looks forward to it the next time. He has begun to realise that shyness is one of those irrational emotions – meeting new people isn't going to cause him any harm. And anyway, he now has social play to help him. Play is one of the great solutions to shyness at this age; two children who don't know each other can join in the same play activity without speaking a word.

Four-year-olds can be shy, but shyness is less frequent at this age. He mixes regularly with other children, and through this his shy feelings have subsided. Whereas before he may have been very withdrawn when meeting someone new, he will be able to handle these situations more easily now – as long as you are with him. If a familiar adult is not with him his level of shyness will be higher. Although his self-confidence is generally high in social situations, it is still fragile; his self-belief can crumble instantly if he feels vulnerable. That's why the most outgoing child can suddenly refuse to enter a room full of other children (even when it contains his friends as well as strangers). The onset of a bout of shyness at this age can be acute, unpredictable and debilitating.

As the child approaches school age he is able to keep his feelings of shyness in check. Many children this age are more concerned about their abilities than they are about shyness. For example, when a five year-old refuses to go along to the classes for gymnastics, his reluctance is based on anxiety that he won't have as good co-ordination as the other children there. And that's quite different from reluctance because of shyness. On most occasions he manages to mix with other children even when a familiar adult is nowhere to be seen. There will be rare episodes of shyness from which he will recover quickly.

By the age of six or seven, most children have developed a strategy for coping with shyness and have minor episodes of shyness depending on the specific circumstances. Adolescence, however, may see a return of shyness as the child becomes more aware of himself and the physical changes occurring through puberty. He is now self-conscious, and could be distinctly unhappy with his physical appearance, resulting in shyness when he is with girls.

Bullying Him Out of Shyness

One way to react to shyness is by trying to force the child into becoming more sociable, rather in the same way that some people believe the best way to teach a child to swim is by throwing him in at the deep end of the pool. However, that head-on approach may not bring the desired results. Let's consider the following example.

The Problem: Jason is four years old and is dreadfully shy at his nursery. Although he has been going there for several weeks, he still arrives in a tearful mood and he still doesn't talk to the other children in his group. When nursery staff discussed this with his parents they explained that he has always been shy. They had just assumed that he would grow out of it and they have become increasingly impatient with him in recent years, finding his shyness irritating. They know Jason dislikes going to nursery but they literally drag him there each morning, hoping to force him out of his shyness. These shock tactics haven't worked, however.
The Facts: Jason was shy even when a young baby, and has continued to be this way as he has grown older. His parents are very caring but have become frustrated by his shy behaviour. However, he can be a very stubborn child, ready to dig in his heels if he does not approve of something. His parents intention of forcing him out of his shyness by placing him in nursery has been ineffective; he is thoroughly miserable there and isolates himself. It is as though he is determined to prove the strength of his shyness and actively resists any pressure or encouragement for him to change.
The Analysis: Forcing the boy out of his shyness is a technique doomed to failure. When confronted by coercion, he simply becomes more entrenched. The situation has developed into a battle of wills between Jason and his parents, with the nursery staff caught in the middle each day; it's no longer about helping a shy child become more sociable, and has become a clash of child against parent. This type of head-to-head conflict is unproductive.
The Solution: Jason's mum and dad need to develop a reasonable, calm plan of action. Their tempers are too heated and their tolerance has worn thin. They should take a more relaxed approach when dealing with their son's shyness. Instead of battling against him, they should try gentle encouragement. They spend too much time reprimanding him when he is shy and not enough time praising him when he isn't shy; and they spend too much time arguing with him about his shyness and not enough time helping him overcome it. If his parents and nursery staff adopt this same strategy, the switch in perspective from a punishment-based approach to a reward-based approach will be a forward step.

Overcoming Shyness - Action Plan

You can help a child of any age beat his shyness by following this action plan:

1. **Validate his feelings.** He may be afraid you'll laugh at him, so talk to him about his shyness. That gets the subject into the open. Let him know that you understand about shyness, that you have been shy too, and that it's all right to be shy sometimes. Sharing your feelings like this makes him feel better.
2. **Set reasonable targets.** There's no point in simply insisting that he becomes talkative and outgoing the next time he meets new children – such expectations are much too high. Instead, set an attainable goal, such as just saying "hello" to another child; he's more likely to experience success.
3. **Discourage shy behaviour.** A shy child often has behavioural mannerisms which reveal his true underlying feelings (eg looks down at his feet, sucks his thumb, fidgets with his clothing). Point these habits out to him and suggest he concentrates on not behaving like that the next time he feels shy.
4. **Give replacement habits.** As well as discouraging behaviour which shows that he is shy, you can encourage the child to adopt behaviour that actually suggests he is sociable (eg smiling when someone speaks to him, making eye-contact with others, looking interested). Practise these with him.
5. **Talk to him appropriately.** Research shows that adults tend to use simpler forms of speech when talking to a shy child (the sort of speech they would use with a much younger child) and this could encourage further immature behaviour from him. When he's shy, therefore, talk to him as you normally would.
6. **Provide small-group activities.** If you know that a child is shy, his worst nightmare will be meeting lots of new children and adults all at once. It makes sense to try to provide social activities that place him in the company of one or two others at most at a time. This will build up his social confidence.
7. **Avoid spotlighting him.** A shy child hates the very idea of being in a situation where everyone stares at him, so avoid this if at all possible. For instance, when in a group, he should not be asked to sing in front of the others or to tell his latest news, at least not without advance notice that would allow preparation.
8. **Provide structure when he plays with friends.** A shy child finds ambiguity and flexibility in social situations very difficult to handle. He fears that he may have to talk to others unexpectedly. When he is with others, he finds it easier when the play activities are well-planned and organised.

9. **Play games requiring more than one player.** A shy child would prefer solitary play activities to avoid mixing with other children. But that's the easy way out. Instead, direct him to games and toys that need another child for them to be played properly; this will encourage him to interact.
10. **Help him feel good about himself.** Let him know that you care for him even when he's shy, but that you are sure he'd have more fun if he spoke to others. Take an interest in his activities, talk to him about them, reassure him that other children like him and look happy when he does mix well.

Q & A

Q. *Is it normal for a four-year-old boy to be shy in front of his parents when he's having a bath? He has suddenly started to insist they leave the bathroom when he washes.*

A. This is perfectly normal. But you are mistaken to think that it is shyness – it's only that the child wants privacy, nothing more. Every child is entitled to have responsibility for his own body, and to decide who is allowed physical (or in this case, visual) contact with him. At this age he has become more aware of his body and that part of growing older involves becoming independent and having privacy. So don't worry about it. You can help him by recognising his right to privacy, and by reminding him you are entitled to privacy too (eg he shouldn't barge into your room without permission).

Q. *Is a shy child always unhappy? I know a young child who is very shy and yet seems to be very happy.*

A. Shyness is by no means the same as unhappiness. There are plenty of shy children – like this child – who have a very enjoyable time; and they may grow into adults who are shy but who are also contented with their lifestyle. Problems arise, however, when a child's shyness gets in the way of things, and has an adverse effect on his development (eg when his shyness stops him from going to his best friend's party and his friend becomes annoyed with him; when he is good at sport but his shyness stops him from attending the local sports club for the under-fives). Other than that, you could justifiably look on a child's shyness as just one more of his individual characteristics.

Q. *I can predict when my child is going to be shy, and so I don't bother involving him in that particular activity. Should I be more insistent?*

A. You are right to avoid confrontations where at all possible. However, this strategy inevitably has two outcomes. First, it encourages his shyness because he is never challenged socially. Second, he has no opportunity to learn how not to be shy. Perhaps an alternative approach would be to involve him in activities that you expect to make him shy, while giving him adequate preparation so that he can cope more effectively. Explain that you know he finds this difficult, but that he can learn ways to behave that will make him feel less shy. He'll probably be willing to have a go if he knows you are working with him, supporting him.

Q. *Surely shyness is good for a child? At least he won't talk to strangers.*
A. That's absolutely right. Shyness can protect a child in certain circumstances, and you certainly wouldn't want to encourage him to become so sociable that he would talk to anyone at all. Indeed you would probably be very worried if he lacked social sensitivity. You have to strike a balance between suggesting to a child that he talks to anyone and everyone and suggesting that he talks to nobody at all. Warn him about the hazards of talking to strangers, especially when he nears school age and is more likely at times to be without adult supervision.

19

Sibling Rivalry

"There are times I get so fed up with their constant fighting with each other. They bicker over the most trivial things. On the other hand, there are times when they can be so thoughtful and helpful to each other."

It would be terrific if brothers and sisters got on with each other all the time, but tension between siblings occurs in every family. In fact, regular bickering is so common between brothers and sisters that most psychologists regard sibling rivalry as normal.

The origins of this form of strained relationships between brothers and sisters in the same family usually lies during the early years. A first born child is knocked off his perch by the arrival of the new baby – before the birth he had parental attention all to himself – and from then on the resentment towards the younger sibling can intensify. Yet it's not just the first born child that can experience sibling rivalry, however. Even second born and third born children can feel resentment towards a new baby, despite the fact that they are already used to living with brothers and sisters. Younger children are likely to experience jealousy too, especially when they think that older brothers and sisters are allowed more freedom, later bedtimes, and more new clothes.

So there is no surprise when the children in a family don't always get on well with each other, especially when they are young. When sibling rivalry does exist, at best it results in a verbal disagreement between the children as they shout at each other, and at worst they raise their hands as they try to thump each other. Parents would be delighted if their children mixed well with each other, but often the reality is quite different. (Of course, there are many instances when bothers and sisters do have a trouble-free relationship.)

Age Gap

The age difference between the first child and second child affects the level of sibling rivalry between them, although remember that every child is an individual. Here are some of the likely effects that different age gaps will have on the first child. These findings signify trends, however, not certainties, and parents should never attempt to plan their family spacing solely in the hope of avoiding some negative aspects.

Age Gap Less Than Two Years
Advantages for an Older Child:
- with such a small age gap, the first child will still be young at the birth and is less likely to feel strong jealousy towards the new baby.
- both children are more likely to become close friends and this bond could well continue into adulthood.

Disadvantages for an Older Child:
- the older child might feel he is not being given enough attention as his parents have to spend so much time caring for the baby.
- because the two children are so close in age they may feel the need to compete with each other at home and school.

Age Gap Between Two and Four Years
Advantages for an Older Child:
- he is old enough to be treated as the 'older brother', and this brings benefits such as staying up later than his younger sibling.
- his daily routine is quite different from the new baby's pattern. This means he can have time alone with his parents every day.

Disadvantages for an Older Child:
- he knows that another child in the family is going to have a practical effect on his life, such as having to share his bedroom.
- he realises the new baby takes attention from mum and dad. This may cause him to feel insecure, and even angry.

Age Gap of More Than Four Years
Advantages for an Older Child:
- he can play an active part in caring for the baby, such as helping with bathing and changing him.
- there is less likely to be jealousy of the baby; both children will have different interests and different friends as they grow up.

Disadvantages For Your Older Child:
- this size of age gap may mean the older child doesn't form such a close friendship with his younger sibling during their childhood.
- his social life may be disrupted because his parents are more tied to the house now; you may not be able to take him to leisure classes.

Breaking The News

Although parents should obviously tell their child beforehand that he's going to have a new brother or sister, a child's sense of time is different from an adult's. He may see no difference between a week and a month, or even between one month and six months. If they tell him in the first few weeks of the pregnancy, he may become bored with the long wait and continually ask them when the baby's coming.

The best strategy is to introduce the idea to their toddler when the pregnancy starts to show in a way that he couldn't help but notice it, probably around the fourth, fifth or sixth month. Tell him calmly, without feeling embarrassed about it. And pitch the conversation at a level suitable for his understanding. Don't be tempted to give too much information – this is not the time to explain the human reproduction process to a young child. Just tell him enough so that he's not confused.

Every firstborn child reacts differently to the news that he is to become an older brother. However, he is bound to be taken aback when he is first told. And who can blame him. Up to this point in his life the older child has had his parents all to himself and he probably expected this way of life to continue forever. No wonder the thought of a new brother or sister fills him with feelings of insecurity and confusion.

Look at it from the child's point of view. He gets all the parents' love and attention, his grandparents probably give him lots of time and love too, and all the clothes and presents are just for him. He doesn't relish any change to the situation. Small wonder, then, that the impending arrival of a new brother or sister makes him feel threatened, insecure and jealous. Talk of a new baby shakes his 'me-focused' world at its very foundations.

When an older child is told of the new baby, he may be very troubled. Parents should not expect him automatically to be happy with the news flash – that is unrealistic. He might be afraid of loss of love and think "Will they love the baby more than they love me?"; he might perceive it as a punishment and think "Why do mum and dad need another baby – have I done something wrong?"; and he might be aware that family resources now have to be split four ways, not three, and think "Where will the baby sleep? Will she get my bed?".

Worrying that a toddler might be upset by the new arrival shouldn't influence the parents' decision to have another child. He'll eventually get used to the idea, sooner or later. And most parents confirm that the pleasure of having a second child outweighs any possible disruption in the early days. The older child will learn in time that his parents love him as much as they did before and that they have enough love for two. In the meantime, however, they should give him lots of reassurance if he does seem troubled by the news.

The child's immediate reaction might be pride, indifference, sulks, tears, anger, silence or delight. Parents need to be prepared for any of these responses, and to treat their older child seriously. Let him ask them any questions at all about the pregnancy and the new baby – either at the time they tell him or later – and always give an honest reply; listen to what he says, accept his feelings even if they don't like them, reassure him that he has nothing to worry about, and don't get cross or irritable if he keeps asking the same things over and over again.

The Birth Itself

An older child needs to be told that he (and his mother) will be going away for a day or so when the baby is born, because in many instances the child stays with his grandparents, a relative, or a close friend at this time. If possible, he should remain in his own house, with someone looking after him. But whatever arrangement is made, he needs reassurance that he (and his mother) will be coming home again afterwards and that 'going away' means only for a very short time. This may have to be repeated until he definitely understands.

Some parents want their older child to be present at the birth itself. Indeed, there are many documented cases in which the baby has been delivered at home because there was no time to reach the maternity hospital, allowing the older child to witness the whole event. Parents with that experience often report how it has brought them all closer together as a family.

A study compared differences in sibling rivalry between children who were present and those who were absent from the birth of a sibling. Parents were asked questions about aspects of their child's behaviour that could be caused by sibling rivalry (eg babyish actions, temper tantrums, taking toys from the baby, saying he doesn't like his new baby, nightmares, sleeping difficulties, and aggression towards mum and dad). The results showed that there were no significant differences between the two groups of children regarding these dimensions of the children's behaviour. The research evidence, therefore, is inconclusive, and the presence of an older child at the birth of a younger brother or sister remains an individual decision for the child's parents.

Parents have a right to exercise choice when it comes to birth arrangements, in conjunction with the professionals supporting the antenatal care. But they should think carefully about the older child's perception of the birth. If he sees mum in pain and discomfort caused by labour and the delivery – even though childbirth is a natural process – then he may have negative feelings towards his new sibling. It's something that should be thought out very carefully.

The First Meeting

If you have an older child and your second baby is due, there is a lot you can do to minimise your older child's jealousy of the new baby, and you can start with their first meeting. Encourage him to think that his younger brother or sister loves him. For example, when he visits the baby in hospital for the first time, make sure the baby has a present for him (one that his mother took into hospital with her), lying in the cot when he arrives. Likewise, let your older child take a gift – preferably one that he chose himself – for the new baby. Of course, this exchange of gifts is totally artificial, and may seem absurd in the eyes of adults. Yet it can help form an emotional attachment between your children from the beginning, and initiate a strong relationship between them.

When you see your older child after the baby is born, you may be shocked by how big he seems compared to your fragile newborn. Suddenly, he seems to be much older than you realised. Don't worry if you find that you feel very protective towards your baby as a result – this is a normal reaction for parents to experience at this stage and will soon pass. Try not to hover too defensively when your older child goes near his younger sibling; although your baby is very small, your first born is likely to be extremely gentle, especially if you are there to offer guidance on how to hold the baby and what to say.

Here are some suggestions for reducing sibling rivalry during the first few days back home, when your family is united once again:

- **if your older child is jealous, don't make him feel guilty.** You may be upset to see your first born child become angry, aggressive, clingy or even babyish himself. But don't chastise him for it. He is having a normal reaction, stemming from his sense of insecurity.
- **don't fuss too much over the baby in the older child's presence.** Although your existing child has to adjust to sharing your attention with the baby, he needs time to get used to it. If possible, try not to fuss about your new baby in front of your older child.
- **try to arrange family outings.** Going out with a young child and a baby is never easy, and requires lots of preparation, but it is worth the effort. Potential feelings of hostility towards the new arrival are reduced when there is minimal disruption to family life.
- **involve your older child in the practical care of the new baby.** Even a young toddler can fetch a clean nappy from the cupboard or bring you cotton wool and cleaning cream. There is always something he can do to help you no matter how small the task.
- **encourage others to give attention to your older child, as well as to your baby.** Most visitors to your house are determined to see the new arrival as soon as they set foot in your house, and your older child may feel very left out.
- **make him feel involved.** Remember that it is his new baby too – he has feelings of pride. There is no reason why he should not be the one to take visitors into the room when they come to see the baby for the first time.
- **have 'quality time' every day.** Nobody would deny that life with two young children in the house is hectic. However, your older child needs a little individual attention every day to remind him that he is special too.

Changes

Sibling rivalry will probably be present at every stage of the children's lives to a greater or lesser extent, no matter how young or old they are. (Of course, when they are adults they can be left to sort it out themselves, whereas parents have to become actively involved as the peacemakers when they are children otherwise the rivalry may increase). However, the way this rivalry is expressed changes as the children grow older. The list below outlines the typical ways in which jealousy between the children in a family is expressed at each age. Bear in mind though that the manifestation of sibling rivalry depends largely on the children's individual personalities, the age of the children and the age difference between them, and the way they are managed at home by their parents. The examples given may not mirror your own children exactly but the chances are that you will see some of these elements reflected in their relationships.

18 Months

(a) He is the older child: Sibling rivalry tends to be at a minimum, because he is so focused on himself and his own needs. His attention will be drawn to his younger sister mostly when she starts to cry. However, he won't show strong resentment towards her.

(b) He is the younger child: A child aged 18 months does not represent much of a threat to older siblings, and so sibling rivalry is not usually a difficulty. If he does find his way to the other children's toys or games, they will be able to use their bigger size to their advantage.

Two Years

(a) He is the older child: A typical two-year-old is alert enough to know that the presence of a younger brother or sister will have an impact on his life at home. He won't notice the effect immediately but he may become attention-seeking or babyish himself.

(b) He is the younger child: Because he is at a peak level of curiosity he likes to explore into rooms and cupboards, even those that are not his. And this can be very annoying for older brothers and sisters, who will not be pleased to find their toys messed up.

Three Years

(a) He is the older child: This age gap is associated with the peak level of sibling rivalry, largely because the child is old enough and mature enough to understand that a new baby will draw attention and resources away from him.

(b) He is the younger child: Older siblings are able to spell out the rules of family life more clearly, and he will co-operative more than before, although he remains self-interested and determined. The three-year-old may be invited to join in games with his older brother.

Four Years

(a) He is the older child: He accepts the reality that there is a new baby in the family, but he won't be entirely happy about it. At times, he might be mean to the newborn, often not intentionally. For instance, his loving hug might become too enthusiastic.

(a) He is the younger child: He probably shows great loyalty to his older brother or sister and may even follow them around like a faithful puppy. On the other hand, there will be times when he forcefully attempts to boss his older siblings about and gets angry with them.

Five Years

(a) He is the older child: He feels good about himself because he is now at school, and is perhaps more tolerant of his younger sibling. However, he may try to dominate the younger one, telling him what to do and how to do it and this inevitably results in conflict.

(b) He is the younger child: He wants to be like his older siblings, perhaps wanting to walk with them to school, and he may not understand why they prefer to go with their own friends. He may be unsettled by the achievements of the older children.

Six Years

(a) He is the older child: Tolerance of younger brothers and sisters is at a premium; the child has his own ideas, his own likes and dislikes, and he doesn't react well to the intrusions of younger siblings. He may try to use the age gap to control the younger ones in the family.

(b) He is the younger child: He will begin to respect the rights of the other children in the family, and realise the reciprocity of relationships (ie if he's good to his older sister, the chances are that she will be good to him).

Eight Years

(a) He is an older child: He begins to perceive himself as "older". While he is naturally protective towards younger siblings, he doesn't want to have to be responsible for them whenever they play outside. The antics of a younger sister may annoy him if he is with his friends.

(b) He is a younger child: He looks up to his older siblings, as long as there is an age gap of at least two years or so. Less than that, the competition may be fierce; more than that, neither is a threat to each other and the eight-year-old will be proud of his older brother.

Ten Years

(a) He is an older child: He cares deeply for his younger brother or sisters, and tries to guide them whenever he can. But he'll have no patience when they don't do as he says. He will be irritated by their mischief, yet he will defend them against aggression from others.

(b) He is a younger child: The child treats his older siblings with respect. He likes his privacy and therefore respects their privacy too. At times he will try to take part in some of their activities, if the age gap is not too great , and he will probably be very well behaved.

12 Years

(a) He is an older child: The fierce independence shown by a 12-year-old means that he has difficulty getting on with the other children in the family. He may have little time for the younger ones, treating them with sarcasm and imitating them when they complain.

(b) He is a younger child. His adulation of older brothers and sisters fades as his confidence and independence increases. Their styles and fashions are unlikely to be his, and as a result he may reject their advice and suggestions.

14 Years

(a) He is an older child: Much depends on the age gap. He probably gets on well with a sibling who is a pre-schooler; he won't feel threatened by the younger child, and will be affectionate to him. With a small age gap, he may be rude to the younger child.

(b) He is a younger child: Since he treats his older brother or sister with respect – because he is greatly interested in their activities and wants to learn from someone who is older – relationships are good. Sibling rivalry is rarely a major problem at this stage of development.

Managing Sibling Rivalry

If you are a parent of more than one child (or you work with siblings in a child-care setting) you'll know that no matter how hard you try, cries of "That's not fair", "She's allowed to stay up later than me" or "He always gets more than I do" will ring out at some time. You may find that most family arguments are caused by rivalry between your children. Sibling rivalry affects every child – although your oldest child is more prone to jealousy, your youngest too will have moments when he is convinced everyone else in the family gets a better deal than he docs.

Although you can't eliminate sibling rivalry altogether, you can attempt control it and to reduce its potential impact on family life. Don't leave it all to chance. Make a decision to **treat your children seriously** because if they feel that you only regard them with shallow amusement, rather than genuine respect, they will soon become jealous of each other. Listen to their complaints when they are expressed. The endless list of gripes and groans that your children have about each other can be irritating, and you may be tempted to dismiss them immediately. It is better to make time to listen to them – you will have to give them attention anyway if they start fighting one another. There is absolutely no point in making your child feel guilty because he is jealous of his sibling. He doesn't do this deliberately so you will gain nothing by berating him with comments like "You're acting like a baby by being so jealous of your sister. You should be ashamed."

Aim for **fairness, not equality**. Most parents make a conscientious effort to be fair to their children, so that each child gets his rightful share of love, time and resources. Of course, this isn't always possible but is a goal worth aiming for. There will be times when one of your children is absolutely convinced he is disadvantaged even though you can see nothing to justify this feeling. It is easy, however, to confuse fairness (ie all your children get what they need) with equality (all your children get the exact same as each other), but this is unsatisfactory and will result in rivalry. After all, equality means dissatisfaction for someone – giving your children the exact same each time (eg when one gets a new book, they all get a new book) will cause one of your children to be delighted (because she wanted a book) and the others to be annoyed (because they didn't want a book). It is often easier and more convenient when all your children need the same item or want to attend the same activity. However, don't force them into this situation. In the long run it's better to meet their individual needs.

There are few things more emotionally draining than having to listen to your children bickering constantly with each. And your response will probably be to criticise them for their negative behaviour – that's only natural. The problem is that your criticism only makes matters worse by getting everyone in a bad mood. Of course, you want to change the situation so that fights are less frequent, but it is possible to **achieve change without criticism** through positive feedback instead of negative comments. There is always a place for criticism in family life – after all, nobody is perfect – yet too much of it can create tense relationships at home. There is a difference between criticising your children and criticising their behaviour. It's better to say to them "Fighting with each other is unpleasant" (ie criticising their behaviour) than to say "You're unpleasant when you fight" (ie criticising your children).

Getting on with others in the family is so important. When siblings don't have a good relationship, they fight about everything. Although children are by nature social animals and seem to have an inborn need for company, they are not automatically experts at getting on with others. There are many social skills that they have to learn and part of a parent's task is to teach these skills to their children so that they all become more competent socially. Encourage your children to **communicate their feelings**. Sibling squabbles often stem from the children's inability to use words to communicate their feelings and ideas; they use fists instead. Ask your children questions about how they are feeling. And provide opportunities for sharing. Many sibling fights start because one or more of the children are unable to share their toys. This can be very difficult for some children. First, explain to your children why they should share, and second, teach them how to share. They will need your guidance. Play games that involve turn-taking. Your children cannot possibly play together peacefully, without fighting, unless they are able to take turns. But this doesn't come naturally as a young child wants to be first for everything. Games give children experience of taking turns.

Comparisons

While it is very tempting to compare brothers and sisters with each other in the hope of inspiring one child by the example of his sibling – this can have the opposite effect and actually de-motivate the children. Sometimes comparisons are generated by the children themselves. Let's consider the following example.

The Problem: Six-year-old Joe is very disparaging about his achievements in school. He desperately wants to gain high marks in any class test and tries very hard, but he is never pleased with his performance. His teacher is delighted with his progress in class, as are his parents. Yet Joe is constantly dissatisfied despite the fact that he is in the top reading group and number group.

The Facts: Joe's family are very supportive and caring. His parents value education and place great importance on school achievements. Aside from Joe, there are two other children in the family, a ten-year-old boy and an eight-year-old girl, both of whom are extremely clever – they were each the top of their class last year. Joe thinks his older sister and brother are fabulous and he wants to be like them. He studies very hard whenever he has homework, gives maximum effort in the class and listens very seriously. Neither his parents nor his teacher have ever compared him to his older siblings.

The Analysis: Although Joe's parents have deliberately avoided comparisons with his older brother and sister, Joe puts himself under tremendous pressure by trying to compete with them. The comparison comes from him, not from anybody else. He admires his siblings and wants to be like them in every possible way, including school attainments. But he is a unique child, with his own talents and abilities, different from his brother and sister. Unfortunately, his desire to match them in terms of school progress has resulted in dissatisfaction and in the long-term is having a negative effect on Joe.

The Solution: His parents can help their youngest child by encouraging him to value his own achievements – whether or not they match those of his older siblings – and by helping him set sensible targets for the future, based on his current stage of development. They should tell Joe that they just want him to do his best in class, to do as well as he possibly can, explaining that they don't compare him with his siblings and that he shouldn't do this either. They could encourage him to take up an interest that his older siblings are not involved in. Although Joe might always want to achieve the same school grades or exam marks as his siblings, he will gradually develop pride in his own abilities.

Q & A

Q. *My two children are six and four years old, and they fight a lot with each other. Are they going to be this way all their lives?*

A. Feelings of rivalry that start off in childhood often do continue throughout adulthood. But as your children grow older – with your help – they'll learn to control sibling rivalry so that it has less impact on their relationship. They'll realise that their jealousy is often irrational; and they'll also realise that having a brother or sister has many benefits that may only emerge after childhood (eg having someone to share feelings with, someone to offer advice, someone to listen to their problems, someone for company and so on). In adulthood, most people recognise that the advantages of having a sibling grossly outweigh the disadvantages.

Q. *I've noticed that my three-year-old son gives his new sister such enthusiastic hugs that she starts to choke. Does he really mean to hurt her?*

A. It is extremely unlikely that he deliberately tries to hurt his sister. He probably loves her, and that is why he wants to hug her so openly. Unconsciously, however, he may feel threatened by her arrival – and although he isn't aware of this deeper sense of insecurity, it is having an effect on his behaviour. The over-enthusiastic hug is a combination of his genuine love towards his sister and his genuine perception of her as a threat. Your son's behaviour is telling you that he is troubled and you should respond sensitively to him. Reassure him that you love him as much as you always did and spend as much time with him as you can.

Q. *How can I help my son stand up for himself? He always gives in to his sister when she wants his toys, even though he seems to be unhappy about it.*

A. There are possibly two angles to this. First, you may have to boost your son's self-confidence so that he can stop being a victim. Remind him that he has nothing to be afraid of and that he shouldn't let his sister have anything of his unless he wants her to. The other angle to consider is that your son may not be as upset as you imagine. Perhaps he takes his sister's toys just as she takes his; this may be their agreed arrangements. What seems unfair to parents, on the surface, may suit the children themselves. So check it out with your son and daughter before taking action. Ask them what agreement they have reached about sharing. You may be surprised with their answer.

Q. *How can I stop my four-year-old son from being disruptive every time I start to breast-feed his baby sister?*

A. Your son obviously feels very jealous when he sees you breast-feeding. And no wonder. After all, you hold the baby very close to you, and she is in direct physical contact with you in a warm, nurturing experience. His disruptive behaviour at that time is probably his attempt to draw attention away from his sister on to himself. Explain that he was breast-fed when he was a baby (assuming that's true), and that he enjoyed it too. Keep him close beside you when you breast-feed; let him watch you, perhaps even lean against you, so that he also has close physical contact with you. And make sure that he has something to do while you feed your baby.

Section 5: Intellectual Development

This section looks closely at a child's intellectual development, both in terms of general learning skills and language acquisition. Chapter 19 considers the source of intelligence and the main influences on intellectual development, while also examining creativity in childhood. It is necessary for you to be aware of the milestones of normal language acquisition, and Chapter 20 highlights these while also tackling the problem of slow language development and hearing difficulties. Chapter 21 focuses on children with special needs and the special challenges they and their families face, and the transition to school is examined in Chapter 22.

20

Intellectual Development

"What amazes me is how a child's intelligence seems to grow so quickly. When she is a toddler she struggles with a shape-sorter, and just a few years later she loves drawing, filling in dot-to-dot books, and jigsaws. The transformation is wonderful to see."

A child's learning skills (her intelligence) develop significantly in the first five years. You can't fail to notice how her abilities to reason, to understand and to solve problems improve so much during this phase of her life.

Probably the best way to define a child's intelligence is to think of it as her ability to learn new skills, her ability to adapt to new situations, and her ability to solve minor problems – these are all learning skills (which is the reason why psychologists prefer to talk of "learning ability", "learning skills" or "thinking skills" rather than "intelligence"). A clever child has a higher level of learning skills – and is able to use them more effectively – than one with a lower level of learning ability.

And don't be fooled into thinking that a precocious, sociable, self-confident child is always more intelligent than someone the same age who is more withdrawn. These are social skills, not learning skills, and reveal little (if anything) about her level of intelligence. A child who talks to adults easily and who has the social mannerisms normally associated with an older child often has these solely because she spends more time in the company of adults. It is a matter of social experience and social training, not her level of thinking skills.

The Source of Intelligence

There is no clear-cut explanation for the source of a child's intelligence. The list below highlights the principal theoretical ideas and their practical implications for helping improve learning skills:

"Intelligence is inherited": Some psychologists claim that up to 80% of a child's intelligence is inherited from her parents in the same way that other qualities (eg colour of eyes, height tendency, weight tendency) are also inherited. Therefore a child's learning ability is directly related to her parents' own learning ability.
Evidence: Identical twins have intelligence levels that are closer than

non-identical twins. In addition, there is a better chance of accurately predicting the learning ability of an adopted child through knowing her natural mother's learning ability than through knowing her adoptive mother's learning ability.

Implications of This Perspective

1. Accept a child's level of intelligence for what it is and do not push her too hard to achieve at a rate beyond her ability. She is born with a fixed amount of inherited intelligence.
2. A child who seems to have a lower level of thinking skills should be given more help to improve than a brighter child. She will require a higher amount of intellectual stimulation in order to improve.
3. A child who is clever does not need support to learn new skills. She will always be clever no matter the circumstances, and will progress irrespective of stimulation she receives.

"Intelligence is acquired": Some psychologists claim that a child's level of intelligence depends almost entirely on her experiences during the early years of childhood. If she is given sufficient stimulation then her learning skills will improve, but if she is under-stimulated then her intelligence will remain the same.

Evidence: Studies have found connections between a child's home environment and her intelligence, for instance, children from middle-class families tend to have higher measured levels of ability than children raised in areas of deprivation. These difference begins to show at the age of two or three years.

Implications of This Perspective

1. Since a child's level of intelligence depends heavily on the stimulation and learning experiences she has at home, she will benefit from a wide range of games and toys.
2. There is no limit to a child's true intellectual potential, she is only as limited as her learning experiences. Parents and carers should expect the highest thinking skills from a child.
3. Have high educational standards for her. Since the learning environment is so influential, it is better for a child to learn in a setting that makes strong intellectual demands.

"Intelligence is interactive": Some psychologists take the view that intelligence develops as a result of the interaction between the learning ability a child is born with and the learning experiences she has subsequently. In other words, the environment nurtures and enhances her basic innate abilities.

Evidence: Many studies confirm, for instance, that parents who play with their child during the pre-school years tend to have more intelligent children, that children who have more toys are often brighter by school age, and that children's learning skills can improve depending on the teaching method used.

Implications of This Perspective

1. Parents and carers should play with a child, rather than just provide learning opportunities. She needs encouragement, advice and support to advance her existing learning skills.
2. Learning experiences should be demanding enough to challenge a child's thinking skills (in order to develop them further) but not too demanding or she will give up.
3. If a child has difficulty learning a new skill using one teaching method, then it is always worthwhile to try a different teaching approach as that may be more helpful.

"Intelligence is learned": Some psychologists claim that intelligence can be taught, just in the same way that the skill of riding a bicycle can be taught. Intelligence is not a unique human characteristic from this perspective; once the important learning skills have been identified, they can be taught to a young child.

Evidence: For instance, you can specifically encourage a child to ask questions when she doesn't understand something, to divide a large problem into smaller components so that she tackles it more effectively, or to be more reflective before answering a question. Thinking skills like these could improve a child's intelligence.

Implications of This Perspective

1. A child's intellectual ability is not fixed, but depends on how well she is taught when she is young. The quality of the teaching process is more significant than her inherited ability.
2. Parents should understand the processes that underlie learning, not just the knowledge a child should acquire. And children should be taught these processes.
3. The learning environment should be challenging. A child does not benefit by resting on the strength of her achievements; she needs to continue learning all the time.

Confusing, isn't it! Each of these different perspectives appears to have supportive evidence, and yet they are in conflict with one another. You will have to decide for yourself which theoretical approach you feel most comfortable with. However, there are several common points shared by all:

- **stimulation.** No matter how clever a child is, she will benefit from being challenged intellectually through a variety of play activities, games and toys. This does not mean she has to "learn" all day, but you should try to create a stimulating environment, one that encourages her to get involved.

- **support.** Children learn best when they feel valued, when they feel someone takes an interest in them, when they feel relaxed. So try to stay calm when a child struggles to learn a new concept – her failure to acquire this new skill is unintentional. She is doing her best, so support her instead of agitating her.
- **expectations.** She will learn best when she is expected to learn. However, when a child is subjected to unrealistic expectations, she may feel so pressurised to achieve that she becomes overwhelmed with anxiety, and consequently fails. Expect every child to improve, but not at a rate that is beyond her.
- **enjoyment.** You probably have problems learning when the environment is tense and unpleasant. A child is no different from you in this respect. Learning should be fun for young children and they should not be afraid of failure. She'll learn best when the atmosphere is relaxed and enjoyable.

The main intellectual skills that a child is expected to have acquired have already been listed in Chapters 2-5, and now is a good time for you to look at these again. You should also read over the advice given in these chapters about encouraging a child's development and about testing these skills.

Self-Fulfilling Prophecy

Young children have an amazing ability to fulfil negative expectations no matter what age they are. For instance, when parents worry that their toddler will be disruptive during a family gathering, this may well happen. Low expectations can also be self-fulfilling. Let's consider the following example.

The Problem: Six-year-old Ruth's parents accept that her ability to learn new concepts and ideas is slower, compared to her older brother and sister. Consequently they don't push her in learning situations; if anything, they do the opposite. They have already explained to her class teacher that she finds learning difficult and that they shouldn't push her too hard; she needs more time to learn, that's all. School staff are now convinced that the more Ruth's parents accept her slow progress, the less progress she makes.

The Facts: Ruth has two older siblings. They are both extremely clever, and both progressed through their developmental milestones very quickly (eg sitting up, first steps, first words). In school, they continue to be close to the top of their classes. In comparison, Ruth's progress has always been slower and she is not able to learn as fast as they do. Her parents take great pains to remind her that she is an individual, quite different from her older brother and sister, and that she should not try to compete with them. She will move at her own pace. Ruth's siblings are aware of their young sister's comparative difficulties; they try to help her with learning tasks.

The Analysis: The developmental progress of the two older children has given Ruth's parents the impression that she is slow to develop. Perhaps she is slow – but her parents don't really know because their baseline of comparison is high (ie the older children's excellent rates of progress). They perceive six-year-old Ruth as having difficulties with learning, and all their behaviour towards her confirms that view (eg they discourage school staff from making learning demands on her, they let her progress at her own pace, they tell her that they don't mind her not being as clever as her older siblings, and so on). Of course, the parents' sympathy and support is well-intentioned, but this approach effectively convinces Ruth that she has a problem with learning. And she now believes it herself. Their predictions have become self-fulfilling.

The Solution: If Ruth is ever to have confidence in her own abilities – whatever these may be – she has to start believing in herself. And that requires her mum and dad (and her teacher) to take a different attitude towards her. This can be achieved in a number of ways, including having higher expectations of her. Difficulties are less likely when they are not anticipated. In addition, comparisons with the older siblings should cease altogether as they simply emphasise the differences between the three children and confirm Ruth's self-image of being a child with learning difficulties. She needs encouragement to progress, not sympathy when she doesn't progress; she needs demanding challenges in school, not learning activities that simply go over old ground. This subtle shift in outlook is more likely to lead to Ruth's progress than a continuation of the existing approach which serves only to maintain her low expectations of herself.

Creativity

Most adults value a child's intelligence more than they value her creativity because they assume that intelligence is a more important quality. However, creativity is connected to the learning process, for instance when a child creates an innovative solution to a problem or when she writes a story to express her ideas.

The connection between intelligence and creativity is unclear. Certainly a child does not have to be clever in order to be creative, although the findings from psychological research indicate that people who have a high level of creativity tend be of at least average intellectual ability.

A child who is genuinely creative in her ideas, thoughts and actions will show the following qualities:

– originality. She will propose new solutions to problems or suggest original ideas. For instance, a young child might decide that her drinking cup can be used to shovel earth in the garden – that's creative. So is a four-year-old's idea of sticking cloth on to her drawing of a doll to make it more interesting.
– usefulness. There's no point in a suggestion that is utterly useless. For instance, a five-year-old's idea that mountain climbers should grow wings in case they fall off is not truly creative because it can't possibly work. However, she would be creative if, for example, she suggested they wear a parachute.
– change. A creative idea looks at a difficulty from a fresh angle. It is the change in outlook that is a sign of creativity. Like the time a young child asked you why earth grows from the roots of flowers. Or the time an infant suddenly realised she was putting the shape in the wrong hole of the shape-sorter.
– multi-purposeful. When a child makes a genuinely creative response, it will have many characteristics. For instance, if she sees that there is no plug for the bathroom sink she may suggest using a towel to block it, and also that the wet towel can then be used to wash her hands and face.

Encouraging Creativity

Every child is naturally creative, no matter what you do, although children vary in their levels of creativity. Here are some tips for encouraging a child to be more creative:

- **respond positively when she is creative.** This doesn't mean that you should squeal with delight when she paints a life-size sketch on the wall of your house! However, try to be enthusiastic when she shows you a drawing she has completed or when she sings a new song she has just made up. Your positive reaction encourages her to continue creating new ideas.
- **let her test out her creative ideas.** Easier said than done, of course, because children under the age of five rarely appreciate the consequences of their ideas. Even so, give her some scope to be inventive. If personal injury is likely, then you should intercede, but other than that it is better to let a child try out her suggestions in practice even though they may fail.
- **help her deal with uncertainty.** Young children frequently prefer to know the outcome of something before it starts; they enjoy predictability. Yet a child who is able to cope with ambiguity is more likely to be creative. So when she asks you "What will happen if I do this?" you could say "I don't know exactly what will happen but we'll have some fun watching you try this out."

- **let her struggle with a problem, at times.** A child learns a lot by example and so it is reasonable for you to show her a solution at times when she can't solve a problem she faces. But it is also reasonable for you to ask her to find a solution herself at other times. This helps her deal with frustration and also is more likely to lead to new and challenging suggestions from her.
- **listen without criticising.** A child who is criticised every time she offers an interesting idea will soon learn not to be creative. Her impulses to be original will be stifled by her anticipation of negative comments. Far better to have an attitude which encourages a child to say what she thinks and feels and to offer ideas that are different from those offered by other children.
- **give opportunities for imaginative play.** Creativity depends on a lively imagination, an ability to go beyond the obvious. And imaginative play is a good way of stimulating this type of thinking in a young child. She might enjoy dressing-up in adult clothes or pretending to be someone else, or she might enjoy clay-modelling which allows her to make new shapes.

Q & A

Q. *What is an intelligence test? Does it reveal a lot about a child's thinking skills and her potential to learn?*

A. Psychologists have identified the key learning skills that are assumed to contribute to a child's intelligence (eg the ability to process visual patterns, the ability to recall previously heard information, the ability to make comparisons), and an intelligence test is a series of small mental challenges that measures these skills. Intelligence tests are standardised, which means that psychologists know the typical performance on these tests for each child of each age. When a young child is given an intelligence test (which can only be administered by a qualified and accredited psychologist) her scores are then compared with the typical scores of a child her age. Not everyone approves of intelligence tests, however. Questions have been raised about their validity and reliability, and consequently they are less popular amongst professionals than they were previously.

Q. *What can I do to motivate a three-year-old who is passive? She has little interest in toys and prefers to sit and look rather than to get involved.*

A. Children vary in their levels of motivation, just as much they vary in their levels of ability. The problem you are experiencing with this child is that even if her intellectual level is very high, she does not use that ability to improve her learning. There is no easy answer to this problem, and you are right to be concerned. There are several strategies you could try. You might, for instance, let her choose the next toy that is bought for her – she'll be more motivated to play with the toy if she has chosen it herself. Make a specific time when you tell her she should play, and select a few toys for her. Then play together with her, at least until she gets started. Your involvement may egg her on. Praise her when she does take a more active role and tell her how pleased you are with her. She may be less passive when she plays with other children her own age.

Q. *What is the best way to improve a toddler's concentration?*

A. Concentration is important for learning because a child who cannot focus on the learning activity in front of her won't sit long enough to complete it. However, concentration is a skill that develops from birth onwards. Even by the time she is a toddler, she would normally flit from toy to toy, activity to activity, at a moment's notice – she feels there is so much to do, so much to learn, that she literally cannot wait. Concentration will gradually improve over the next few years. In the meantime, you could help her by involving her in activities that do require concentration. For instance, tell her a short story, and when she indicates that she is about to move off, give her a cuddle and encourage her to listen to a little bit more; when she finishes playing with a toy, gently encourage her to play with it for a little longer – but avoid confrontations.

Q. *How important is play for a child's intellectual development?*

A. There are many ways in which play contributes to a child's development, eg it encourages her to mix with other children, it provides a forum for using her imagination, it allows her to release emotions, it shows her the boundaries of her abilities, and it increases her self-confidence. And it also enhances her learning skills. So the educational dimension is only one aspect of play. Remember she needs to engage in many types of play, not just play that has an educational component. Too much of the one sort of toy or game will bore her; she needs variety.

21

Language Development

"I used to be worried about Robin's language development, but I realise that was silly. He uses language so effectively now, to tell me things, to ask me things, and to talk to his pals."

There are several theories to account for the way that a child learns language, and you should think about how they fit in with your own view because the view you hold of language development influences the way you interact with children.

Probably the least likely theory is the one that claims a child acquires language through imitation, that he picks up words and sentences simply by imitating those around him. This theory rests on the observation that a young child who lives in a household where only French is spoken will speak French, and his accent will also reflect the accents of those around him. While this might be able to account for the early stages of language acquisition up to the period of 18 months to two years, it can't account for the wide variety of sentences that a three-year-old child makes, often ones that he has never heard before.

The theory that language is inborn is more plausible. It proposes that each child is born with the ability to speak and to use language, that he already knows how to recognise language from all the other sounds in the environment. One of the amazing features of children's language development is that most progress through the same stages, in the same order, at roughly the same time in their lives. This suggests a natural growth process, in the same way that his bones grow. It is as though a child's language growth follows an innate blueprint.

In contrast, another plausible theory claims that language is learned, because adults in the child's world reinforce specific words, thereby encouraging the child to use them. In a typical day, a child hears thousands and thousands of spoken words, some of which he does not understand. If one of these words (eg "spaghetti") is accompanied by an action or object that motivates him to focus on that word (eg the arrival of a plateful of delicious spaghetti) then the chances are that the child will learn the meaning of the word. And there's also learning by association. If a child regularly hears you say you are exhausted when you flop down in a comfortable chair for a brief rest, then he'll soon learn the meaning of the word "exhausted" by associating it with your actions.

The most convincing theory is that language develops as an interaction between innate ability and environmental stimulation. A child does not grow in isolation. He is affected by his environment, and in turn he has an effect on that environment. It is a constant cycle of action-reaction-action. Through this process, his speech and language skills progress impressively from birth onwards. A child raised in a family in which there is open discussion is more likely to have good language skills than a child raised in a family with limited spoken communication.

Age by Stage

Each child progresses at his own rate with speech and language, but the list below gives an approximate age-by-stage account of language acquisition during the early years, along with helpful suggestions.

Three months: He listens more closely when he hears a noise; for instance, when a bell rings gently he will become quiet and listen to it. He can now probably make two distinct sounds, such as "goo" and "la" and he'll use these in a way to attract adult attention. He also enjoys listening to music and songs.

How To Help

1. Provide a range of sounds for him to listen to, including songs, rhymes and poems. When you change him or feed him, talk to him all the time about what you are doing, even though he cannot fully understand what you say to him.
2. Respond to his vocalisations. At this age, he coos (in other words, he makes gurgling types of noises). These sounds may appear to be early words but they don't have any meaning. Even so, smile at him and talk back in response.
3. Sing him a lullaby in order to soothe him to sleep. Even though you may think you have a dreadful singing voice, you'll be amazed how calming your lullabies can be. The baby feels safe with you, and your voice reassures and relaxes him.

Six months: His babbling sounds are more consistent, and he may synchronise his babbling sounds with your speech, almost as if he is taking turns in a conversation. He can produce at least four or five different sounds and can accurately turn his head towards the source of a particular sound in order to hear it better.

How to Help

1. Allow a pause every so often when you talk to him. This gives him an opportunity to make sounds at the times he wants. Through this he learns about the interactive nature of language, and that he can play a part too.

2. When you hear him use the same babbling sound consistently (for instance, he says "eh" every time he sees you), smile at him and show you are pleased with the recognition. This will encourage him to continue addressing you this way in the meantime.
3. Read him lots of stories. He will love sitting on your knee, being held tight to you, while you softly read him an interesting children's story. The pleasure from this type of experience harnesses his interest in spoken language and books.

12 months: The child may be able to use up to three or four clear words, although some children don't reach this stage until several months later. He will also be able to follow basic directions given to him. Hearing is usually sharp at this age. He may start to talk to himself when playing with a toy on his own.

How to Help

1. When he does use a word appropriately to describe an object, respond in a way that lets him know that you understand the message he is trying to convey to you. He'll talk more when he realises speech is purposeful.
2. Expect the child to join in when you sing songs to him. Of course, he is not able to recite all the words accurately but he may attempt to sing the last word at the end of each verse of a familiar song. He loves this activity.
3. Give him simple commands which you expect him to follow. For instance, ask him "Give me the cup please." He is old enough to understand the meaning of your request and to carry it through to completion.

18 months: He uses around 50 different words, either singly or combined into two-words phrases. Most of the words are nouns, referring to specific familiar objects or to people whom he knows well (eg his siblings, his pet dog, his friend). He understands simple requests as long as they are clearly expressed.

How to Help

1. Look at him and make eye-contact when you talk to him as this helps him focus attention on your comments. And encourage him to look at you when he talks to you. If necessary, move into a new position so that he can see you.
2. Don't rush him. Toddlers can be frustratingly time-consuming when they want to say something, either because they are unsure of the exact words to use or because they can't talk well enough. Either way, he needs time to speak.
3. Help him expand his vocabulary by telling him the names of different objects, especially those that he uses regularly. Use words as they

arise, for instance, instead of saying "put your toys away" say "put your toys in the cupboard."

Two years: Vocabulary is almost 200 words now, and although most of these are still nouns, many of them are general rather than specific (eg "car", "doll"). He also begins to use pronouns. Speech is clearer; however he still makes minor errors such as "tat" for "cat" – these are normal mistakes and will pass in the next few months.

How to Help

1. Be supportive. Mistakes are part and parcel of a child's speech and language at this stage so avoid making too much of a fuss of these natural errors. If you continually correct him, he'll soon lose his confidence and become reluctant to speak.
2. Since he learns from the language he hears around him, provide a good model of language for him to imitate. For example, if he says "Daddy car" when he hears a car outside, you can reply by saying "Yes, that's right, dad's car is outside."
3. Use your normal style of language when talking to a two-year-old (as opposed to a simpler type of "baby" talk) but try to speak more slowly using less complex sentence structures so that he can tune in to your speech more easily.

Three years: He uses upwards of 1,000 different words, and understands a lot more than this. Sentences are longer, containing many verbs and adjectives. Most of the earlier "baby" mannerisms have been dropped. He asks questions whenever he is unsure of something, and he likes to chatter away to you whenever he has an opportunity.

How to Help

1. Ask the child to tell you about a programme he has just watched on television. This forces him to choose words carefully and helps him see the purpose of language. Listen to him and nod approvingly when he replies appropriately.
2. Be patient and tell him the meanings of any words that he does not know. You may find his questions about word meanings irritating because of their frequency, but this helps the child extend his vocabulary further.
3. Listen when he wants to talk to you. Whether or not you have other children too, the chances are that you and he are kept busy for much of the time. But he still needs to have lots of time for discussion and questions with you.

Four years: A four-year-old has a spoken vocabulary of approximately 1500 words. His speech begins to resemble adult speech in the way it communicates his feelings and ideas. He uses the past tense and other word endings, asks you lots of questions, and gives very long accounts of incidents that have happened.

How to Help

1. Encourage him to talk about his drawing. He loves representing people, objects and ideas on paper – even though these may not be immediately recognisable to you – and will take great pleasure in telling you all about them.
2. When he does speak to you about something, help him keep a relevant line of conversation instead of allowing him to drift off tangentially. A four-year-old can easily lose the thread of a discussion if he isn't given a gentle reminder from you.
3. Ask him questions that are open-ended. Closed questions (that is, those that only need a "yes" or "no" answer) require little linguistic effort for a reply. However, open-ended questions (eg "Why do you like your friend?") are more challenging.

Five years: Estimates of vocabulary size at this age are very difficult to make but he probably has a minimum of 2,000 words. He uses language well and appropriately. He has also learned many of the social conventions of language such as not interrupting when another person speaks. The child communicates well with others.

How to Help

1. Seek his views on various minor matters, such as which jumper he would like to wear tomorrow or what film he would like to see. He'll enjoy taking part in these discussions and will have a positive contribution to make.
2. Answer his questions as best you can. But you can also tell him that there are some questions that don't have easy answers (for instance, "What happens when you die?" or "Where was I before I was born?"). Avoid discouraging him.
3. Remind him to make eye-contact when speaking to another person. The social actions accompanying speech are increasingly important, now that he has reached school age. He should look at the other person when talking to them.

When He Won't Listen

The ability to listen is important. If he doesn't listen properly then he won't tune into what others are saying. He will also miss instructions. Let's consider the following example.

The Problem: Alan is four years old and he is not a good listener. His parents often have to ask him several times to do something before he responds. They don't think he deliberately ignores them, just that he isn't listening properly. Even when he gives them his full attention, he still misses out minor details. His parents are worried that this will cause difficulties for him when he starts school the following year. However, no matter what they do, Alan's listening skills fail to improve.

The Facts: He has always been a restless child who is easily distracted. Even when he was an infant, he was always on the go, flitting from one activity to another and not paying attention to people who spoke to him. In addition, Alan's house is noisy - the television is usually on from morning until night and his older siblings often play loud music in their rooms. When Alan does not appear to listen to his parents, they tend to get very angry with him but this doesn't have any effect.

The Analysis: Alan's difficulty with listening skills has been a problem for several years, not just one that has arisen recently, and it has never been tackled with sufficient effort. His parents have grown to accept him as a child who doesn't listen, and they tolerate this from him, except when at times they lose their temper with him. Poor listening skills have now become a habit for this four-year-old boy. There are lots of distractions at home which add to the difficulty.

The Solution: Alan's parents should consider a more systematic approach to helping improve his listening skills. The first stage should be to eliminate as many distractions as possible. For instance, before making a request to him they should ensure that he looks at them – not elsewhere – and that background noise is eliminated (eg the CD player or television is switched off). And they can ask him to repeat their comments or request, to verify whether or not he has heard them properly; this encourages him to take a more focused approach. They could also consider some games that will help him establish more effective listening skills, such as "When I went on holiday I took with me..." where a new item is added to the list each time, or closing his eyes and trying to identify sounds that he hears. These will prepare him for the listening demands of the infant classroom.

Is He Slow To Talk?

If a child does have a problem with his speech development you are most likely to notice it when he is between the ages of 12 months and three years, because this is the time when his language skills are expected to bloom. Before convincing yourself that a child's speech is not as advanced as would normally be expected for someone his age, bear in mind that there is a huge variation in the speed of language learning and that these variations are usually perfectly normal.

When a speech and language difficulty does not respond to support from a child's parents and carers, advice from a speech therapist may be needed. This professional has been specially trained in communication skills, and is able to diagnose accurately and treat speech and language problems in childhood.

Once the therapist has observed and assessed the child's speech patterns, she may recommend a course of action that combines direct input from the therapist (perhaps on a weekly basis) and from you, or she may decide that no direct involvement is needed at present. Referral to a speech therapist can be made by the family doctor or through a local child health clinic. Every child who is referred for speech therapy automatically receives a hearing test because there is a firm link between impaired hearing and language problems in children.

Hearing Difficulties

Hearing loss is common in childhood, though it is difficult to detect if mild or intermittent. Hearing loss can be present from birth or it can occur later. Lack of hearing has an adverse effect on language learning, because the child is unable to hear clearly what is said to him. And if he can't hear comments, instructions or ideas, then he cannot act on them properly nor use them to extend his existing knowledge. In addition, a child with a hearing problem frequently has associated behavioural problems, arising from frustration at his inability to communicate easily.

You may not realise that a child has a hearing difficult although you may suspect there is something wrong. Here are the signs to look for:

- the child insists on music and television being played loudly. It may be that he simply enjoys loud noises, but if he has a hearing difficulty then he may say he can't hear when you turn down the volume.
- he does not react when you talk to him. Again, he may deliberately choose to ignore you. But his consistent lack of response may be a sign that he does not hear clearly and so does not turn round to look.
- the child watches your lips closely as you speak. A child who can't hear properly will unconsciously teach himself how to lip read. He does this automatically and thinks this is what everyone else does too.
- he appears isolated when playing in a group of children. His poor hearing means that he has difficulties talking to other children and responding to them; he becomes remote from his peers.
- speech patterns are distorted. Since the child does not hear sounds properly, his speech sounds are distorted. For instance, he may omit the ending of longer words, and use "sh" and "s" interchangeably.
- he is slow to develop language. He may have a more restricted vocabulary than you would expect given his bright and alert appearance, and his use of grammar may be less complex than expected.
- he is restless and easily bored. So much of play involves hearing. Lots of toys generate sounds, and if a child doesn't have this type of auditory feedback then it is not surprising that he loses interest.

You can "test" a child's hearing in very basic ways if you think his hearing may be impaired. For instance, when he is sitting quietly watching a television programme, stand behind him so that he cannot see you. Then gently bring a ticking watch from behind him towards his left ear then his right ear – he should react quickly, by turning his head round to look at you long before the watch is level with his head. However, the best course of action is to arrange for a full hearing assessment.

Q & A

Q. *How can I make a four-year-old be more communicative with me? Even when I know he is worried about something, he doesn't talk to me.*

A. Children vary in the extent to which they talk about their feelings. One child might be very open, willing to relate his news to include the slightest details, while another might prefer to keep himself to himself. It is probably best not to put much pressure on him to speak to you, because the more pressure he feels then the more he will be reluctant to talk to you and your colleagues – a confrontation can develop and that will not be productive. Instead, make sure that he has plenty of opportunities to talk to you. And keep on asking him about his experiences, about his friends and play activities, and indeed about anything you want. But do this gently. Maybe he will always be uncommunicative, though keep trying anyway.

Q. *Will a hearing aid help a child with a hearing problem to hear properly?*

A. The child's audiologist will have given his parents a full explanation, and possible some explanatory leaflets as well. Certainly he should wear this device if it has been recommended for him. Hearing aids are increasingly sophisticated and have become smaller (and therefore less noticeable and less obtrusive). However, wearing a hearing aid does not mean that a child hears spoken words in the same way that a hearing person does, but it will make the sounds much clearer for him. Children under the age of five often need to be persuaded to keep the hearing aid on because they are embarrassed about it. Along with his parents, try to convince the child that he should persist wearing it, emphasising the benefits that it brings.

Q. *My toddler hasn't started talking fluently yet although he is nearly two years, and I think this is why he loses his temper so easily. What should I do to help him?*

A. This is the age when children are more prone to temper tantrums anyway, so it may be that the child's bursts of rage are more to do with establishing his independence than with poor speech development. Yet, his lack of speech could be causing frustration. Assuming you already provide plenty of language stimulation, there is no need to do anything more at this stage. He will probably catch up soon enough. In the meantime, until his language skills progress, keep a close eye on him and encourage him to try to communicate with you. If you sense he is becoming frustrated, calm him down and talk to him slowly; this will help settle him.

Q. *What do you do with a child aged 21 months who won't be quiet? He prattles on and on all day, without a break.*

A. Do absolutely nothing. He is at that wonderful stage where he has discovered the magic of spoken language. He realises that he can generate his own speech and that this brings many advantages, such as gaining attention, making requests, and speaking to others. Unlike adults, the child does not take this for granted; instead he intends to use language whenever possible because he enjoys it so much. Perhaps the most effective strategy at this point is for you to listen, and to respond when you think a response is called for. You'll probably find that a lot of his speech isn't directed at anyone in particular and he probably doesn't expect an answer from you. When he is a few months older, you can try to focus his speech slightly, for instance by asking specific questions, and you can remind him to stay on track when he answers.

22

Special Needs

"I know a child who has special needs but I don't really understand what that means. To be honest, I'm uncertain how to act with her. I think she only has a problem with talking but I'm not sure the extent of her difficulties."

All children have a range of psychological needs; the need to be loved, the need to be physically cared for, the need to feel secure, the need to have self-confidence, the need to have structure and consistency in life and the need to mix with other children. A child whose psychological needs are not met will experience emotional difficulties. For instance, a child who is not loved will have difficulty forming stable relationships in adulthood. A child who is denied the opportunity to mix with other children will experience later difficulty in establishing social relationships. And a child brought up in an environment of instability at home will be unable to cope with the demands of school. It is the parents' job to ensure their child's psychological needs are satisfied.

But there are some children who have special needs in addition to those described above, needs that arise because the child has atypical development. At one stage, psychologists and child care professionals described these children as 'handicapped' or 'subnormal'.

So a child who is paralysed from the waist down, or who has weak muscles, or who requires crutches to move around, was described as 'physically handicapped'; a child who is completely blind, or who has limited vision in both eyes, or who has cataracts, was described as 'visually handicapped'; and a child who cannot keep up with her school work, or who has Down's Syndrome, or who fails to learn to speak, or who never develops enough to be able to sit up unsupported, was described as 'mentally handicapped' or 'mentally subnormal'. These labels were used to categorise children with developmental problems.

However, this form of labelling is no longer used. Now, children with developmental problems are described as having 'special needs'. This change in terminology, though, is not simply a substitution of one label for another. It occurred for the following reasons:

- the terms 'handicapped' or 'subnormal' do not reveal anything about the child's strengths, only her weaknesses. They indicate that she has some type of difficulty, but not the practical effect of that difficulty. A child may be unable to walk, and yet might be confident and determined, able to use elbow crutches to move around the room. Labelling this child 'physically handicapped' focuses on her physical difficulty, and tells nothing of how she copes with that difficulty.

- the terms 'handicapped' or 'subnormal' are too general and fail to recognise essential differences between children. They suggest that all 'handicapped' or 'subnormal' children are the same and need the same sort of help. Yet that is not the case. One child might find school work so difficult that she cannot learn in normal-sized classes and requires individual teaching. Another child might be unable to feed and toilet herself, and be unable to speak except in monosyllabic sounds. Labelling both these children as 'mentally handicapped' or 'mentally subnormal' fails to differentiate the individual level of development that each child has.
- the terms 'handicapped' or 'subnormal' suggest the difficulties are all-or-none, that a child is either handicapped or she is not handicapped. There is no such clear cut division. Child development occurs on a continuum from normality to abnormality, and virtually all children lie at a point between these two extremes. Children with special needs therefore share many common features with all children. Labelling a child as 'handicapped' or 'subnormal' suggests she is radically different from other children, when in fact she is simply at a different point in the same developmental continuum.
- the terms 'handicapped' or 'subnormal' do not indicate what sort of measures would help the child overcome, or at least cope with, her developmental difficulty. They only state that she has a problem. Two children may be 'visually handicapped', but one might have no vision at all and need to learn Braille, whereas another child might have limited vision and need to read using magnifiers. Labelling both these children as 'visually handicapped' fails to say what specific help these children need.
- the terms 'handicapped' or 'subnormal' encourage people to focus on the child's condition, rather than on the child herself as an individual. They suggest there is homogeneity amongst children with special needs. That is far from the truth. For instance, many people assume that all children with Down's Syndrome are the same because they have very similar facial features and ostensibly similar levels of development. Yet, if you have the opportunity to get to know a child with this genetic condition, you will soon realise that the child is a unique individual with her own personality, her own ideas, her own sense of humour and her own level of abilities. She is a child, not a combination of genes. Labelling the child 'Down's Syndrome' is an accurate description of her genetic condition but it encourages people to view her in stereotyped ways.

Shifting the emphasis away from 'handicap' (considering the child's weaknesses only) to 'special needs' (considering ways in which the child can be supported so that her development is least impaired by her difficulty) allows each child to be treated as an individual. It is also more likely to lead to the child receiving the necessary help.

Raising A Child with Special Needs

The following guidelines may be helpful for parents of a child with special needs:

- find out as much as you can about your child's difficulty and the possible impact it might have on her development. Realising your child has special needs is upsetting and you will take time to adjust. But the feelings of worry many parents have stems from lack of knowledge of the child's likely future development. Request specific information from those working with your child.
- if you don't have confidence in professionals supervising your child's development, ask to be referred to someone else. If you feel uncomfortable with any of them, or you feel unable to trust their judgement, or if you lack confidence in them, ask to be referred to someone else. You are entitled to do that, and no professional would want to work with a client who is ill-at-ease with them.
- contact other parents who have a child with difficulties similar to those of your child. You will benefit from sharing your worries with someone else, and you will be able to pool your experiences. This can usually be done through organisations specifically formed to help parents. Many parents find this form of optional contact useful in clarifying their understanding of their child's development.
- remember that your child with special needs has the same psychological needs as other children. She needs just as much love, security, care, acceptance and comfort. She also needs structure in her life. You may be tempted to 'spoil' her because you feel sorry for her as a result of the difficulties she is experiencing. However, long-term over-indulgence will not be in her best interests.
- bring up your child with special needs in a way that maximises her potential. All parents want their child to achieve to the fullest of her ability, whether the achievements are at school, with friends, on the sports field, in music, or in art – and the same should apply to a child with special needs. No matter the extent of her limitations, the child needs to be given opportunities to encourage full development.
- try to adjust to uncertainty. Specific predictions are virtually impossible to make. This means that many of the questions you want to ask about your child who has special needs – such as if she will ever be able to talk, if she will ever walk by herself, or if she will require spe-

cialised education – in many instances cannot be answered with any certainty until the child is older.

- don't assume that because your child has special needs that somehow she has a natural affinity to interact with other children who have special needs. This common assumption has absolutely no evidence to support it. Your child with special needs should be given as much opportunity as possible to mix with other children of normal development, in the playgroup, nursery and school.
- remember that there is a difference between a disability and an impairment. A disability only becomes an impairment when it seriously interferes with the child's development. A physically-disabled child can lead an active and stimulating life, minimising the effect of her disability. However, parents of a physically-disabled child may be so protective that the child's self-confidence is reduced.

Schooling for a Child With Special Needs

In previous decades, children with special needs were automatically educated in segregated special schools. These school – often situated in isolation away from ordinary schools – offer smaller classes, more experienced and specially-trained teachers, auxiliary staff to provide the child with additional help in non-educational tasks, and possibly specialist physiotherapy and speech therapy. Those additional facilities allow the child to receive a specialised curriculum tailored to her individual educational needs. Extra teacher attention means the child can be given more help than she could in an ordinary primary school class.

Yet years of segregated special schooling produced remarkably little experimental evidence to suggest children with special needs progress any better in these schools than they do in ordinary schools. Indeed, one of the drawbacks of segregated special schools is that they reduce the child's involvement with normal children – and this can impair her social development.

The combination of these factors has reversed the trend of special schooling. Now, local education authorities seek to include a child with special needs into her local school, before considering the possibility of segregated special school. Of course, there are some children whose development is so severely impaired, to the point where they require constant care, that their needs cannot be met in an ordinary school. However, there is an increasing awareness and acceptance that many children with special needs can cope in their local school as long as they are given the necessary support.

There is no reason why a child with learning difficulties should have to attend a special school in order to receive individual teacher attention and additional learning support. In most cases a child's special needs can be met in the ordinary school if adequate resources are provided. Likewise, there is no reason why a pupil in a wheel-chair, for instance, should not attend her local school. If the school is flat, having been built on the level, then it will be ideal. If the school has some steps, then a ramp can be fitted by the local authority. Should the child need physiotherapy, this can be given at her home after school hours. This reduces the justification for segregating special needs pupils from other pupils.

As a parent, you may feel your child with special needs would be better off at a segregated special school, with its guaranteed extra resources and its protective environment. You may reject the idea of inclusion on the basis that the child will not receive the help she needs, and that she will be abused by the other children in the school. That still remains your decision. However, at least parents are now offered a choice. Make your choice of schooling only after detailed consideration of which school can best meet your child's educational, social and psychological needs. Take your time and do not let yourself be rushed into any decision; you need to be happy with your selection.

The Family

By necessity, a child with special needs becomes the focus of her family. This is perfectly understandable. Practical circumstances dictate this and the parents have little choice in the matter. Of course, parents of a child with special needs are under tremendous pressure, but they usually receive help. There will be psychologists and paediatricians, social workers and welfare officers, health visitors and physiotherapists, all willing to support the stressed mother and father. The danger, however, is that the other children in the family may get left out. All children need parental attention.

Psychological research confirms that when a child in the family has special needs, the other children (compared to those in families where there is not a child with special needs):

- have a higher level of antisocial behaviour
- may be anxious they will develop the same problem
- are more likely to have a mild emotional difficulty
- often feel neglected
- are expected by their parents to do more about the house
- frequently complain that their parents expect too much of them
- experience parental pressure to be 'normal'

If you have a child with special needs in your family, here are some suggestion in order to avoid potential pitfalls when dealing with your other children:

Unreasonable Demands

Caring about each is an important part of family life. Just as you and your partner look after your children and attend to their needs, it is perfectly reasonable for you to expect your children to develop understanding and concern towards people other than themselves. Within reasonable limits, this form of responsibility can increase your children's maturity. For instance, expecting your five-year-old to pour a drink for her brother or sister at the same time she pours a drink for herself is reasonable. Actions like that encourage her to become less self-centred. But a child who feels her life is taken up running errands for the rest of her family, or who feels that she is constantly being asked to do more than her friends are asked to do in their families, will react against this. Children with a sibling who has special needs often report such feelings. An abnormally high level of domestic responsibility will cause siblings to resent a child with special needs. To avoid making unreasonable demand:

- **listen to their complaints.** Your first reaction might be to dismiss out of hand your children's groans about being asked to do too much. Listen to what they have to say, take their comments seriously, and judge whether or not they have a point.
- **consider your children's daily schedules.** Even though your children may not be aware of it, they may be in a position of being asked to do too much. Make sure they have enough time to play with their toys at home and to be with their own friends.
- **share out household chores fairly.** Your oldest child doesn't always have to be the one who sets the dinner table because you are busy bathing your child with special needs. Your younger children should be expected to play their part around the house too.
- **be honest with your children.** Let them know that you are aware of their feelings eg "I know you don't like having to carry the shopping in from the car every day, but it means I have more time for your sister". This acknowledges your children's emotions.
- **give them an unexpected break.** Even when they are extremely helpful and supportive, there's no harm in announcing that they can have a day off. That special treat makes them feel more positively about the situation.
- **explain that they are helping you.** Your children may not realise the impact of their support for you, so tell them "Your tidying up means that I can play longer with your sister, and that is going to help her learn to talk". They'll feel better after this explanation.

Feeling Neglected

You have a limited amount of time to spend with your children, and simple logic dictates that the more children there are in your family then the less time there is available for each individual. Most children learn to adapt to this situation without undue concern. When one of your children has special needs, however, she is likely to demand more of your attention. This doesn't happen because you love her more than the others, but because she can't function without this extra attention. Yet the net effect of this is that her siblings may feel neglected; they may feel that they come second in the list of family priorities. Your other children may not be mature enough to see things except from their own point of view. They may feel uncared for or that you love them less than you love your child with special needs. Another common feeling in siblings is that their parents only show interest in the achievements of the child with special needs. All of these feelings can increase sibling rivalry. To avoid your other children feeling neglected:

- **make time for each of your children.** Although your child with special needs takes up a lot of your time, try to arrange things so that you have a few minutes every day to talk to each of your other children on their own. They need this 'quality time' with you.
- **don't focus all family activities around your child with special needs.** Let the other children choose the family weekend outing, even though their choice might not exactly suit your child with special needs. They deserve to make choices too.
- **take them along with you when possible.** They will probably enjoy being with you, even if they are only accompanying you and their sibling on one of her medical appointments. Your other children will enjoy having the opportunity to talk to you and to be with you.
- **demonstrate your interest in their achievements.** Make a fuss when one of your other children makes progress, such as managing to complete a difficult jigsaw. Every achievement merits your interest, not just those of your child with special needs.
- **tell them why you have so little time.** Explain to them that you are so busy with their sibling that you have less time for them. But emphasise that you love them just as much and that you would do the same for them if they ever needed your help like this.
- **make plans for the future.** Your children will love to plan future activities with you, whether it's a day out or a longer family holiday. Even if they feel sorry for themselves now, planning like this makes them feel involved with you, and with each other.

Resenting Dependency

Most children with special needs are slower to reach the milestones of independence than other children their own age. Basic skills such as taking that first step, saying her first word, and achieving bladder and bowel control take longer to acquire. Depending on the nature of your child's specific developmental problem, she may never acquire these skills at all.

This means that she probably retains her dependence on you for longer than normal and your other children may resent this. Their attitude towards their sibling will fluctuate, however. At times, they will be extremely caring and helpful, trying hard to encourage her to make progress and showing great pleasure when she does. And your child with special needs will thrive on this attention from her siblings. At other times, though, they will be annoyed with her – and possibly resent her – because her lack of independence interferes with their plans. To avoid them resenting their sibling's dependency:

- **don't put an unnecessary burden on them.** Of course, all your children should help each other, but each of your children has a right to their own life. Try avoid asking too much or disrupting their plans because of the demands of your child with special needs.
- **give them knowledge of their sibling's problem.** Lack of knowledge causes distrust; the more your children understand the nature of their sibling's problem, the less likely they are to resent her. Secrecy strains family relationships.
- **ask them to teach new skills to her.** Your children will take great pleasure from trying to teach her, for instance, how to complete a small jigsaw, how to take her first step, or how to sing a nursery rhyme. Their active involvement reduces resentment.
- **point out that they are dependent in some ways too.** Remind them that they too need your help at times and that they are not entirely independent themselves. After all, they need you to run them to after-school activities, to choose their clothes etc.
- **emphasise that she isn't deliberately having difficulties.** There's no harm in telling them that their sibling didn't choose to have slow development; she would rather be like her brothers and sisters. Being dependent, therefore, isn't something she necessarily enjoys.
- **encourage your child with special needs to be independent.** No matter what level of development she is at, there are things she can do for herself, so let her do them. You may feel very protective towards her but she needs to do things on her own wherever possible.

Unrealistically High Expectations

Even during the pregnancy, parents start to form ideas about what they hope their child-to-be will be like and what they hope she will achieve. However, when a child has special needs, she may be totally unable to attain these pre-birth expectations. Without realising they are doing so, her parents may compensate for her difficulties by projecting unrealistically high expectations onto her brothers and sisters. Siblings of a child with special needs often comment that their childhood was a time of pressure to be somebody that they were not. For instance, they may feel they were expected to come top of their class in school, to be extremely popular with the other children, or even to win prizes at sport. In addition, their parents often expect them to be 'normal' in every way, and deviance in any form isn't tolerated. No wonder that sibling rivalry thrives in these circumstances. To avoid having unrealistically high expectations:

- **accept that each of your children is an individual.** In every family, every child is different, with her own particular strengths and weakness – no two children follow the same developmental path at the same rate.
- **avoid the argument "You should count yourself lucky".** True, your other children don't have difficulties similar to their sibling with special needs, but that doesn't mean they have no difficulties at all. Reminding them of their siblings problem doesn't help.
- **don't overreact to their misbehaviour.** Your children are going to be naughty at times, as is your child with special needs. The fact that they have a sibling with special needs doesn't mean they will always behave just as you would like them to.
- **have expectations appropriate to your children's abilities.** There is no point in expecting your other children to make great educational achievements in school unless they have the ability to do so. You can't make them have talents and skills.
- **analyse your own motives.** Think about the standards you set for your other children and decide whether or not you are being reasonable. Satisfy yourself that you are not asking too much simply as a way of compensating for having a child with special needs.
- **expect the same standards of behaviour from all your children.** Your child with special needs requires discipline as much as the others. Expect the same level of good behaviour from her as you do for her siblings – this benefits all of them.

Family Characteristics

The way your other children react to their sibling with special needs – and the degree of sibling rivalry that develops – also depends on other factors too. First, there is the age of the child with special needs. A sibling who is much older than her will have been aware of her difficulties right from the start, and will have been involved the moment she came back from the maternity hospital. A sibling who is much younger than her is unlikely to show any real understanding until she reaches school age, but by then the seeds of resentment may have been sown.

The sex of the sibling has an influence. Research data suggests that girls are more likely to have a difficult emotional reaction to having a sibling with special needs than are boys, and are more likely to harbour feelings of resentment. Lastly, there is the severity of the child's developmental difficulties. The greater the problems of the child with special needs, then the greater the emotional impact on her siblings; children seem more able to adjust to a sibling with special needs when her difficulties are physical rather than intellectual.

It is important to encourage your children to talk about their sibling's difficulties. This type of communication usually does not happen spontaneously; they may be embarrassed or confused. Suggest to your children that they talk about the effect their brother or sister has on them personally. Give them information about the nature of their sibling's problem. Anxiety frequently stems from misunderstandings or lack of knowledge about the condition that is affecting their brother or sister with special needs. Limited explanations are better than none at all.

And let your other children express their fears honestly. It's not a crime to admit fear at having a brother who is blind, or embarrassment at having a sister who has learning difficulties. Let your children come to terms with these feelings by expressing them to you within a caring family environment. You should also prepare them for hurtful remarks from other children. Point out that others probably don't understand the problems of a child with special needs, and might make insulting comments – knowing these remarks stem from ignorance not malevolence, may reduce your children's anguish.

Overprotective

Research studies have found that parents are significantly less likely to be firm when managing their child with special needs than they are when dealing with the child's siblings. It's as though parents are instinctively protective towards a child with special needs. This is not always a helpful approach to take. Let's consider the following example.

The Problem: Eight-year-old Hannah has cerebral palsy which results in her having difficulties with walking and climbing stairs. In addition her speech is affected; her words are often slurred and hard to understand. In recent years Hannah has become very cheeky to her parents, especially when she can't have her own way. They find her behaviour embarrassing. Hannah's grandparents have told her parents that they are spoiling her but they don't agree. They are unhappy with her cheeky behaviour but assume this is a just a passing phase.

The Facts: Hannah has two devoted parents who will do anything for her. She is their only child and they spend all their free time with her. The difficult early years, in which Hannah received intensive physiotherapy and speech therapy, made the family very close to each other. Her parents at times feel sorry for their daughter, and are extremely upset by the difficulties she experiences. They feel that life is hard enough for

Hannah; consequently they want to do everything they can to make all her experiences very enjoyable. They are reluctant to reprimand her for misbehaviour.

The Analysis: The reality is that Hannah is spoiled by her parents. They allow her to be cheeky and to misbehave in other ways because they feel sorry for her; they believe she has enough to deal with having cerebral palsy and don't want to make her unhappy by setting firm limits at home. But Hannah's cheekiness will only increase, eventually making her unpopular with her peers. Her parents are too protective.

The Solution: The only way the situation will change is if Hannah's parents have the set same of behavioural standards for her that they would have if she did not have special needs. It's time for them to set reasonable limits on her behaviour, to praise her when she behaves well and to be prepared to reprimand her when she misbehaves. This strategy will not do Hannah any harm; on the contrary, it will provide a structure and consistency in her life that she needs. Feelings of pity and concern are natural, as is the desire to protect Hannah from any further upset. Yet those feelings alone won't promote her positive development; she also needs to have clear standards for her behaviour.

Scapegoat

Having a child with special needs in the family can at times be a convenient scapegoat for every family problem. It's easy to use the child as the explanation for all arguments and difficulties that occur – that saves having to look at other alternatives for resolving the family tensions. To identify whether or not this form of scapegoating occurs in your family, ask yourself the following questions.

Do you automatically assume that every family difficulty is caused by having a child with special needs in the family?
Do you think relationships in your family were better before your child with special needs was born?
Do you feel that the atmosphere at home is much less strained when your child with special needs is out of the house?
Do you often find that you have to spend so much time with your child with special needs that you have no time left for anyone else?
Do you have a more enjoyable time on family outings and day trips when your child with special needs doesn't accompany you?

If you answer 'no' to most of these questions, then it is unlikely that you are unfairly scapegoating your child with special needs. However, if you answer 'yes' to these questions, then the chances are that you are scapegoating your child with special needs to explain tensions at home.

Q & A

Q. *How early can a child's developmental difficulties be detected?*
A. Much depends on the nature and severity of the child's condition. Many physical conditions such as spina bifida and severe cerebral palsy can be evident at birth, whereas other conditions such as learning difficulties or specific language disorders may not emerge until the child is at the toddler stage. The earlier the child's special needs are detected the better because that means she can be given suitable stimulation and support at a younger age.

Q. *My five-year-old child has learning difficulties and I have a choice to send him to a special school or his local school. How can I decide?*
A. You are faced with a difficult choice. Visit both schools in order to determine what they could do for your child. Speak to the head teacher and have a good look round the schools, making sure that you see the actual class your child would be in when he starts there. Ask about the level of learning support provided for children with special educational needs and about the typical curriculum for pupils at your child's stage. Get full information about the whole range of curricular activities offered to pupils.

Q. *What can be done with a slow toddler who shows no interest in toys? She just sits there passively, staring but not doing.*
A. Some infants with special needs are slow to react – they lack that curiosity and determination to explore which is typically associated with a child this age. Like this toddler, they prefer to watch rather than get involved. To tackle this pattern of behaviour, bring the toys, games and puzzles over to the toddler and show her how to play with them. Gently place her hand on the play item if necessary and give her lots of praise and encouragement. Your interest and guidance is just what she needs to stimulate her enthusiasm for play.

Q. *I am convinced that my two-year-old has a problem with her development but my doctor told me that I'm fussing about nothing. What can I do?*
A. Consider the possibility that your doctor is correct. Perhaps your child's development is within normal limits. If you are not convinced by your doctor's reassurance on this occasion, however, sit down and write a list of your specific worries about your child. Note particular examples of her behaviour that cause you concern in order to provide evidence of your views. Then make another appointment with your doctor and calmly and reasonably go through the list with him. Ask for referral to a specialist professional who deals with developmental difficulties. Your doctor will listen to you.

23

Starting School

"He starts school after the summer and I'm both excited and terrified about this. He look so small in comparison to school-aged pupils and yet I can see that he is ready to move on from his nursery."

The transition from pre-school provision to infant school is one of the biggest steps in a young child's life. At best, it signifies the beginning of a positive stage in his development, one which brings educational stimulation and endless opportunities for personal and intellectual growth. At worst, however, it can signify the beginning of a negative stage in his development, one which is marked by tension and insecurity, unsatisfactory relationships with other children and adults, and a lowering of self-esteem. (In many instances, the same applies when a child changes from one infant school to another – the same pressures exist).

When you think about this transition from a child's point of view, it's not surprising there are lots of pupils who have problems starting school. There are so many changes to be made, changes which represent a departure from the pre-school world he knows. And this element of change isn't just felt by a child who has spent his previous years at home; it is also felt by a child who has attended a playgroup, a nursery, or a childminder because none of these match the infant school environment exactly.

Readiness For School

A child's readiness for school can be improved by focussing on strategies for coping specifically with the impact of the changes between nursery and school. Let's take a closer look at some of the specific changes associated with starting the infant class. Your awareness of these factors means that you can prepare the child for them:

Factor 1: The school building

Playgroups usually function in one room, and even large nurseries occupy two or three large rooms at most. And these rooms are frequently self-contained in one small building. Toilets will be close by, and every pre-school facility will be used only by children who are relatively close to each other in age. Compare that with the infant classroom of a large primary school; even though the first class may be self-contained, it still functions as part of a larger school.

How to encourage readiness for the school building:

1. Give the child a chance to become familiar with his new school building, before the school term. Take him round the rooms he is likely to use, including the toilet, dining areas, and playground.
2. When visiting the school with him, make sure he is aware of the areas that are designated for infants and those that are designated for older pupils. He should see all of these areas.

Factor 2: The curriculum

Tremendous strides have been made in nursery education in recent years in order to match the pre-school curriculum with that of the infant class activities, and there is clear overlap between what children learn in these two phases of their education. Yet there are many instances where this does not apply, creating the possibility of confusion in the young child's mind. And, of course, there are many under-fives who never set foot in nursery before they start school. An unfamiliar infant curriculum can be daunting for a new pupil.

How to encourage readiness for the curriculum:

1. Make sure the child has some experience of the sort of classroom activities he will meet in his new school. If you are at all in doubt, talk to his teacher who will be able to advise you on suitable tasks.
2. Try to become familiar with the sort of work carried out in the first infant class so that you can introduce him to the range of materials and programme of study he is likely to meet there.

Factor 3: The expectations

Fortunately, the distinction between caring for pre-school children and educating pre-school children has become blurred. No longer are child-minders seen as simply baby-sitters, no longer is nursery seen simply as a care facility, and no longer is school seen simply as a place where children experience formal education. However, expectations of children in school tend to be different from (and more demanding than) those in the nursery. There is more structure, higher expectations, a longer day, and a greater need for independence and personal responsibility.

How to encourage readiness for expectations:

1. Encourage the child to become independent and less reliant on adults. Help him master basic tasks such as putting his coat on, dressing and undressing (eg for PE), and eating lunch.
2. Give him practice working in small groups with others. This will improve his listening and social skills, his concentration, and his ability to respond to group, rather than individual, instructions.

Factor 4: The pupils and teachers

Compared to nurseries, playgroups and childminders, infant schools have many more pupils and far fewer adults to look after them. Each child has more peer-group relationships to deal with than ever before. In addition, a new infant pupil moves from being the oldest child in the nursery (ie at the top of the 'pecking order') to the youngest child in the school (ie at the bottom of the 'pecking order'). And there is less individual adult attention available for children in school than there was for them at the pre-school stage.

How to encourage readiness for the pupils and teachers:

1. The more opportunities he has to mix with other children his own age – in both formal and informal settings – then the more ready he will be to mix with his classmates in school.
2. Explain to him in advance that although he is in the oldest group in nursery, he will be in the youngest class at school. But reassure him that he has nothing to fear from this shift in age groupings.

Factor 5: The routine

Of course every infant class strives to have a happy and industrious atmosphere. But routine is still an essential aspect of the infant-school day, more so than in a nursery or playgroup. Routine provides a structure to the day's activities and gives children the opportunity to plan ahead. Each pupil is expected to be aware of – and to follow – the routine within his particular classroom, and within the other areas of the school. Inability to cope with this more formal routine could cause a child to have problems organising himself and his workload.

How to encourage readiness for the routine:

1. In the few months before starting school, try to structure the child's day so that there is an element of regularity. Ask him to predict some of the activities later that morning or afternoon.
2. Give him practice in planning for anticipated activities. For example, if he knows you are taking him swimming, ask him to prepare his swimming gear well in advance of your expected leaving time.

Personality Counts

Ask any infant teacher to list the characteristics of pupils who are most likely to thrive in an infant class; although she is likely to mention educational features such as "intelligent", "competent" and "good use of language", the chances are that these will not be top of the list. Instead, personality traits are more likely to be in first place, especially during the first year at infant school.

That doesn't mean that a child's intellectual ability isn't important for achievement in school, just that settling in to the infant class can depend more on a child's emotional characteristics. Of course, a child's ability has an influence on his success at school. But his **positive attitude** towards learning, and towards school in general, will determine whether or not he uses that ability. A positive attitude shows through in many ways, including a general enthusiasm for educational activities within the infant classroom, a desire to please the class teacher, a willingness to try hard at every assignment presented to him, and a desire to tell you all about his experiences when you collect him at the end of the school day.

A child who has a low level of **self-confidence** will have an uphill struggle settling into the infant class. Psychological research confirms that children who are lacking in self-confidence tend to do less well at school than would be expected on the basis of their intellectual ability, tend to make derogatory remarks about anything they do even when these achievements are of a satisfactory standard, have greater difficulty making new friends with the other children in their class and are very defensive when relating to adults.

Having good **listening skills** is a fundamental part of learning but is not something that comes naturally to all children. An infant classroom has a lively atmosphere, as the young pupils begin the formal learning process. There is so much that they have to listen to, including instructions from the teacher and from each other, new information that has to be absorbed, and ideas and feelings expressed by others. It is also important to **ask questions** as one of the main ways children learn during the pre-school years is through inquisitiveness. Children frequently bombard adults with questions such as "Why is the grass green?", "Who makes dogs have a tail?", "How many sweets am I allowed?" and "Why is rain wet?". By asking those sorts of questions, a child is able to extend his knowledge and understanding of the world around him. True, many of the questions asked by a young child are unanswerable (eg "Why is the sky blue?") but they shouldn't be discouraged. Asking questions is also a means of expressing his ideas and feelings (eg "What will happen if the teacher gets angry at me?", "Why is he crying?", "Will I be all right in the playground?" etc).

So much of the learning process in the infant class involves children working together, usually in small groups, in order to solve a particular puzzle or to complete a joint task. That means a child not only has to be able to co-operate with all his classmates when required to do so by the teacher, he also has to **respect** them and to be prepared to listen to different perspectives even if these clash with his own. Parents spend a great deal of time discouraging anti-social behaviour in children but they should also spend time encouraging children to be kind, considerate and caring. The atmosphere in any infant class is determined by the attitudes of the pupils towards each other, and a considerate child will find the infant class much more enjoyable.

Every child shows aggression sometimes, whether it's physically (by hitting, kicking or biting) or verbally (by screaming, swearing or insulting). That sort of behaviour – even though it is often shocking – is normal in childhood. All children get angry now and then, and aggression and anger are two emotions that are closely intertwined, but **control of aggression** is important. Hostile behaviour is not acceptable in a school, no matter how young the pupil is, and will always be frowned upon by the child's teacher. So the more you can discourage a child's willingness to react aggressively during the pre-school years, then the more likely he is to settle in to the infant class.

Concentration

A child who can't concentrate will not be able to progress much in the infant class. And it doesn't matter how much he enjoys the activities, he must be able to concentrate in order to learn. The key dimensions of concentration include:

Active Focus

Whereas a young baby attends to something only when it captures his attention by moving across his line of vision, a school-aged child actively searches and explores his environment. His powers of attention are more dynamic and he can actively choose what to concentrate on.

How To Improve Active Focus

When out shopping in the supermarket with the child, ask him to find one item in particular (eg a bag of flour). Encourage him to walk up and down the different aisles until he is able to locate it, and remind him only to look for that item.

Systematic Search

Watch a young baby pick up and examine, say, a rattle. You'll notice that he does this in a very haphazard way and will only look at one or two sections of it. However, a school-aged child explores an object more systematically. This means he can discover more about it.

How To Improve This Skill

Ask the child to find a particular magazine that you have been reading, telling him only that it is somewhere in the house. Encourage him to search for it systematically (eg from room to room), rather than going from here to there without any overall search plan.

Selective Tuning

Young babies are not good at filtering out information. They try to look at everything they see and hear. However, a school-aged child is more able to focus his attention on one specific aspect of a situation, and this means he can pick out the key sources of information.

How To Improve This Skill

Teach him how to cross at a pelican crossing, paying special attention to the flashing 'green man'. From the child's perspective, the crossing contains thousands of fascinating things to look at, but you should encourage him only to focus on the lights themselves.

Ignore Distractions

Concentration is not just about attending to something in particular, but also involves blocking out potential distractions. For instance, a school-aged child can only concentrate on the infant teacher's voice when he is able to shut out the other noises in the classroom.

How To Child Improve This Skill

Ask the child to think of, say, as many different animals as he can. While he does this, talk to him about his favourite television programme. Encourage him to keep thinking of the different animals, even though you are saying things which may distract him.

Maintain Concentration

When a child starts school, he should be able to concentrate on an educational task until it is complete. If he can't, he will not progress as well as he should and he will find that he continues with an activity long after the others in the class have started on something else.

How To Improve This Skill

Tell him to colour in a drawing, and time how long he persists (eg two minutes). The next night, tell him to continue with the activity for a little longer (eg two minutes and 15 seconds); praise him when he achieves this. Gradually increase the amount of time each night.

Memory

This is the means through which a child stores information, and then retrieves it later when he wants to use it again. Learning cannot take place without memory. If a child didn't have any memory of his previous experiences then he wouldn't have any basis on which to build further understanding of the world around him. Lack of memory would mean, for instance, that a child wouldn't know where he had left his books and that he wouldn't remember from one moment to the next that hot things burn. Children who have difficulties with their memory skills often experience learning problems when they start school.

When a child sees, hears, tastes, smells or touches something, this information is held in his short term memory for a few seconds. If it is important to him, it will be passed into his long-term memory so that he can recall it whenever he wants. If the information isn't important, it won't be transferred into long-term memory. Short-term memory, therefore, is the 'clearing house' for information, while long-term memory is the 'store house' for information. Ask a child what he ate for lunch last Tuesday – the chances are that he won't remember very clearly. But ask him to recall his last birthday party – the chances are he'll remember all the minute details.

Your memory differs from a young child's memory in a number of ways. For instance, you have already stored a great deal of background information in your memory and this helps you remember new things. If you are shown six chess-pieces for a few seconds before they are covered up (eg a knight, a king, a queen, two pawns and a bishop), you will remember them accurately. However, if a five-year-old is shown the same pieces, he probably won't remember them accurately because he doesn't have the background knowledge of chess-pieces that you have.

And you use strategies when memorising things. For example, you use rehearsal (repetition) when trying to remember a new telephone number, and this improves your memory. A five-year-old child doesn't use rehearsal like this. As well as this, an adult's short term memory is bigger than a child's. If a list of 20 unrelated words is read to you at the rate of one per second, you may remember seven, eight or even nine of the words whereas a typical five-year-old would recall only three or four.

A school-aged child improve his memory by using the following 'memory strategies'. He can practice these himself, once you have shown him how to use them:

1. **Rehearsal**. A child can increase his recall by using rehearsal (repetition of the information). He is more likely to remember a group of objects, if he has spoken the names of the objects out loud several times while trying to memorise them. Test this for yourself: place a tray of 20 common objects in front of the child, let him look at them for a minute, remove the tray and ask him to tell you the ones he can remember. Repeat this activity with another set of objects, but this time specifically encourage him to say the name of each object loudly, many times, while the tray is in front of him. He will remember more from the second tray.
2. **Organisation**. Information is easier to recall when it has been stored in memory in an organised way. Try this: compile a list of twenty objects (eg five foods, five pieces of clothing, five modes of transport, and five pieces of furniture), putting them in a random order. Give the child this list, let him look at it for one minute, then remove it and ask him to tell you how many he can remember. Then repeat the activity with a similar list, only this time put the objects into their categories, so that the child sees four groups of items. The chances are that he will remember more of the second list because the organisation is better.

3. **Retrieval**. A child's ability to recall from a previously-learned list can improve when categories are suggested to him. To demonstrate this, give him the first jumbled list of objects (as before) without mentioning any of the categories, then note how many he can remember. Do the same with a second jumbled list, but this time – at the point when you ask him to recall the list – suggest that the objects can be grouped into 'things around the house', 'things that help you move', 'things you eat' and 'things you wear' and that he should remember them in these categories. His efforts with the second list are more successful than with the first.
4. **Imagery**. Young children rarely use visual imagery spontaneously as part of their memory, but they can be taught this technique. One way is to imagine a familiar scene (eg a room in the house) and incorporate the objects to be remembered. Give the child a list of four things you want to buy at the supermarket (eg tin of soup, packet of soap powder, loaf of bread and pint of milk). To help him remember these unconnected items, he could imagine a scarecrow with a head that is the packet of soap powder, a body that is a loaf of bread, holding a point of milk in one hand and a tin of soup in the other. He needs to practice this technique.
5. **Rote**. Learning by rote ('off by heart') used to be a popular technique in infant classes for helping pupils retain key pieces of information, such as the words of a song or multiplication tables. Although it is not used widely nowadays, it remains an efficient way of committing to memory essential segments of information. Pick a song that you would like the child to sing, and ask him to learn five verses. This will seem an impossible task to him at first, but if he learns one line at a time – until he can recite it by rote without having to think about it – then he'll soon learn the whole song, and will be able to sing it to you without any difficulty.

Not A Good Start

Despite the best of intentions and adequate preparations, a child can struggle to settle into school. Very quickly, his excitement can drop along with his motivation and he may start to complain that he does not want to go back to school. Lets consider the following example.

The Problem: Five-year-old Cal has been at school for a couple of months now, but his pleasure in being a school pupil has slowly diminished. He comes home from school looking pale and tearful, as if he has cried from the moment he left home. He refuses to take any school books out, insisting that he never has any homework. Cal doesn't talk to his parents about what goes on in school. A couple of times recently he has mentioned that he feels sick in the mornings and asked to stay in bed. His parents are worried; they never had any difficulties with their older daughter when she started school and so they assumed Cal would thoroughly enjoy the infant class.

The Facts: Cal attended nursery for two years before moving to his present school but his best friends attend a different school. He does not make new friends easily because he is rather shy; he needs time to get to know other children before he becomes sociable and communicative. Many of the other pupils in his class, however, were pals before starting there this term. Cal's older sister is several classes ahead of him. He rarely sees her, even during intervals, preferring to spend all her time chatting to pupils her own age. Cal is afraid to discuss school with his parents at the end of the day. He thinks they will be angry with him for not having a good time.

The Analysis: Cal is experiencing social difficulties because he has no particular friends at school. The existing relationships are hard to break into, and he feels isolated and alone. Lack of support from his older sister adds to his distress. He genuinely feels ill in the morning; his anxiety at yet another miserable day ahead transforms into real physical feelings of nausea. His parents don't realise what could be troubling him. Like many children his age, Cal's self-confidence is fragile and it has taken a dip following his difficulty making new friends.

The Solution: As their son is not very communicative, Cal's parents need to discuss their concern with the class teacher – she will probably be able to explain that he hasn't made friends since starting in his class and that this could be the underlying difficulty. Next, the parents have to help boost Cal's social confidence by reassuring him that he will settle in soon, by asking him to invite classmates over to his house to play at the weekend or after school, and by encouraging him to be more talkative to the other children. His class teacher can also involve him more in group activities in the classroom. These measures will gradually improve Cal's social life in school.

Learning Style

Every child has his own distinctive way of learning in the classroom. One child might always be the first with an answer to the teacher's question, giving his answer before he has fully thought out all the possible responses. This impulsive learning style often leads the child to give an incorrect response because he doesn't think enough before offering his answer. Another child might prefer to reflect more on the question before committing himself, despite his desire to offer the correct answer to the teacher. This reflective learning style is more likely to lead the child to the appropriate response.

And learning style also affects a child's progress in school. For instance, a child who is learning to read has a variety of ways he can interpret a particular word, and, until he becomes a proficient reader, he has to think about these different interpretations before reading the word aloud. The dimension of reflectivity-impulsivity becomes relevant at this point. One research study assessed a group of children who were about to learn to read, in terms of how reflective or impulsive they were. When the children's progress with reading was assessed a year later, the researchers found that children who had been assessed as having a reflective learning style at aged six were better readers a year later, compared to the children who had been assessed as having an impulsive learning style.

That's why it is important to encourage a child to take his time when working on an educational activity. Reassure him that it's better to get the right answer than it is to be the first to answer – accuracy is better than speed. Encourage him to check over his work, even though he is satisfied that it is correct, and to think about his responses in class before he makes them. In the long term, this will benefit his learning.

Q & A

Q. *What should a child be able do for himself by the time he starts the infant class?*

A. Many infant teachers expect pupils to be reasonably independent by the time they start school. The typical five-year-old pupil can take off his coat and hang it on the cloakroom peg, manage to go to the toilet without help, separate well from his parents when they drop him off at school, follow group and class instructions given by the class teacher, take off his outdoor shoes without help, find his way round the school building, eat his lunch properly, give clear answers to any questions posed by the teacher, and concentrate on any learning activity. He can practice most of these skills at home with support from his parents.

Q. *My five-year old regularly complains that he is bored with the work the teacher gives him in class. What should I do?*

A. A child who is under-stimulated in school will be bored no matter how much he likes the other children and his teacher. Every child needs to be challenged educationally and intellectually. If you are convinced that your child is genuinely bored through lack of challenge, then raise this with his teacher. Explain why you think this, and give the teacher lots of examples to support your claim. (Don't be put off by a teacher who tells you are have an over-inflated view of your child's ability.) Ask the teacher for 'extension materials' – work at the level your child can cope with, but varied – so that you can use this with him at home. Rather than accelerating your child through the curriculum, extension materials provide variety at the same level and ensures your child's learning skills are fully consolidated before he moves on to the next stage.

Q. *If a child is being bullied at school – even at the age of five or six years – what should his parents do?*

A. Bullying in the infant class is more common than most parents realise. A victim often withstands this form of abuse without telling his mother and father because he is afraid that disclosure will make the bullies pick on him even more. (Girls are just as likely as boys to experience bullying in school, though bullying of girls tends to involve verbal violence while bullying of boys tends to involve physical violence.) The prime responsibility for eliminating bullying in the infant school rests with the teachers and every school has a preventative programme that the teachers use with young pupils. Parents must always report incidents of bullying to the class teacher who will then take appropriate supportive action.

Q. *What are useful activities to help develop a child's writing skills before he has actually started school?*

A. Suitable pre-school activities for this purpose include drawing, colouring in of basic shapes, completing dot-to-dot patterns, tracing round the outline of a shape, completing a pattern that has been half-drawn already, pretend-writing in the sand tray, scribbling randomly in a blank drawing book, and completing maze puzzles. Pencil grip is important too. He should hold a pencil by gripping it between his thumb and first finger, with his second finger supporting it about two centimetres from the tip. This takes plenty of practice.

Section 6: The Older Child

This section considers the development of children during the middle and later years of childhood (that is, from around five to adulthood) and the ways that they differ from younger children. Chapter 24 looks at middle childhood (that is, from approximately five to ten years) examining techniques for communicating effectively with them and how to deal with their occasional difficult behaviour. You should be aware of the changes that occur during adolescence, and Chapter 25 highlights these while also tackling the issues of gender relationships and uncooperative behaviour.

24

Middle Childhood

"I must admit that children often change once they start school. I have seen my child transform from an outgoing pre-schooler into a surly ten-year-old child. At times she seems so different from that child I used to know."

Once the pre-school years are over, children often change in unexpected ways. Many parents find this process amazing, occasionally wondering whatever happened to that sensitive, affectionate child they used to know. A quiet, sedate child can turn into a boisterous school child between the ages of five and ten years, and a co-operative, gentle child can become awkward, grumpy, moody and hard to handle.

This transition can occur for a number of reasons, including:

- **confidence.** Attending school is a big boost to a child's self confidence. As far as she is concerned, she's no longer a baby any more. Being at school, just like her older brothers and sisters, makes her feel good about herself and she starts to become more assertive.
- **independence.** She is much less dependent on adults than she was before. She makes decisions for herself and learns to cope with the hustle and bustle of school life every day. This increases her sense of independence and she may become less co-operative.
- **comparison.** The typical child in this age group compares herself with others in her class. If these comparisons are favourable (eg she reads better than most others) then she'll feel good about herself, but if comparisons are unfavourable, she may become moody.
- **friendships.** Her friendships will fluctuate regularly at this age. Her best pal one day might be her arch enemy the next. This ever-changing set of relationships can at times upset the child and may make her hard to handle.
- **difficulties.** Whether the child is bright or not, she may have problems coping with the demands of school. There are plenty of children who have difficulty learning new concepts, despite plenty of enthusiasm and as a result, they can become troubled.

These are only some of the many reasons why a child who attends school can begin to show a change in behaviour. Don't be surprised if such a change occurs, but remember that there are plenty of children who make the transition to middle childhood without any difficulties whatsoever. That's why it's best not to anticipate problems, as they might not occur. But it's best to be prepared anyway.

Nine and Ten Years

Caring for a child who has reached the age of nine or ten can be even more hectic. She has so many extremes of emotion, it's almost as though she is riding on a roller-coaster. One day she looks as if she is the happiest child in the world, and the next day she sobs her eyes out. All it takes to unsettle her happiness is a phone call from a friend to confirm that she is not invited to a party. One day she appears full of doom and gloom, convinced that she is the stupidest pupil in her school, and the next day she bursts with belief in her own ability. All it takes is a high grade in a class assignment to make her feel so good. One day she proudly wears her brand new leather jacket, and the next day she refuses point blank to put it on ever again. All it takes is a friend to say that denim jackets are better.

High And Lows

Emotional development during these middle-childhood years is full of highs and lows. You find yourself reading the expression on her face very closely in order to determine whether she is in a good mood or not. And if you pluck up the courage to ask her how she feels, you run the risk of her snapping sharply at you with the accusation that you are always prying! You end up feeling as though you can't win.

Be reassured – this is normal. The older child you know is no more volatile than any other, and her roller-coaster of emotions is all to do with her and nothing whatsoever to do with you. Her stage of development means that she experiences new emotions, new ambitions and new self doubts, and these are hard for her to learn to control at this stage. In addition, her confidence is very easily rocked, leaving her open to unpredictable mood swings which take her to extremes of behaviour. She can be very difficult to be with at times because she appears so unsettled and irritable.

Another significant factor to consider is that now she is influenced by people other than her parents. More than ever before, she wants to be part of the group of friends her own age – this becomes extremely important to her. Of course, she still loves her parents and values their opinion – and she still needs them to love her, care for her and support her – yet she also values the opinions of her peers. So you might find it is more difficult to cheer her up than it was a few years ago, because her feelings are closely connected to those of her friends.

Ten Tips For Good Communication

One of the most common complaints of parents with children this age is they are so hard to communicate with; it's as if they develop the ability to switch off. For instance, the minute you question a nine-year-old about her behaviour while coming home from school, her eyes may glaze over with that bored expression, as if to say "I'm not going to hear you." Or perhaps you have discovered that when you want to discuss the antics she gets up to, she just seems so hard to connect with. And you don't know whether there is something wrong with the way you are trying to talk to her or if she has simply made up her mind not to listen. There are often barriers to communication with an older child.

Yet many of these barriers can be broken down once you recognise them. Here are some tips to help you communicate more effectively:

1. **Give the child enough time**. You can't expect a hurried conversation or a quick criticism to grab her attention. Like anyone else, she needs time to think matters over and to discuss your comments with you. When you do have something you want to say to her, make a special time for this. That shows you want her to listen.
2. **Listen to the child.** She will always want to explain her side of the story to you. And she expects you to listen. Seeing you pause to hear her explanation of events, or just her opinion, sets a good example and makes her more inclined to listen to you. Listening should be reciprocal so that both of you can express your ideas.
3. **Use suitable language.** You may be tempted to patronise a child when expressing a point of view, by talking down to her. But she will switch off completely if she thinks you treat her like a younger child. Nor do you need to speak slowly and clearly, as if that is the only way she could ever understand you.
4. **Be honest with her**. Rather than falling into another confrontation, you might say in a calm voice "I know you won't like what I'm going to say but I'm going to say it anyway. It's important to me and I want you to listen, just as I know you like me to listen to you." This strategy won't work every time, but it is worth a try.
5. **Avoid regular criticism.** Repeated criticism of her difficult behaviour (eg she shouts at her bothers and sisters) will be ignored eventually. She gets used to negative comments and learns to cope by not listening. This tempts you into giving her even more extreme criticism in the hope of getting through to her.
6. **Offer solutions**. An older child will start to listen if you offer solutions instead problems (eg "One way to clear up the room is by tidying up one area at a time, clearing up bit by bit"). She'll soon realise that you have helpful suggestions to make, not just complaints – and she'll learn to pay attention.

7. **Find something positive.** No matter how many moans and groans you want to express to a ten-year-old about her behaviour, always find something positive about her behaviour to praise. Negative remarks are less likely to get a negative response from her if they are sprinkled amongst a wider array of positive comments.
8. **Don't give up.** The regular "deaf ear" is enough to drive you to despair. In fact, you might even be tempted to give up trying to communicate with her altogether, on the grounds that it is not worth the effort. Resist that plan of action because it leads nowhere except to a total breakdown of communication.
9. **See life through her eyes.** Suppose she accuses you of nagging her. Consider her accusation. Most people would define "nagging" as a constantly repeated request, in a whining, annoyed tone. "Asking" would be defined as a reasonable request, accompanied by a justified explanation, in a pleasant tone.
10. **Consider reaching a compromise.** For instance, your child might like to watch television the moment she comes through your front door, even though her brothers and sisters want to do their homework in peace and quiet. A compromise allowing her to watch television at agreed times would be a good starting point.

Expressing Her Feelings

Communication is a two-way process. Try to create an atmosphere in which she feels able to express her feelings. Effective communication with an older child involves being able to listen as well as being able to give advice. Listening to her isn't always easy, however.

To be a good listener, you have to **let the child speak without interruption**. There aren't many adults able to sit silently without butting in while a child lists a catalogue of incidents or anxieties. Your instinctive response may be to say something before she's had a chance to finish –if you do, she will be reluctant to talk to you so openly the next time.

She needs to know that you understand what she tells you, and that you are concerned and supportive; so **show empathy and understanding**. The best way to do this is to look at her directly as she's talking to you, to avoid any other distraction, and to make appropriate facial gestures that reflect your concern. And **think before you react**. If you give an immediate answer to every problem that's raised, you'll create an impression that her difficulties are trivial and easily solved. Far better to pause for a few moments after she has told you everything, and then to make a comment about how you realise it must be so difficult for her. This demonstrates that you care.

Try to **look for reasons**, rather than pass judgement. For instance, if she tells you that she is in trouble because she was caught pinching a pencil from another pupil's desk, you may be tempted to reprimand her straight away – and of course, this reprimand would be thoroughly justified. Your first step, however, should be to ascertain why she took the pencil. Adopting this long-term approach while dealing with an older child on a day-to-day basis will mean that she is more likely to express her feelings openly to you when she is upset. Create a general climate of listening and communication in your house so that it doesn't just happen when she is in bother.

The Wall of Silence

Despite all your best efforts at establishing open channels of communication between you and an older child whom you mind, you may still be faced with a wall of silence at times. Bear in mind that she won't respond to a display of temper from you; so stay calm, even though you may be filled with frustration.

Of course, time is scarce for individual children when you have more than one. If possible, however, try to find a few minutes for you and her to sit down together on your own without any interruptions from your other children or from a telephone call, to talk about her concern. Do this in a way that is obvious, in order that she knows you are taking her seriously; and make sure any other children in the house are aware that you want peace and quiet at this time. This gesture of your respect for her may be just what she needs to feel confident enough to discuss her anxieties with you.

Once the two of you are seated in chairs, preferably facing each other, tell her that you can see she is worried about something and that you know you can help her. Avoid statements which appear challenging or provocative, for example, rather than saying to the child "Spit it out, the sooner we get this over with, then the sooner we can get back to normal" it would be better to say "I know this is difficult for you, but I'm sure you'll feel better when you've talked to me about it."

A caring, physical gesture, such as taking her hand gently in yours, or putting your arm softly round her shoulders, can help her feel more able to express her feelings. You might find that she starts crying in response – if she does, comfort her and calm her. In many instances, a release of tears like this is necessary before there can be a release of words.

And be prepared for long silences. An older child might not really believe you when you explain that you want to listen, and one way of testing this is by sitting in silence. From her point of view, if you are genuine you'll be ready to wait until she's ready to speak. On the other hand, if after a minute you become impatient and tell her "You'll need to hurry up because I've better things to do than sit waiting for you" then she'll maintain her lack of communication indefinitely.

Even if you can only manage this for a couple of minutes each day, she will eventually begin to tell you what's wrong. Bit by bit, her account will slowly emerge. The longer you listen without interruption, the more she'll say to you, although you need to give her plenty of time. Once you are satisfied that you have heard the full story, suggest (not insist) possible ways forward; she might think your ideas are great or she might reject them instantly. That's her choice. Let her decide whether or not to accept your advice, and listen to her own ideas.

Between the two of you, you'll work towards an effective solution. All it takes is time, patience and a willingness to listen. Having successfully tackled the problem together this time, the child's stubborn refusal to express her feelings will be less likely the next time she faces a crisis. She will be happier to discuss things with you instead of keeping all her concerns and anxieties to herself.

Respecting Rights

An older child has the right to choose whether or not to be communicative with you, however, so consider the following strategies as well:

- **let her know that you accept her right to privacy.** Within realistic limits, she should be able to have some privacy at home. She may prefer at times to be alone in her bedroom. And don't read her private diary when she carelessly leaves it lying around. Tell her that you understand she wants to keep some matters private now that she's older, but add that you are always there to listen if she wants to talk.
- **don't push too hard.** The more reluctant she is to talk to you about something, the more you might push her to talk. This will not work. You cannot force a child to reveal her innermost feelings, no matter what you threaten her with. If you try too hard, then she will become even more distant from you. When you see the shutters are down, leave the conversation alone for a while. Return to it another time.
- **talk to her about things in your life.** Just because she has decided to be less open, you don't have to follow the same course of action. Indeed, if you do, nobody will speak to anyone in your house! Talk to her about the main events in your life and about everyday matters. This keeps the channels of communication open even though she doesn't participate in discussions at the moment.
- **make sure she knows you are there for her.** Tell her repeatedly that there may be times when she wants to tell you something that you may not want to hear (eg she got into a fight with another child at school) but that you would rather she tell you than keep it completely secret. And the fact that she says little about her daily life should not stop you from asking her about it.

Challenging Behaviour

A child in this middle-childhood stage of development has a mind of her own. She is no longer willing to accept everything an adult says and can be very challenging. Let's consider the following example:

The Problem: Ten-year-old Tanya makes her own way home after school, and meets her younger brother and sister there as well as her mother. Her father arrives home around six o'clock in the evening. But by then, her mother is in a foul mood, as are her two younger siblings. Tanya has become so objectionable and surly recently, complaining that everybody at home annoys her and being rude about her mother's clothes, ideas and conversation. It's as though she is deliberately rude. Her father urges everyone at home to be patient with Tanya.

The Facts: Like her friends, Tanya is one of the older pupils in the school and as a result she has been given more responsibility by her teacher. She and her schoolmates play a key part in school life. Tanya is achieving well at school; recently she gained top grades in a reading and maths assessment. Her younger brother and sister look up to her, and her parents expect her to help them with their homework when necessary. Mum and dad are so pleased with their oldest child's marks in class that they have rewarded her with a later bedtime. All in all, Tanya feels very pleased with herself at the moment. People who know her describe her as a good-natured child.

The Analysis: Tanya's new found success and responsibility both at home and in school has increased her self-confidence. She has also realised that being older makes her more powerful in comparison to the younger children. She likes this feeling and hence she exercises authority over her siblings. At this age, Tanya has begun to establish her individual identity, becoming increasingly aware of her unique qualities and characteristics. Testing her parents' limits of discipline is her way of proving how different she is from them; as far as Tanya is concerned, this rude and challenging behaviour shows that she has her own ideas and that she doesn't want to do exactly as other people say.

The Solution: Her parents are happy for Tanya to develop her individual identity, though they would much prefer it if Tanya could achieve this goal in a less confrontational way! To help her reach a better balance in her relationship with other children and adults, her parents should acknowledge that this is a stage many children go through. This doesn't mean Tanya's behaviour is acceptable, just that it shouldn't be taken personally. Second, the normal standards of discipline and respect for others at home should be maintained, despite the girl's pressure to change. Tanya should be reminded regularly why it's so unpleasant to be on the receiving end of her rudeness. And thirdly, the adults in her life should emphasise that she should treat others the way she would like to be treated. The narrow perspective of a ten-year-old can lead her to forget that relationships are reciprocal, and therefore she must not think her challenging behaviour is acceptable. Her parents should react calmly in the face of Tanya's rudeness, continually suggesting that she use a less hostile approach.

Q & A

Q. *Whenever I suggest that my nine-year-old does something like washing her cup, she gets angry at me and refuses to co-operate. What should I do?*

A. Keep asking her, and don't lose your temper. Explain that you are not going to stop asking her to tidy up simply because she shouts at you. Discuss with your child why you want her to wash her glass (or whatever activity she challenges you about), giving solid practical reasons (eg it is her responsibility, your other children are expected to do the same). If you take a calm, reasoned – but persistent – approach, you'll find that she eventually co-operates even though she may do so with a grudging attitude.

Q. *How can I help a ten-year-old who is terribly upset because she hasn't been selected for the school hockey team?*

A. Her confidence has taken quite a knock, and although there will be other opportunities for her to play in the school team, she is too upset to think that far ahead. You need to help her re-establish her self-esteem. By all means be sympathetic to her distress but encourage her to remember the other positives in her life, such as her friendships, her other sporting activities, and so on. This will help the child put her lack of success with the school hockey team into a broader perspective.

Q. *What should I say to a ten-year-old who mixes with a crowd of troublemakers that regularly get into bother?*

A. It's always difficult to discourage a child from having a particular friendship because the danger is that the more you try to break the relationship, the more desirable the friend becomes in the eyes of the child. And at the age of ten years, a child thinks she is more than capable of choosing her own pals. Approach the subject calmly and tactfully, having clarified the reasons why you are unhappy about her pals. Put this evidence to the child; rather than presenting it as an ultimatum, however, suggest that she thinks about what you have said. Talk about the subject again a few days later and listen to her own views. This is probably the most effective strategy because it treats the child with respect and avoids unnecessary confrontation.

Q. *The topic of drugs often comes up with my children. They ask me lots of questions that I can't answer. What should I do?*

A. Learn more about the subject yourself. Go to your local library or your local health centre. There are plenty of leaflets available, written specifically for adults to help them talk about drugs to children, and you should try to get copies of these as soon as possible. Once you have a reasonable knowledge base, you will be able to give your children more informed replies to their question. And that can only be in their best interests.

25

Adolescence

"He is so concerned with his appearance. Last year when he came to me from school, his shirt-tail was hanging out and there was mud all over his trousers. Now it's a different story. His clothes are immaculate and he always looks in the mirror."

Puberty is the phase of physical and psychological growth that signals the end of childhood, as the growing child's body begins to take on adult shape, size and sexual potential. Statistics confirm that the onset of puberty usually takes place between the age of nine and 14 years, although there is considerable variation

Many factors influence the timing of this phase in a child's life, such as gender (eg girls usually enter puberty younger than boys), genetic background (eg sisters tend to reach puberty at similar ages, when compared to girls from different families), body weight (eg short, well-built children often begin puberty earlier than their slimmer peers) and nutrition (eg with better nutritional standards, children experience puberty earlier than they did 50 years ago).

The Signs Of Puberty

Changes during puberty can be seen in three areas of a child, each area overlapping with the others. Firstly, there are the **physical changes**. There is a rapid increase in weight and height, caused by an increase of hormones in the bloodstream (oestrogen in girls and testosterone in boys). This happens months before any outward signs of puberty.

You'll certainly notice the surge in the child's appetite at this stage in his development! Suddenly, he's never away from the refrigerator, even though you might have fed him a huge meal an hour earlier. Suddenly, he clears his plate no matter how much food you load on to it. Suddenly, he snacks throughout the day without getting fat. And his clothes don't fit so well. Trousers that were a perfect length when bought for him a month ago are now too short. Shirts and jumpers become stretched and too tight and shoe size also increases.

These physical changes don't always occur smoothly and in harmony, and the typical adolescent is often unhappy about the way his body shape alters. For instance, some boys grow very tall and thin, making them feel awkward; some girls develop breasts which they consider to be disproportionate to their body size. The torso section of the child's body is the last to grow so he may appear to have long legs and a short waist. With some children, the two halves of the body grow at slightly different rates. Fortunately this balances out quite quickly, but for a month or two one breast might be larger than the other, or one foot larger than the other, making the adolescent feel very awkward.

Sexual Maturity

The second area of change during puberty is **sexual maturity** which occurs alongside the physical changes. Most significantly, the sex organs become larger in boys and girls so that by the time puberty has ended, their bodies are capable of reproduction.

With a girl, the event that signals her fertility is her first period. With a boy, the equivalent sign of sexual maturation is ejaculation, that is the discharge of fluid containing sperm. This might happen during sleep (known as a 'wet dream') or by masturbation. Without sufficient prior understanding, the growing child may become confused and distressed. Fortunately, most parents are able to talk about sexual matters with their children nowadays, making misunderstandings less likely. But they can still occur.

There are other more visible signs of sexual development during puberty. Body shape approaches that of adulthood. Boys becomes taller, with broader shoulders, while girls develop wider hips as their body naturally adapts for their subsequent ability to have children. A girl's breasts begin to develop, a process which will continue for several years. Breast growth is a frequent cause of dissatisfaction for girls because of their belief – created by social and media pressures – that there is an ideal breast size and shape. She may need reassurance that she is attractive and that her body shape is 'normal'.

With boys, a clear change related to sexual maturation is heard in the voice. During puberty, a boy's larynx grows, causing his voice to become deeper. One day he talks in a high tone, a week later he greets you with a voice that sounds as though it is hoarse. This process of change in voice tone rarely happens smoothly, resulting in a stage where his voice may sound rather squeaky. This can result in embarrassment and fear of ridicule from his friends. Again, reassurance may be all that is needed to restore his self-confidence.

An adolescent's hair becomes coarser and darker as puberty progresses. As well as this change, boys and girls start to experience hair growth under their arms, on their face (hardly noticeable with girls), and in the pubic areas. This change may be welcomed or perhaps feared. Facial spots may appear, much to the child's distress.

Psychological Changes

Puberty is associated with **psychological changes** too. The child's peer group assumes greater importance in his life and he begins to form attitudes which are the same as others his own age – in other words, what his parents say to him is less relevant than what his friends tell him. He wants to be like them, to dress like them, to listen to the same music as them and to be part of their group. But he still needs adults in his life. This tussle between dependency on mum and dad (he loves them just as much as he did when he was younger, even though he is more argumentative now) and the need to establish his own independence, is the emotional hallmark of this period. The best help to give a child during puberty is to reassure and support him as his body changes in a way that can be frightening and confusing for him.

The Adolescent Concern With Appearance

For most children in this age group, physical appearance is extremely important. Part of this concern with physical appearance stems from the natural process of peer-comparison which dominates adolescence. The child wants to dress like his friends, wear his hair like his friends, and be as good looking as them. And if he thinks that he cannot achieve these standards of physical appearance, then he feels miserable about himself. This is normal, and he requires support and encouragement to lift his self-confidence during these periods of self-doubt. Boys and girls are equally susceptible to these pressures.

However, there is another factor that intensifies an adolescent's desire to spend hours preening himself in front of the mirror, namely, social and cultural pressure. The growing child is constantly bombarded by advertisements, television programmes and movies which create a link in his mind between looks and success, between body shape and achievement, between smart appearance and intelligence. The media's non-stop message to adolescents is that physical attractiveness is all that matters, and that other personal traits – such as caring for others, a sense of humour, and the ability to work hard – don't matter at all. This has an impact on growing children.

Perhaps this obsession is inevitable, but it has the effect of making young people think that they have to be beautiful and attractive (with perfect teeth, perfect hair, a perfect body shape and a perfect facial structure) before they can think positively about themselves. And the truth is that many young people cannot match this idealised view of beauty, no matter how long they spend preparing themselves in front of the mirror. As a result, they think badly of themselves and have low self-esteem. And this can only lead to their unhappiness.

An adolescent can collapse in a flood of tears because a small spot has suddenly appeared on his chin the day before his best friend's party. It's the end of the world as far as he is concerned. A survey involving children between the ages of ten and 14 years questioned young people about their views on beauty and body shape. (Boys were not included in the study.) The results revealed that:

- girls as young as ten years say they diet because they are unhappy about the shape of their body, even when they are not actually overweight.
- children who diet often think dieting is essential in order to have an attractive body and that if they didn't diet their body shape would be distorted and horrible.
- there are very few girls in this age group who are genuinely overweight; most diets are due to a perceived need to lose weight, not a real need.
- in many instances, young people who diet seriously also have parents who themselves diet seriously, which confirms that children are affected by their parents' behaviour.
- when dieting becomes extreme it can have a severely detrimental effect on the child's body, including a delay to the onset of puberty and a restriction on bone growth.

Other surveys have shown that boys between the ages of ten and 14 are also vulnerable to pressures about idealised body shape and physical attractiveness, although for boys the emphasis tends to be on physical skills and physical strength rather than good looks.

How You Can Help

Here are some suggestions to help an adolescent develop a healthy interest in the way he looks without becoming obsessed by his 'imperfections', so that he has a positive sense of self-worth:

- **talk to him about physical appearance.** Explain that you are pleased he takes an interest in how he looks. After all, there is nothing wrong in a child taking a pride in his appearance, spending time on making himself look good. Yet he needs to strike a balance
- **broaden his perspective.** It will be worthwhile reminding him that his friends like him for reasons other than his appearance. Of course the way he looks and dresses is important but there is more to friendship and popularity than that.
- **encourage him to think about non-physical characteristics.** Ask him why he likes his best friend. The chances are he will reply giving examples of his friend's pleasant nature, his sense of humour and so on. Point out these have nothing to do with appearance.

- **suggest a sensible diet if he is at all concerned about his weight.** Extreme diets are unnecessary and unhealthy at any age. If a child does want to lose some weight, then he should simply cut out sweets, crisps and fizzy drinks.
- **make sure he has enough exercise.** Along with a sensible diet, a basic regime of exercise will help a growing child achieve a pleasant appearance. Walking occasionally instead of using the car, or taking up a leisure sport is all that is required.
- **listen to his complaints.** Be patient with him even though you can't actually see the blemishes he complains about. Calm him down, hear what he has to say, and then try to find a solution (eg suggest he brushes his hair a different way).
- **discuss the pressure of advertising.** It may be helpful to talk to him about the reality of adverts, about how they portray people in an artificial light. This encourages him to maintain a sensible perspective, instead of wanting to conform to media images of beauty.

Sexual Awareness

For most adolescents, sex is both intensely fascinating and intensely embarrassing. By this age, the child typically has already gained basic knowledge about sex – either through school-based education programmes, friends or parents – and he may be reluctant to ask an adult direct sexual questions. However, if the topic does arise in conversation, always give an explanation about sex that sets it within the context of a loving, stable relationship. (Of course, you know sexual intercourse often occurs in a casual, non-loving relationship, but that should left until a child is much older.)

In this transitional stage of a child's life he may experience his first 'crush' – in other words, his first romantic attachment towards someone of the opposite sex. (Boys are as likely as girls to form a crush.) He could have a crush on a particular girl at his school (even if she hasn't spoken to him at all), on a girl he has known all his life and yet whom he previously never thought much about, on a female teacher whom he sees regularly in school, or even on a pop-star or television character.

However ridiculous such an attachment may appear through your adult eyes, it will be very real to the child. So treat him seriously. Although crushes tend to be very temporary and may last only a few weeks or perhaps only a few days, they are very vivid and intense for the adolescent. It's not 'love' in the more mature adult sense of the word, but it is strong and it will occupy his thoughts for much of the time.

Here are some reasons why adolescent crushes are so common (though there are plenty of children who don't go through this phase):

- **maturation.** Previously, opposite-gender relationships have not been particularly attractive – younger children generally prefer to play with children of the same sex. However, the physical and emotional maturation of the adolescent at this point in his life means that he is now more aware and interested in the opposite sex.

- **imitation of adults.** The child wants to be like an older person. And part of being an older person, as far as he is concerned, is having affectionate relationships with those of the opposite sex. Just as he imitates other aspects of adult behaviour (eg wanting more independence), he also imitates this aspect.
- **self-discovery.** As an adolescent develops he learns more about himself. Having a crush on someone is another experience in which he discovers about himself (eg how he communicates with girls, and how attractive he is to girls). This is a new and exciting opportunity for him, and is one he can share with his friends.
- **safety.** One of the benefits of some – though not all – adolescent crushes is that they are safe because the focus of the crush is often unattainable. For instance, he can claim to be in love with the latest pop star, or with one of his friend's mother, but unconsciously he knows this relationship has no chance of becoming a reality.

Coping With Crushes

If an adolescent reveals that he has a crush on someone, or if you happen to discover this by chance, **don't make fun of him**. And don't tell him he is much too young to behave like this – such a tactic will only drive a wedge between you. (Thinking back, you'll probably recall that you had lots of crushes too.) **Treat him with respect** when you discover he is infatuated with someone. Listen to what he says, be sympathetic and reassuring, and offer him advice if you think that is appropriate. His feelings at the time are genuine; they matter to him, and he deserves to be taken seriously by you. Remember that boys and girls have crushes.

Whether or not you approve of such crushes, **there is little you can do to discourage them**. While there are times when a child develops a crush on someone because his friends also have a crush on the same person – in other words, as a result of peer pressure – in most instances, a crush just happens and is unplanned. Nor is he likely to be harmed by it. If you do try to force him out of it, perhaps by cajoling him or by giving a reprimand, the crush will probably become stronger instead of dying out naturally.

However you may want to **put reasonable limits on his behaviour**. For instance, you can encourage him to continue with his normal routine so that he still does his homework, eats meals, talks to his friends and siblings and so on. And you could suggest that he does not dress in order to impress the focus of his attraction. He may need these guidelines. Structure helps him cope with his confused feelings.

The very nature of the adolescent crush means **that it will pass almost as quickly as it appeared**. He may go from one crush to another – this often happens at this age. Try to create an atmosphere in which the child feels he can talk to you about anything, so that he won't want to conceal important parts of his life from you. Treating his crushes seriously but sensibly will enhance your relationship with him and will increase the likelihood that he will talk to you about opposite-gender relationships in the future.

Managing Failure

The fragile nature of the adolescent's self-confidence means that failure can be devastating, whether it is failure in the classroom, failure in relationships or failure in sports. Let's consider the following example:

The Problem: Twelve-year-old Pat is experiencing a run of poor marks at school. He has had at least one test a week for the last four or five weeks and his grades have progressively worsened. By the time he arrives home at the end of the school day, he is sad and uncommunicative. Pat's parents try to cheer him up but this doesn't have any effect. They have even found him crying a few times, as he held his test paper in his hand. He has become very anxious about going to school, and he often complains to his parents that he wishes he didn't have to go back there.

The Facts: Pat is a clever child who has previously had high achievements in school. However, the broad range of the curriculum is proving demanding and he has a problem getting through the volume of work each week. Pat does not have a study plan, lurching from one week to the next as the work piles up. At home, he shares a room with his younger brother – this five-year-old is enthusiastic and noisy, so Pat has little peace and quiet when trying to study.

The Analysis: Like many children, Pat is struggling to adapt to the demands of his secondary school. And the more challenging it becomes for him, the more overwhelmed he feels. Repeated failure in class tests is having a cumulative effect. He is now locked into a downward spiral in which his reduced self-confidence results in low test scores which reduce his self-confidence even further. The lack of a coherent study plan, and the lack of a quiet study area, only makes matters worse. Pat is caught in a rut, from which he sees no escape.

The Solution: The adults in his life need to give him clear advice. First, he needs to develop a more structured plan of homework and home study. His parents can help him with this. Suppose, for instance, he normally spends around two hours on homework each evening. They can suggest that he splits this time into two 30-minute study periods with a short break and a snack in between. Then they can make sure he sticks to that structure. Second, they can find a quiet area at home for him to study, away from their other children. This planned approach to the problem of coping with schoolwork, coupled with reassuring and supportive comments, could be sufficient to slowly turn the situation round so that Pat gains more favourable grades in future school tests.

Nag, Nag, Nag

The unpredictable moodiness of the adolescent means that you may find yourself nagging at him, for instance, because he makes such a mess of the house, because he doesn't do his homework, because he demands to play his music loudly or because he expects you to do everything for him. However, there are ways of changing his behaviour without resorting to nagging. Here are some suggestions for tackling this situation:

1. **Think about your level of criticism.** No sensible parent deliberately sets out to nag a child all the time; it's one of those habits that slowly creeps up without you realising it. Stand back and consider how much criticism you make of your adolescent.
2. **Criticise behaviour, not the child.** There is a difference. It's better to say to a child "This room is very untidy" (ie criticising his behaviour) than to say "You're a slob for leaving this room in such a mess" (ie criticising the child himself).
3. **Understand his point of view.** You may feel frustrated because he isn't helpful to his younger siblings. Before nagging him about this, check out the reasons for this behaviour. Maybe they have been annoying him and this is his way of managing without getting angry.
4. **Admit you don't like nagging.** Tell the adolescent that you hate being put into the position of having to nag at him. He will respond more positively when you say "I hate when I have to get on at you like this. Let's try to sort things out together."
5. **Point out the positives.** Rather than constantly criticising him for the negative aspects of his behaviour, highlight the positive aspects. For instance, you might say "It's a pity we are arguing at the moment because you were so well-behaved last week."
6. **Make suggestions.** Sometimes a child locks into a pattern of behaviour because he cannot see any other alternative. For instance, maybe he shouts out as this is the only way he can get attention. Try to suggest other ways he could behave to achieve the same goal.
7. **Set attainable targets.** Once you have identified a way in which you would like him to change, set a small achievable target. Explain to him all that you want him to do at this stage is, for instance, to say "hello" to you when you open the door to him.

8. **Praise him when he meets this target.** As soon as he achieves this small goal that you have set together, praise him for doing so well. He'll benefit from your interest and encouragement. Then set a new target, one step ahead of the previous one.
9. **Aim for gradual change.** The chances are that the adolescent will not change completely overnight, so have realistic expectations of him. Any progress he makes with your support will be slow and gradual, step by step over a period of weeks rather than days.
10. **Take stock.** Once progress is underway, sit down with the child and talk about how you are both working together. For instance, you could say to him "Things are so much better now that we have been able to talk together and sort it all out."

Q & A

Q. *I suspect that our 12-year-old son has a girlfriend but I'm not sure. Should I challenge him about this?*

A. If you are reasonably sure that he does have this relationship, then of course you should speak directly to him about it. Tell him your suspicions, without making him feel guilty about it. Explain that you would rather have honesty in your relationship than pretence and concealment. Your discussion may be just what he needs to have the confidence to discuss the matter more openly with you.

Q. *How can I discourage an adolescent from having such a materialistic attitude? Everything is "I want".*

A. This attitude is common amongst children this age and stems more from his desire for social acceptance than it does from any deep-rooted belief in the acquisition of goods. He wants that expensive jacket and those expensive trainers so that he will be like his friends. An adolescent seen by his pals wearing clothes that are not the height of fashion can experience social difficulties. Remind him that personal traits are more important than material goods, and suggest that if he really wants an item, then he can save his pocket money until he has enough to buy it himself.

Q. *Is it true that all adolescents are troubled?*

A. Although the teenage years are thought to be a time of storm and stress, serious emotional difficulties during this period are the exception rather than the rule. Detailed investigations have confirmed that most children in this age group are calm, predictable and clear-headed – although if you happen to have a moody adolescent at home, you might not find this result very reassuring! Another surprising fact to emerge from research is that there is often agreement between adolescents and parents on politics, religion and education. They frequently share the same values. So disagreement on the major issues are far less common than you might suppose.

Q. *Whenever I ask him about what he does at nights, just to make conversation, he gets annoyed with me. How can I make him understand that I care for him, that I am not prying?*

A. Be honest with him. Explain that you are genuinely interested in his life at home, and that he doesn't need to feel so threatened by your questions. Let him know that you recognise he has a right to have privacy but at the same time point out that he likes to chat to you about the things you have done. Relationships are reciprocal and you only have the same expectations about him in this instance as he has of you. This type of approach may help him adopt a more reasonable attitude to your questions.

Useful Addresses

Accident Prevention
British Red Cross Society, 9 Grosvenor Crescent, London SW1X 7EJ (020 7235 5454) www.redcross.org.uk
Child Accident Prevention Trust, 18-20 Farringdon Lane, London EC1R 3AU (020 7608 3828) www.capt.org.uk
Royal Society for the Prevention of Accidents (RoSPA), 353 Bristol Road, Birmingham B5 7ST (0121 248 2000) www.rospa.co.uk

Adoption & Fostering
Barnardo's, Tanners Lane, Barkingside, Ilford, Essex IG6 1QG (020 8550 8822) www.barnardos.co.uk
British Agencies for Adoption and Fostering, Skyline House, 200 Union Street, London SE1 0LY (020 7593 2000) www.baaf.co.uk

Asthma
National Asthma Campaign, Providence House, Providence Place, London N1 0NT (020 7226 2260) www.asthma.org.uk

Autism
National Autistic Society, 276 Willesden Hospital, London NW2 5RB (020 7833 2299) www.nas.org.uk

Bereavement
Compassionate Friends, 53 North Street, Bristol BS3 1EN (0117 953 9639) www.tcf.org.uk
Cruse Bereavement Care, Cruse House, 126 Sheen Road, Richmond, Surrey TW9 1UR (020 8940 4818) www.kvg.pwp.blueyonder.co.uk
Foundation for the Study of Infant Deaths, Artillery House, 11-19 Artillery Row, London SW1P 1RT (020 7222 8001) www.sids.org.uk
SANDS (Stillbirth and Neonatal Death Society), 28 Portland Place, London W1N 4DE (020 7436 7940) www.cafamily.org.uk

Brittle Bones
Brittle Bones Society, 30 Guthrie Street, Dundee, Scotland DD1 5BS (01382 204446) www.brittlebone.org

Cancer
Children's Leukaemia Trust, Clict House, 110 Cannon Street, London EC4N 6AR (020 7433 1997) www.childleuktrust.org.uk
REACT (Rapid Effective Assistance for Children with potentially Ter-

minal illness), 270 Sandycombe Road, Kew, Richmond, Surrey TW9 3NP (020 8940 2575) www.react-kew.demon.co.uk

Cerebral Palsy

Conductive Education, Cannon Hill House, Russell Road, Birmingham B13 8RD (0121 449 1569) www.conductive-education.org.uk

Scope (formerly The Spastics Society), 6 Market Road, London N7 9PW (020 7619 7100) www.scope.org.uk

Child Abuse

The Children's Society, Edward Rudolf House, 69-85 Margery Street, London WC1X 0JL (020 7837 4299) www.the-childrens-society.org.uk

NSPCC, NSPCC National Centre, 42 Curtain Road, London EC2A 3NH (020 7825 2500) www.nspcc.org.uk

National Children's Bureau, 8 Wakely Street, London EC1V 7QE (020 7843 6000) www.ncb.org.uk

Children In Hospital

Action for Sick Children, Argyle House, 300 Kingston Road, London SW20 8LX (020 8542 4848) www.hantsweb.org.uk

Coeliac Disease

Coeliac Society, PO Box 220, High Wycombe, Bucks HP11 2HY (01494 437278) www.coeliac.co.uk

Cystic Fibrosis

The Cystic Fibrosis Trust, 11 London Road, Bromley, Kent BR1 1BY (020 8464 7211) www.cftrust.org.uk

Diabetes

British Diabetic Association, 10 Queen Anne Street, London W1M QBD (020 7323 1531) www.diabetes.org.uk

Juvenile Diabetes Research Foundation, 25 Gosfield Street, London W1W 6EB (020 7436 3112) www.jdf.org.uk

Down's Syndrome

Down's Syndrome Association, 155 Mitcham Road, Tooting, London SW17 9PG (020 8682 4001) www.dsa-uk.com

Dyslexia

British Dyslexic Association, 98 London Road, Reading, Berks RG1 5AU (0118 966 2677) www.bda-dyslexia.org.uk

Dyslexia Institute, 133 Gresham Road, Staines, Middlesex TW18 2AJ (01784 463851) www.dyslexia-inst.org.uk

Early Education
British Association for Early Childhood Education, 136 Cavell Street, London E1 2JA 9QY (020 7539 5400) www.early-education.org.uk
National Association for Gifted Children, Elder House, Milton Keynes (01908 673677) www.nagcbritain.org.uk
National Association for Special Educational Needs, 4/5 Amber Business Village, Amber Close, Amington, Tamworth, Staffordshire B77 4RP (01827 311500) www.nasen.org.uk

Education (General)
Advisory Centre for Education (ACE), Aberdeen Studios, 22 Highbury Grove, London N5 2DQ (020 7534 8318) www.ace-ed.org.uk
Centre for Studies on Integration in Education, 415 Edgeware Road, London NW2 6NB (020 8452 8642) www.connections.gcal.ac.uk
Reading/Language Information Centre, Reading University, Bulmershe Court, Earley, Reading RG6 1HY (0118 931 8820) www.ralic.rdg.ac.uk

Enuresis
Enuresis Resource and Information Centre (ERIC), 34 Old School House, Bristol BS15 2DB (0117 960 3060) www.enuresis.org.uk

Epilepsy
British Epilepsy Association, New Anstey House, Gateway Drive, Yeadon, Leeds LS19 7XY (0113 210 8800) www.epilepsy.org.uk
National Society for Epilepsy, Chesham Lane, Chalfont St. Peter, Bucks SL9 0RJ (01494 601300) www.epilepsynse.org.uk

Haemophilia
Haemophilia Society, Chesterfield House, 385 Euston Road, London NW1 3AU (020 7380 0600) www.haemophilia-soc.demon.co.uk

Health
Family Planning Association 2-12 Pentonville Road, London N1 9FP (020 7837 5432) www.fpa.org.uk

Hearing Impairment
British Deaf Association, 1-3 Worship Street, London EC2A 2AB (020 7588 3529) www.britishdeafassociation.org.uk
Cued Speech Association, Bay View, Stoke Fleming, Dartmouth TQ60QX (01803 770 944) www.communicationsforum.org.uk
National Deaf Children's Society, 45 Hereford Road, London W2 5AH (020 7229 9272) www.ncds.org.uk

Hyperactivity
Hyperactive Children's Support Group, 71 Whyke Lane, Chichester, West Sussex PO19 2LD (01234 551313) www.hacsg.org.uk

Learning Difficulties
MENCAP, 123 Golden Lane, London EC1Y 0RT (020 7454 0454) www.mencap.org.uk

Meningitis
National Meningitis Trust, Fern House, Bath Road, Stroud, Gloucester GL5 3TJ (01453 768000) www.meningitis-trust.org.uk

Muscular Dystrophy
Duchenne Family Support Group, 37a Highbury New Park, Islington London N5 2EN (0870 606 1604) www.dfsg.org.uk

One Parent Families
Gingerbread, 7 Sovereign Court, Sovereign Close, London E1W 3HW 020 7488 9300) www.gingerbread.org.uk
National Council for One Parent Families, 255 Kentish Town Road, London NW5 2LX (020 7428 5400) www.oneparentfamilies.org.uk
Single Parent Action Network, Millpond, Baptist Street, Easton, Bristol BS5 0YW (0117 9514231) www.hantsweb.org.uk

Parenting
Meet A Mum Association (MAMA), Waterside Centre, 26 Avenue Road, London SE25 4DX (020 8768 0123) www.mama.org.uk

Pregnancy and Childbirth
Association for Post Natal Illness, 145 Dawes Road, Fulham, London SW6 7EB (020 7386 8885) www.apni.org
National Childbirth Trust, Oldham Terrace, Acton, London W3 6NH (020 8992 2616) www.nctpregnancyandbabycare.com

Research/Statistics
Department of Social Security, Correspondence Unit, Room 540, The Adelphi, 1-11 John Adam Street, London WC2N 6HT (020 7712 2171) www.cas.gov.uk
Family Policy Studies Centre, 9 Tavistock Place, London WC1H 9SN (020 7388 5900) www.fpsc.org.uk
National Foundation for Educational Research (NFER), The Mere, Upton Park, Slough SL1 2DQ (01753 574 123) www.nfer.ac.uk
Office for National Statistics, 1 Drummond Gate, London SW1V 2QQ (0845 601 3034) www.statistics.gov.uk

Sickle Cell Disease/Thalassaemia
Sickle Cell Society, 54 Station Road, Harlesden, London NW10 4UA (020 8961 7795) www.sicklecellsociety.org
UK Thalassaemia Society, 19 The Broadway, Southgate Circus, London N14 SPH (020 8882 0011) www.ukts.org

Special Needs (General)
British Psychological Society, St Andrew's House, 48 Princess Road, East, Leicester LE1 7DR (0116 254 9568) www.bps.org.uk
Child Psychotherapy Trust, Star House, 104-108 Grafton Road, London (020 7284 1355) www.edinburgh.gov.uk
Disability Information Services, Harrowlands Centre, Harrowlands Park, Dorking Surrey RH4 2RA (01306 875156) www.diss.org.uk

Speech Impairment
Association For All Speech Impaired Children (AFASIC), 69-85 Old Street, London EC1V 9HX (020 7841 8900) www.afasic.org.uk
British Stammering Association, 19 Old Ford Road, Bethnal Green, London E2 9JP (020 8983 1003) www.stammering.org

Spina Bifida
ASBAH (Association for Spina Bifida and Hydrocephalus), ASBAH House, 42 Park Road, Peterborough PE1 2UQ (01733 555988) www.asbah.org

Syndromes
Children's Liver Disease Foundation, 36 Great Charles Street, Birmingham B5 6DR (0121 212 3839) www.childliverdisease.org
Fragile-X Society (National Coordinator), 53 Winchelsea Lane, Hastings, East Sussex TN35 4LG (01424 813147) www.fragilex.org.uk
Guillain-Barre Syndrome Support Group, LCC Offices, Eastgate Holdingham, Sleaford, Lincs NG34 7EB (01529 304615) www.gbs.org.uk
Marfan Association UK, 5 Aldershot Road, Fleet, Hampshire GU13 9NG (01252 810472) www.marfan.org.uk
Prader-Willi Syndrome Foundation, 30 Leopold Street, Derby DE1 2HF (01332 365 676) www.pwsa-uk.demon.co.uk

Visual Impairment
Royal National Institute for the Blind (RNIB), PO Box 173, Peterborough PE2 6WS (0845 766 9999) www.rnib.org.uk

Index